Eber & Wein Publishing's

Who's Who
in American Poetry

John T. Eber Sr.
MANAGING EDITOR

A publication of

Eber & Wein Publishing

Pennsylvania

Who's Who in American Poetry: Vol. 3

Library of Congress
Cataloging in Publication Data

ISBN 978-1-60880-415-3

Proudly manufactured in the United States of America by

Eber & Wein Publishing
Pennsylvania

Who's Who
in American Poetry

The Stab of Maybe

This is no home
But a sterile operating room
Under general anesthesia
Yet sensitized
We muster our bid before the razor's edge
Hoping this cut will be more precise

You are no lover
But a volunteer for the needy
Bearing capsules of benevolence
You go the rounds
Letting your heart bleed when it's necessary
Dropping the empty cup at the door

I am no man
But a white gown showing crimson stains
Constant desire for assurance
And fulfillment
Waxes and wanes while I am writhing in pain
Punctured by the stab of maybe

Jeffrey Magnuson
San Diego, CA

Grand Prize Winner

My Personal Reality

We are all unique
Yet we are all one.
To be sure there is no one mother mold.
It is the Divine in us that makes us whole.
I can see clearly what I believe.
What I think is what I am
And what I have been
Is who I am.
No argument from me
That it is done unto me
As I believe.
No beginning, no ending, only now.
I flow in God's presence and power
Preparations set in motion
For the results I expect to achieve.
For certain I am that I am what I believe.
And for our choices, great and small
Responsibility is the price
For the freedom we achieve
For it is done unto us as we believe.
The positive choice leads to peace, fulfillment.
The negative, to conflict and despair.
For it is done unto us as we believe.
When the transition between birth and death
Makes you ponder.
Just remember: It is done unto us as we believe.

Jean Hurst
St. Simons Island, GA

Jean Hurst has served in a variety of roles throughout a career that spans academe, the arts, and the business community. A native of Georgia, Jean Hurst has had many achievements affirmed personally, professionally and socially. Her credentials include a PhD in dramaturgy from Florida State University, master of fine arts in speech and drama from the University of Georgia, bachelor of arts in English from Mercer University, as well as several areas of post-graduate work from Furman University, San Jose State, Northeastern University, and University of Georgia. She and her late husband, artist/sculptor/art professor emeritus Ralph Hurst, became founding members of the Community Foundation of North Florida, and together and individually supported numerous charitable efforts as well as both visual and performing arts.

Deserve

I don't deserve you.
I don't deserve the things you do.
We smile for the world.
And I dream of you.
Why me? I can't imagine.
No one understands
Why we do what we do.
Or who we are.
Or why we are.
We were.
Why were we?
Who were you?
Why did you do what you did?
No one understands.
Why me? I don't understand.
I can't sleep tonight.
I try to smile but it fades into tears.
I never did anything to deserve what you did.
I never did anything to deserve you.

Sydney Lewis
Valley City, OH

[Hometown] Valley City, OH

Extinguished Candle

Extinguished is the candle glowing within,
Like a ferocious wind destined to win.
It creates a question whether it had ever been,
Or just exhausted after consumed as a tasty gin.
Undoubtedly, revival may be difficult to begin.

Just like hand-blown glass and the human heart,
The light is fragile and spirit invaluable from the start.
Glowing laughter and happiness are lifeless on the crash cart.
Likely never again be grazed as by Cupid's dart,
Future life unsweetened, bitter and tart.

Like winter snow, the candle falls cold.
Destruction, vengeance and violent actions are told.
Mimicking an incurable disease of deadly black mold,
Rebellion against our creator's intentions is evilly bold.
It promotes America's current and eternal blessings to be sold.
Sinful fallen Satan seemingly is our owner when darkness we hold.

The United States, God once held dear,
We were a babe in swaddling wrap and God was near.
We respected and were obedient to our creator and held no fear.
Being separated from us, God sheds many a tear.
From us His prodigal children, He is waiting to hear,
But won't wait much longer, that is very clear.

B. J. Boal
Des Moines, IA

[Occ] insurance (in between gainful employment); [GA] never or not yet occurred

Frozen Heart

There is darkness behind your eyes
Your past has damaged your spirit and tainted your soul
Forever broken, but not beyond repair
I see the darkness dancing in your eyes
I feel the pain in your stare, and I long to save you
To bring you back from the shadow that has consumed you
Pull back the veil that you have hidden yourself behind
I want to be the reason for your smile and laughter
To softly kiss away the anger that resides in you
Wash away the rage that boils deep inside of you
I can see the light behind the darkness in your eyes
It dimly seeps around the edges and pierces the veil
There is happiness buried deep down inside of you
It's been trapped behind the wall you have put up
It's been hidden for so long yearning to be released
It is winter in your heart now and it is oh so cold
I will be the sun to melt the snow
I will be the hammer to chip the ice away
I want to thaw your frozen heart
But most of all I want to be the one to save you
Take my hand in yours, and I will lead you to salvation
I can see the ice melting now...summer has come

Brittany Phillips
Howell, MI

[Hometown] *South Lyon, MI; [DOB] December 28, 1990; [Ed] college; [Occ] parts manager at a body shop; [Hobbies] drawing, writing, playing guitar; [GA] being a published poet*

A friend once confessed to me all the things that had happened in his past. This poem was inspired by that. I felt his anger and felt love growing. I wanted to be the one to save him from the pain and to be the one to make him happy. I think the ice is melting now, and summer is coming for him, and it is because of me. This makes me smile.

Love

Love should be never-ending,
beginning long before the wedding,
and lasting well beyond this life,
for both the husband and the wife.

It can actually be for all eternity,
if we love with great sincerity.
Love should also be very forgiving,
focusing less on getting and more on giving!

There are many ways to express our love,
ranging from great big kisses to little hugs.
No matter how you do it, though,
the message sent is that we love them so.

We don't share these emblems with everyone,
only with those with whom we have great fun!
Yes, we find happiness with those we hold most dear,
and experience great joy whenever they are near.

Curiously, it may take months to show that we care,
but it only takes a few seconds to cause great despair!
So be sure to cherish each other as much as you can,
and never utter words that could hurt your biggest fan!

Thomas S. Parish
Topeka, KS

[Hometown] Topeka, KS; [DOB] January 24, 1944; [Ed] BA in psychology, MA in clinical psychology, PhD in human development/developmental psychology; [Occ] life coach; [Hobbies] writing poetry and dancing; [GA] in 2005, I was recognized by the International Biographical Centre in Cambridge, England, as "One of the Top 100 Educators in the World"

People often go into psychology in order to better understand themselves and/or others. Writing poetry, however, certainly helps me to also better understand myself and others, particularly as I focus writing odes that specifically describe my perceptions of them. In addition, writing poetry is exciting, insightful, and fun for me as I seek to share ideas about the key concepts around which our lives often evolve, e.g. our work, familial happiness, and love!

Song in Aslan's Sanctuary

Bethlehem is the glory of Aslan, our loyal aristocrat.
Sing and shout; Aslan, Aslan, Aslan!
Bethlehem is the story of Aslan, our royal aristocrat.
Sing and shout; O Lamb, O Lamb, O Lamb.
Aslan's revelation from the sanctuary of seven angels;

"Great and amazing are your deeds;
O Lord, God Aslan.
Great and true are your way,
O King of the nation!
who will not fear, O Lamb,
and glorify your name;
For you alone are holy,
All nations will come and worship you,
For your righteous acts have been revealed."

History of his mystery is His song in His sanctuary.
Holy, holy, holy.
Mystery of his history is His song for our eternity.
Worthy, worthy, worthy.
Song in Aslan's sanctuary is exaltation!
O Lamb, O Lamb, O Lamb.
Sanctuary in Aslan's song is for all nations!
Aslan, Aslan, Aslan.
Song in Aslan's sanctuary is revelation!
O Lamb, O Lamb, O Lamb.
Aslan's sanctuary is Aslan's creation!

Timothy A. Wik
Elkins Park, PA

[Hometown] Elkins Park, PA; [DOB] September 29, 1959; [Ed] high school graduate, some college; [Occ] general labor via job agencies; [Hobbies] poetry, movies, music; [GA] publishing a book of poetry

My interest in poetry goes back to 1982 when I published a poem titled "Paradise Won." About five years later, I published a book of Christian sonnets. I have contributed poems to publishers over the years. Most of my poetry is literally, symbolically, or allegorically poetry. My poetry is inspired by combination of previous poetry published and scripture verses from the Bible.

This Little Girl of Mine

For Susan: this little girl of mine on the occasion of her sixtieth birthday
August 26, 2015

Tho' not of my loins, this little girl of mine
She is no longer the little girl
Who crawled onto my lap for a goodnight kiss
Her hair still wet from her evenin' shower
She snuggled in my arms, just before bed time
Trying to stay up just a wee bit longer
Did she think she was fooling her old man?
I cared not, holding her tightly
I miss those days
But it was pure bliss for
She was this little girl of mine

Now a grown woman
She still calls me Daddy
Many years have passed
I miss those days of long ago
Did I ever tell her often enough
How much I love her
Did I ever tell her?
I'm so proud to call her still
This little girl of mine

Joseph M. Laino
Mineola, NY

[Hometown] Bronx, NY; [DOB] June 5, 1937; [Ed] BA degree; [Occ] retired; [Hobbies] writing, model railroading; [GA] my children

My children and grandchildren are very important to me during these advancing years. My fondest wish is for their happiness. This poem is for my daughter who worries about me constantly. My son who lives with his family in Virginia calls me two to three times per week to, as he says, "check up on me." I have several nieces, nephews and friends who telephone or stop by to help me. My grandson telephones from his course to discuss sports. I am, indeed, a lucky man!

God's Favorite Color

What is God's favorite color? I asked myself
the other day.

I was outside in the morning, and all at once,
I thought I knew—
God's favorite color has to be blue!

"Yes," I said, "God's favorite color has to be blue!"

Blue as the sky looking up that day, as blue as the sky!
I knew it was true!

God's favorite color has to blue!

What do *you* say? Do you think it is true?

Yes, God's favorite color has to be blue!
Just look at the sky, and you shall see.

It has to be true, God's favorite color is *blue!*

Sandra Weaver Gillespie
Evans, GA

[Hometown] Evans, GA; [DOB] March 29; [Ed] BS in education; [Occ] retired teacher; [Hobbies] cooking, writing, family; [GA] president of freshman and junior high school classes

I am married to Rev. Bob Gillespie, a retired Methodist minister. I have been a retired teacher for some time now. I attend church regularly, with my husband. This poem was inspired recently when I looked up and saw the beautiful blue sky.

Horrors of War

Sadness and sorrow
Grief and despair
Confusion and worry
All too much to bear.
Embraced in a hope
Too tight to resist,
Choked up in sadness
For one who is missed.
Feelings, emotions,
Overwhelming strife
For husband or son
For daughter or wife.
The pain and the sorrow
Then soar to new heights
As one who was fighting
Is ripped from war's sight.
Why must this happen?
Why so much hate?
The horrors of war
Control someone's fate.
The family then clings
To ones they hold dear,
Hoping that someday
All wars disappear.

Lynn Ruoff
Houston, TX

[Hometown] Houston, TX; [Ed] master of arts, Stephen F. Austin State University; [Occ] professional artist; [GA] exhibited my art in New York, Santa Fe, NM, and other galleries in the US, Canada and Europe

The Summer Storm

A distant rumble
A flash of light
A summer storm
Is coming tonight.

Roosting birds huddle close
Trees bend and sway
Hang on tight
A summer storm is on the way.

Fireflies compete
With the lightning so bold.
Their time to shine
Is a sight to behold.

A gentle pitter patter
Becomes a mighty roar.
The thirsty earth
Gratefully accepts the thunderous downpour.

All is quiet
The summer storm has passed
With a weary sigh
It's back to sleep at last.

Carolyn Fuller
Anna, IL

[Hometown] Anna, IL; [DOB] August 8, 1942; [Ed] high school education; [Occ] homemaker; [Hobbies] reading, poetry, observing nature; [GA] a fifty-two-year marriage

Freedom

The gift of freedom is the greatest treasure
There's nothing else to which it can measure

To confiscate another's wealth—is that fair
Take from those who do—give back to those who don't care

What is yours is not mine
Be it today or any other time

Share a thought that cannot be bought
Extend a hand—write in the sand

Throw away a kiss—one you'll not miss
Be yourself each day—keeping slavery at bay

Mary Miller
Belvidere, IL

An Artist's Delight

As I look up toward the sky
Many white clouds are floating by:
Some are large and some are small,
Each resembling a cotton ball.
In between a soft shade of blue
Giving an impression of a brooklet running through:
Combination of blue and snowy white
Along with imagination is an artist's delight.

Rhoda Osheroff
West Orange, NJ

Happy Retirement

All the bells and whistles at the Burlwood Bar...
A dozen or so people hold glasses up to me; I've come so far.
They throw a nice party and tell me its time to go,
but really, this work's all I know—I want to stay.
They say I'm too old, it's time to go anyway.

I notice the time on my wrist of gold,
where'd it all go?—Oh, how much I've sold...
I know not my wife, my children stranger still;
was I there for them? Yes, like cash in the till.

What am I doing here? A bar is not my scene.
I'm not a drinker, nor reveler, just a teetotaler,
like that funny English chap, Mr. Bean.
No one here will miss me...

Early to home, maybe my wife will kiss me?
My driveway has a strange car in my usual spot;
a peek in the window reveals my wife's passion is hot.
Their sweat and wild hair attests that they've been at it awhile.
Should I break them up? Cause a scene?
Maybe shame my wife with scheming guile?
Does forever-love exist? Her happiness still matters to me.
I'm the problem; not there for all her needs, you see...

Happy retirement! My work is done.
Nothing remains . . . tires drone, Benny Goodman fades;
speeding along, I hear the curved fence break.
The car sails into the waiting arms of purgatory;
how extraordinary . . .

S. Grimm Bagley
Coalinga, CA

Betrayal

Have you ever been caught red handed?
Have you ever been betrayed?
Oh what a hurtful feeling of dismay.
Betrayal is low-down
dirty and not very pretty.
Sorry does not always
work at first, but it's hard
to regain that trust!
The trust that took many years
to build, and now it appears
to be going downhill.
Betrayal is a joykill!

Gloria J. Roberson
Queens, NY

[Hometown] Queens, NY; [DOB] February 18, 1954; [Ed] MS in education; [Occ] elementary teacher; [Hobbies] travel, jumble puzzles; [GA] when I retire

I am a school teacher in NYC about to retire in June 2016 with thirty years of service. This poem was inspired by what the title portrays...betrayal. However, life goes on and you don't let it get you down because soon you will rebound. I have learned to forgive, but not to forget. Writing helps me to vent, mend, and heal. I have been writing poetry for over thirty-five years.

Nature's Balance

White puffy clouds drift across bright azure skies,
Casting shadow upon the glistening White Sands.
On the horizon, purple sierras rise up to greet them.
Tall pines extend their welcoming arms,
Soliciting cool drinks of crystal drops.
When the clouds do not answer, showing their treasures,
Drought invades the land!
All life weeps in bereavement,
For sunshine must be complemented with clouds
Bestowing rain to balance the gift of life.

Dorothy Schultz
El Mirage, AZ

Dorothy Schultz lives in El Mirage, AZ. Growing up in New Mexico in the '40s and '50s, she often visited the White Sands, and the mountains between Sands and Roswell, NM where she lived. During the 1950s New Mexico experienced a drought similar to the one that the Southwestern United States is currently experiencing. Dorothy witnessed the impact that the drought had upon the environment and the increase of forest fires and the destruction of the beautiful woods where she loved to hike. Rain was an occasion to go outside and experience it.

We Long for Love

We long for that sweet poison,
long for that sweet drug,
though we know it shall destroy us,
still we long for love,
for the one form of poison,
which never seems to be strong enough.

Victoria E. Jones
Bridgeville, DE

Creature Called "Man"

Lord, it's really hard to understand
This creature you made and called a man
He seems so stubborn and hard to please
When a woman just tried to put him at ease
By being honest, true and sincere
And showing him he's the one she wants to be near!
To hold him and love him and see him through strife.
Giving all of these simple but important things to life!
Still this creature warns "Don't get serious!"
Thus driving a woman till she's nearly delirious;
Wanting to give of herself all she can
Then backs away shouting "You aren't tying down this man"
Show him a female—loud, insincere and wild
And right away they are just like a child...
Who sees all the candy in a candy store;
And no matter how much they have,
Think they gotta have more!

Daisyann Fredericks
Canajoharie, NY

[Hometown] Canajoharie, NY; [DOB] January 27, 1935; [Ed] twelfth grade; [Occ] clerical work; [Hobbies]
sewing, writing poems; [GA] balloon ride with daughter and grandson

The poem "Creature Called 'Man'" was the result of an experience in my life many years ago—the person
who inspired it kept in touch from wherever he lived and always said he "wished he'd married me!" (His loss.)
We remained friends the rest of his life! He passed away five years ago.

Round and Round

Round and round and round again,
Stuck in the same old cycle that I've always been
This time it will be different is constantly what I'm told,
This time things will be better, just you wait and see

Now I've been compliant, I've done as I was asked
I've been given instructions that I've obeyed,
Round and round and round I go,
When will this cycle ever end?

Round and round and—
No I'm done
No more that's it, I'm through
Maybe it's giving up, who knows
Judge if you want, I really don't care

After going round and round and round some more,
The cycle ends now, forever—
I'm done.

Izzy Allen
Danville, NH

[Hometown] Danville, NH; [Ed] GED

Self-portrait

My father was a descendant of Noah who lived in one of the two cities called
Heaven on Rarth—Hangzhou, in the Middle Kingdom.

Another descendant of Noah lived in the other city called the Heaven on Earth—
Suzhou, in the Middle Kingdom. It was my mother.

They met, got married, and raised a family on the shore of the famous literarily
West Lake in Hangzhou, an ancient capital of China.

I was born one spring night after my mother woke up from dreaming of a little
tiger that followed her home.

I was the third son and the weakest of five siblings, a sister and four brothers.

I did survive typhoid, wars, drowning, riding accident, target shooting,
tuberculosis, and car accidents.

I was lost in the underworld of Buddhism as a child monk until God found and
brought me into His Kingdom.

I was a refugee, student, soldier, veteran, graduate assistant, research officer, senior researcher,
professor, minister, author, columnist, editor, radio host, satellite TV evangelist, and a poet.

I earned a BS, MD, PhD, and FAIC and my name has appeared on a few
international "Who's Who" lists.

In fact, I am nothing, but I am a child of God through His Grace, the redeeming
blood of Jesus Christ, and the power of the loving Holy Spirit.

I married a preacher's daughter and we have two children, one daughter and one son.
Thank God and praise His Holy Name!

Micah Leo
Vista, CA

*[Hometown] Hangchow; [DOB] April 18, 1926; [Ed] PhD; [Occ] Christian writer, preacher; [Hobbies]
poems; [GA] being God's child*

*I was a soldier during World War II, a student of science, an editor of two monthly magazines, a doctor of
philosophy, a professor of chemistry, a fellow of American Institute of Chemistry, a minister of Gospel, the
president of a theological seminary, an author of several books, a columnist for two newspapers, a winner of
the poets' choice, a member of the International Poetry Hall of Fame, the founder of Christ Society of Poets,
and presently the editor-in-chief of the* Psalms Today, *a bilingual quarterly in both Chinese and English.*

Weep

Drifting off to sleep I silently weep
No sounds, not one little peep
Wondering why this silence I keep
Depression locked inside so very tight
Won't allow you to see my flood of tears
Crying for all of my lost years
What a doormat I have become
Around you, my heart is now numb
Never wanted more than affection and love
Regret losing my whole being, my soul for you
My heart is deeply battered and bruised
Grabbing my extra pillow I cover my face
I clench my teeth and grip it tight
For me, there is not any freedom
I weep

Joann Elizabeth Meyer
Eagle Lake, MN

[Hometown] New Ulm, MN; [DOB] October 26, 1972; [Ed] culinary school; [Occ] lunch cook; [Hobbies] cooking, baking, reading, writing, fishing, traveling, giving back to those who helped me

I have always enjoyed reading and writing many poems. During my abusive marriage, I wrote to express my feelings. I once had medication for depression and for my enlarged heart. After leaving everything but my children behind, I found myself, and in the process stopped all medications and took back control of my mind! Unless anyone has been abused they don't fully know how amazing it feels! My teenagers are safe here and we embrace love. We help feed the hungry and donate time, clothes, and our hearts when needed. When in doubt, love.

Tiny Stream

Trickle trickle tiny stream
bubble bubble over rock and stone
swift and swifter round the curves
babbling buddy streams join on in.

Down from the hills the waters flow
over the falls cascade wet waters
crash and splash on solid rock
soaking all the playing running people.

Andy D. Anderson
Springfield, OR

[Hometown] Albert Lea, MN; [DOB] August 24, 1930; [Occ] lifetime career in aviation industry as mechanic, electrician, flight engineer, quality control inspector, working in all areas of the world; [Hobbies] baseball during my youth, golf during middle age, tennis in senior years, hiking in my super senior years, writing and publishing stories and poems, painting landscapes with watercolor, volunteering at my church and art center

Writing for me is merging my written words as bolts go into nuts. I then build bridges for the readers to cross over into my fantasy world. Next I guide them along each paragraph trail through the woods of my imagination. My wish is that they enjoy and grasp the story I created.

Beauty of the Soul

Foliage dense with sturdy branches
Stands the oak on yonder hill,
Giving birth to thoughts of grandeur
When all is silent and is still.

Birds nest among its branches
Squirrels play among its leaves,
Beauty reigns supreme in springtime
When 'tis kissed by gentle breeze.

Who can make this awesome wonder
God's creation to behold?
The Great I Am in glorious rapture
Creates beauty for the soul.

Bettye S. Blankenship
McMinnville, TN

I am an eighty-two-year-old retired teacher. I am a widow, the mother of one son who is a physician and two grandchildren. I have an MA in home economics, which I taught in secondary school for thirty years. I have three loves in my life—they are God, family and country. My greatest achievement in life is being a Christian.

Sense of Self-worth

To fill a void, all search for worth and value:
In human heart, there stirs an inner yearning
To look for love, acceptance and esteem,
A sense of value, attention and self-worth:
A struggle, an aspiration, and a dream.

Some look for worth in pleasing others;
Like leading actors on a world stage,
They hope for praise, appreciation,
Attention, focus, and congratulation,
Acceptance, love, and close association.

Some struggle for worth in work and challenge,
Like Sisyphus pushing a boulder uphill;
Accomplishment, career, reward and merit,
To strive for success and high achievement,
To earn the gold or crown and wear it.

Consider this: True worth begins with life;
God treasures His unique creation;
He loves, accepts, forgives, and understands;
To fill our void, the search begins and ends in Him;
He knows our face, our heart, our feet and hands.

Kenneth Swan
Marion, IN

[Hometown] Vincennes, IN; [DOB] April 10; [Ed] graduate degree; [Occ] teacher; [Hobbies] outdoorsman, hunting, fishing, traveling; [GA] family

The search for significance is really a search for truth—discovering yourself and ultimately discovering God. The search for truth is not an end in itself, but much is learned along the way. The journey rewards the effort. Yet there has to be a destination—knowledge of yourself (which gives us understanding of others) and knowledge of God. Scripture informs the search. Faith and commitment provide direction. What inspired this poem was my observation of others, particularly the youth who struggle so hard to find themselves and define themselves.

Lyph

Torn.
Born.
Forlorn.
My mother was torn.
I was born.
Now I'm forlorn.

Christina Moody
Murray, KY

[Hometown] *Fulton, KY;* [DOB] *December 25, 1978;* [Ed] *master's in mental health counseling;* [Occ] *Internet researcher;* [Hobbies] *walking, reading, movies;* [GA] *my children*

Poetry is my passion. I love to move people as it moves me.

Ma Is a Gem

In her youthful eyes
her pa is a king and
her ma is a gem.
Domestic violence...will not
detour her strength.
Her horses are her best friends and
her beautiful ocean waves
carry her the distance.
Oohh...the blossom of a gorgeous
flower is an island, courageous child.

C. Denise Simmonds Medina
Edison, NJ

Untitled

He was studied
while sitting there
as others walked by
welling up inside
unable to share
though much in need,
no one stopped or seemed to care
all continued to pass by
all consumed with their own I
seeded depression kept them there
emotional pain deepened the lock,
hours, days, months and years
humanity eludes this soul
multitudes question why
these tortured beings long to die
differences embed the whole
eruptions of depth spew fear,
without magic of one spark
a fire cannot survive
so let us give where others lack
willingly ignite and cause contact
light up connection to be alive
stirring embers to overcome dark.

Deborah Lynn Davey
Becket, MA

[Hometown] South Hadley, MA; [DOB] April 11, 1954; [Ed] high school, college, Institute of Children's Literature; [Occ] retired; [Hobbies] writing, drawing, reading, crafts; [GA] motherhood

In April 1954, Deborah Davey was born at Westover Air Force Base, Chicoppe. South Hadley is her hometown; both are in Massachusetts. After Deborah Williams-Davey became widowed, she studied classes through Institute of Children's Literature and devoted herself to dream of becoming a published author. Her desire was to share diverse experiences and provide hope to others. Motherhood was the greatest joy and responsibility. She enjoyed teaching children in church, was active in many other faith activities, and volunteered often in many lived communities.

The Rose

Through troubled times love
　　does not die,
It simply seems to question
　　why.
Where are the words to just
　　express.
The heartfelt answers to
　　this stress?
　　　　　　　And so it was....
He couldn't say "I love you"
He gave her a long-stemmed
　　Rose of red.
He couldn't say "My love is true"
But the red rose said it
　　instead.

Betty Manley
Deer River, MN

[Hometown] Deer River, MN; [DOB] February 21, 1930; [Ed] two-year state teacher's college; [Occ] retired daycare; [Hobbies] gardening in earlier years, writing poetry and short stories; [GA] some good impact on young lives

Marriage can experience difficult times, but with love it can survive. My poem is about this. The worst a marriage can endure is the death of a child. Our eight-year-old son walking home from church one June day was hit by a truck and died instantly. That was the winter of my life. Our marriage survived and we had fifty-three years together. We loved children. We had three sons, including the one we lost, and we adopted a little girl. We were foster parents and ran a daycare. I enjoy reading and writing poetry and short stories. I now live with a son and his wife in beautiful northern Minnesota.

Eber & Wein Publishing

Reality's Dream

Sink deep into the cold dark night.
Where fantasies and nightmares take flight
and one loses sight;
resisting the temptation of light.

Where dreams are saved in hourglass sands
that slowly slip through naked hands.

Where eyes are closed deep in thought
and inner peace is sorely sought.

There is no waking of this dream,
only other realities never seen.

Please shake me and wake me
from this crazy world of mistakes.

This make-believe land of water and sand;
where the dominant species is called....*Man.*

In this place where I cannot wake, I do not care.
For then I realize the dream is real
and that life is the true *nightmare!*

Robert J. Vogt
Schenectady, NY

[Hometown] Schenedtady, NY; [DOB] February 2, 1969; [Ed] BS in graphic design; [Occ] airport cashier; [Hobbies] drawing, writing, photography; [GA] being published here

With a college degree in art, my first love is drawing, and writing is but one hobby. Although I must confess in college I got better grades in my creative writing elective class than I did most of my drawing classes. Imagination is my biggest talent, and I'm very creative in whatever I put my mind to. Influences on my writing came from Dr. Seuss and Edgar Allan Poe at a very young age. I liked the weird and creepy words that rhymed. Although I know poems don't have to rhyme, in my opinion it isn't a poem unless it rhymes. It makes it more of a challenge. I also feel a poem should give an opinion or make a statement for the observer to think about.

Rose Petals

The rose petals are unfolding in a bizarre way He
said let's rip them off so the rose will look normal
She said I've done that too often to too many people
How can he learn when his ears only work one way
Cavemen noted causality and started the wheel rolling
If I had a paintbrush I would paint a violent still life
Apples and peaches together yet far, far apart
It says nonfiction so he believes it
Beauty is only voice deep
I will not promise anything on the grounds
It may eliminate me
So speckle your eggs you robin rust
While he and I linger in lust
Light reflects differently off different people
If my myths are destroyed I am destroyed
Overwhelming loneliness surrounded by the crowd
No one saying anything, all speaking too loud
My best talent is my ability to confuse myself
To be a revolutionary is an admirable thing
But who wants to be admired when they're dead

Barbara Steinhauser
Parker, CO

[Hometown] Parker, CO; [DOB] 1953; [Ed] MFA in writing for children and YA; [Occ] freelance writer; [Hobbies] yoga, babysitting my granddaughter; [GA] birthing three healthy children

Recently, I returned to Minnesota to place Mom in a memory care unit. This meant preparing our home of fifty-seven years for sale. In the process of cleaning out rubbish, I came upon a collection of verses I had gifted my parents while in college titled I Owe You Nothing, Nothing, Nothing—So Here for You Am I! *The poem "Rose Petals" unifies many of the ideas present within that collection.*

An Ode to Deadliest Warrior

A show that aired on Spike TV did not last long enough
It managed to combine good fun with scientific stuff

Two men who never met before are going head to head
They only have one goal: to make their adversary dead

One man we hear from on the show is Geoffrey Desmoulin
Betimes he tells the audience who he believes will win

He places cameras all throughout to use on every speed
For data as the weapon experts make the dummies bleed

The next is Armand Dorian, a doctor in L.A.
His job here is no different from a basic working day

He looks at all the damages to use as information
The data gathered here is used inside a simulation

The third is a computer guy; this fellow's name is Max
And now you know all 3 of them, so sit back and relax

Chris Oczko
Conklin, NY

Janet: The Love of My Life

Not Parkinson's nor any heart incision
Could ever drive us apart
No knife could ever pierce the space
Reserved for you in my heart

Thanks be to God for pulling me through
I've surely been blessed once again
My new life began some four years ago
As I let the words flow from my pen

I've been lifted from hell and I'm halfway to heaven
Let's take a brief pause from that ride
I don't believe I'd have made it this far
Without having you by my side

It's been over a quarter century now
Since the day we tied the knot
Soon after came the love of our lives
The birth of David-Scott

There've been ups and downs, there've been highs and lows
But no storm we couldn't weather
No matter what the obstacle was
We managed through it together

Now as the days continue to pass
We can look at each other with pride
And no matter what the future may bring
That knot will always be tied

David L. Dyer
Grosse Ile, MI

Six years ago, at age sixty-eight, I developed Parkinson's disease. Next, I had open-heart, triple-bypass surgery. This was a calling from God. While seemingly on my death bed and knowing I had a story to tell my brother, Dr. Wayne Dyer, renowned author/speaker uttered these words to me: "Do not die with your music still in you." Those words prompted a visit to the Vietnam Memorial, where I traded my alcohol addiction for sobriety in honor of all those lives that were taken. The lack of alcohol produced insomnia, which in turn put a pen in my hand.

A Lullaby Prayer

I hold you in my arms tonight—
Outside, the iv'ry moon glows bright,
To your nurs'ry, a fair, night light
Shines through the pane and calms your fright.

I rock you gently as I sing
Of One who made the moon: a King.
Tightly, your tiny, soft fingers cling
To me while I hum, then softly sing:

"The stars, dear one, that shine so clear
First shone the fourth day, now in here.
Who made them: the Lord, I love and fear;
I pray, you too, will love Him, dear.

Darling, rest well, this peaceful night
And know that God has sent His Light:
The Light to cleanse your soul, pure white,
And shed the chains of eternal night."

Heidi Ann Hildebrandt
New Richmond, WI

[Hometown] New Richmond, WI; [DOB] November 28, 1994; [Ed] Double Eagle Academy; [Occ] domestic engineering apprentice; [Hobbies] writing, reading, knitting, crocheting; [GA] will be when I marry and rear godly children

As a young lady reared and educated in a godly, biblical home, I have been taught and encouraged to fulfill God's highest calling for me as wife and mother. Currently, I spend my days at home under the guiding hands of my parents while I grow in the Lord and trust Him to provide me a godly husband in His good time. Even now, I pray a prayer similar to the one in the poem, that the children he and I will have will love Jesus and follow Him.

The Poets

We are here to make stories, to laugh and/or cry—
We are here together and everywhere,
To take and make those grand adventures like untold fantasies.
Discussing the possibilities on taking bold choices.
We are men, women and children,
At a variety of different ages and nationalities,
Creatures with minds that are capable of most anything;
Emotions that wrought, keep us on the boundary of sanity
And yet, could easily destroy our very being,
Letting us dwindle in shame and darkness—
Putting our minds into something which we could not escape its grasp;
Insanity.
Although is it not what makes it the more sincere, more beautiful?
For the world we live in will also be our end!
Ah. But think of the many ways a story can unfold,
Blossoming to new life, an innocent pure blood youngling.
What begins as a fresh start, slowly endearing the way into maturity
Shaping. Morphing. Sculpting.
There, is it when the beginnings get tough.
We are here and everywhere
Telling mysterious stories and thrilling tales,
From adventures we have taken part, as well other folk.
We are the storytellers,
Writers…
The poets.

Ezekiel J. Watkins
Renton, WA

[Hometown] Renton, WA; [DOB] January 2, 1989; [Ed] high school; [Hobbies] games, fishing, writing

It's Autumntime

Each morning has a haze,
And weather simply says:
"It's Autumntime!"
Pumpkins out on each farm,
Gather day by day charm;
It's Autumntime!
Jack Frost soon comes to call,
In coat of white for fall;
It's Autumntime!
Artists in this nation,
Lack no inspiration;
It's Autumntime.
Now fill the old wood-shed,
Get ready far ahead;
It's Autumntime!
Lovebirds will take a walk,
Admire bright leaves and talk;
It's Autumntime!

Roy G. Price
Los Angeles, CA

[Hometown] Tyler, TX; [DOB] January 24, 1934; [Ed] a bit of college; [Occ] retired at present

My Own Worst Enemy

In this dark cave
I call my mind
A path is paved
And a coil unwinds

In this dreary place
Where sin and madness play
Joy and love race
Without further delay

In my own cage
I am my own worst fear
But diminish the rage
And my heart starts to clear

In that filthy jail
When I lose all hope
A light will prevail
And I grasp a rope

In this crumbling room
That crashes to the ground
There is no longer any doom
Because I have been found

Leah Murfin
Quincy, IL

[Hometown] *Quincy, IL; [DOB] July 28, 1998; [Occ] sophomore, Quincy Notre Dame High School*

My name is Leah Murfin. I am sixteen years old, and I love writing poetry. Inspiration can strike me anywhere, at any time. I enjoy reading, writing, music, and hanging with my friends. I am honored to be accepted into this book, and I hope you enjoy my poem.

Signs

When we lay in the grass looking up at clouds
that were dragons or lambs or elephants,
calling out the shapes aimlessly because
we were too tired to run anymore,
there was no meaning in it beyond the moment…
not like the Etruscan priests in blood to their elbows
leaning over the sacrifice, eyeing the curling entrails.
Did the bulging liver mean victory beyond the Apennines?
Not like the old gypsy poking at her tea leaves
and suddenly crying, "His hand will heal!
Jango will play again."

Omens come to those shriveled by disappointment
or when time is running out.
So avoid looking above the horizon
at those ectoplasmatic shapes of arms or feet
or open mouths or eyeless heads.
Even now the map of Africa appears
like nothing but a torn heart,
one side eaten away by the gnashing of tectonic teeth,
a brokenhearted land
where the women…I think I can see them
…walking their pathways, bravely seeking God's blessings…
are ignoring the signs.

Cynthia Newgarden
Plattsburgh, NY

[Hometown] Chicago, IL; [DOB] September 23, 1925; [Ed] BS, MA in English; [Occ] English teacher; [Hobbies] reading, quilting, traveling; [GA] reciting my poem translated into Greek

As a widow, my greatest joy is my family. I've had eight children and now twenty-two grandchildren. They are all truly wonderful. If asked, they might call me a news junkie. The world calls to me. Years ago, I wrote a poem supporting the Greek war relief. This new poem is a response to the terrible news coming from West Africa. In addition to poverty and frequent injustice, people in Africa must now face the threat of the ebola virus while trying to carry on—day by day. My heart goes out to them.

Der Obstverkäufer

Aufgepasst, aufgepasst;
The Survivor, 2299
Overdosed on magic today
Day tripping and wishing
To be some life exchange
Rather than be remembered as
The boy with a bag of iron oranges,
Holding an apple and wasp
In the harvest of cherry angiomas,
And other benign events.
But never forget jester-day,
When his fire burned
Into our brightest hopes,
Standing in the angry orchard
With an atomic smile,
Pretending to be a star.
Life becomes very long,
And some children never taste citrus.
Oh this slave heart,
Would these aneurysms finally burst?

Michael Anthony Kolbash
Tucson, AZ

[Hometown] Wayne, NJ; [DOB] December 10, 1992; [Ed] BS in physiology, BA in German

We'll Make It Through, Sunflower

Broken promises rest easy in the lines of her palms
Words flow easy for her when sung in a song
Written by someone she's never met, never seen
Except on the pages of a magazine
He begs her to see her beauty. "You're a queen."
He continues to whisper with the beat of the music,
"You're more than just a girl marked with bruises."
His words hit her harder than anything
She listens to his voice content on believing
But he's telling her she's beautiful and amazing
Yet when she looks in the mirror she feels worthless and defeated
She picks out every flaw, every scar
She's the only one who sees through her performance
To hid the broken girl within.
She walks away from the mirror with a clouded mind
And listens one more time as hot tears roll down her face
His voice cuts through the dark
It wraps around her to block out her doubt
Her tears dry as the song finally fades out
He sings the last lines and she's finally able to believe him
"You'll make it through this, you're not alone, darling.
I'm here for you, always."

Georgia Sroka
Decherd, TN

[Hometown] Winchester, TN; [DOB] December 29, 1997; [Ed] high school; [Occ] student; [Hobbies] music, writing, reading

I'm a high school student trying to fight my way through life. The thing that inspired this poem was music. Music sometimes is the only thing that can break through my walls and make an impression on me.

I Love You

I love you until the end of time. I love you because you are my best friend.

I love you because the world would be cold if I didn't have you by my side.

I love you more than rain and shine, but most of all, I love God for putting us to comfort and protect one another from good or evil ways of people in this world.

I'm inspired as a woman to love you; only you.

So if you asked me if I made the wrong choice, I'd say what God would say: it's good.

Nina Chaney
Davison, MI

[Hometown] Pontiac, MI; [DOB] February 9, 1987; [Ed] associate's degree in liberal arts, bachelor's degree in human biology with a minor in computer information systems; [Occ] receptionist; [Hobbies] writing poetry, reading sci-fi and romance novels, walking, volunteering with Home & Hospice when I can; [GA] three hundred hours of community service through commitment to service at University of Michigan–Flint campus; recently graduating in human biology with a minor in computer information systems at the UM–Flint; also completing my studies at Oakland Community College where I received my associate's in liberal arts

What inspired my writing of poetry is the observance I have been exposed to over the course of my entire life—the amusement I longed for through my journey of good or bad times—whether a bad breakup or simply wanting to be loved as we all do. I want to help those who've fallen learn to view it as a lesson of life but still overcome.

When I Was Turning Fifty

When I was turning fifty,
A friend of mine once said,
All the troubles with growing old
Are looming just ahead.

Soon you'll have the aching joints,
Your memory begins to fade;
Soon you'll have more pills than friends,
Then you start the bathroom parade.

So pay some attention to this tale
And dry up all those wasted tears;
Your hair turns white and your teeth turn yellow,
Welcome to the Golden Years!

James W. Mayou
Mashpee, MA

[Hometown] Mashpee, MA; [DOB] June 21, 1949; [Ed] associate's degree in engineering; [Occ] part-time merchandiser, Kellogg's; [Hobbies] baseball cards, writing poetry, bowling; [GA] marrying my wife, Nancy

I love writing poetry. Many of my poems are patriotic but occasionally I write about love and humor. I wrote the poem, "When I Was Turning Fifty," for a good friend who was turning fifty. I wanted to poke fun at growing old and also poke fun at the golden years in general. Growing old has its ups and downs but it is just another page in your life.

The Beach

Searching for seashells along the sandy beach,
I see another; I stoop and reach
For the loveliest shell to give my friend.
I see another shell, and I bend
To pick up another pretty shell.
When I see my friend I've a lot to tell.
The waves gently invade the shore,
Uncovering seashells while I pick up more
Different sizes and textures of shells today;
On the beach I find I could stay.
The waves gently cover my feet;
Then the waves slowly retreat.
I can see my footprints on the sand;
Then the waves come back to the land.
Now they're starting to pound the shore.
They pound, retreat and pound once more.

Ava Hill
Eldon, MO

Rescued

My Lord, it seems that, once again, You've answered my deep prayer,
And all my constant daily pleas, for help from my despair.
My Lord, I give You all the glory, You deserve such praise and more!
You're such a loving Father, whom I love so and adore!

My Lord I'm just so deeply awed, each time You show me love,
For every time You show me how, You're watching from above!
You know me as no other one, and every deep desire,
You know I need You in my life, in all that does transpire!

When I recall the brokenness and the pain I suffered through,
For all I learned to believe in, came crashing Lord in two!
'Twas then, my Lord, as You know, I felt my life had died,
I felt I could not carry on, nor did I want to try.

'Twas then I crawled to You, my Lord, like a crippled child I'd come,
Confused at how my life had changed, so empty, broken, and numb!
With a heart so deeply broken, a soul with scarce a flame,
With joy completely vanished, a life so wracked with pain.

You rescued me, Lord, from a pit of despair, and bathed me in mercy and grace,
You cradled me in compassion, Lord, and dried the tears from my face.
You held me as a frightened child and nourished me back to health,
You filled my soul with such a fire and a faith of more value than wealth.

I know I can never repay You, Lord, no matter how hard I try,
So I shall always be grateful Lord, for Your mercy in saving my life!

Darlene Ware Horzepa
Ormond Beach, FL

I'm so grateful and humbled for this great opportunity to touch the souls of all who hear or read my work! My goal in life is no different than any other believer in Christ, to reach out and touch the souls of all who hear the message of God's love and forgiveness. As John T. Eber Sr. says, "We're leaving our heartprints and legacy for future generations to come." I'm a single mother living in Florida with my greatest achievement, my twenty-six-year-old son. My dream has always been to publish my own book and, until that happens, I'm grateful to have them published one by one. Eventually, the right publisher will see its potential and make this dream come true! Thank you, Eber & Wein for believing in my gift and helping me touch the souls who need it most!

Seeds

Saturday morning I planted some seed
Didn't follow instructions I had no need

What does it matter God will take care
When the garden is prolific I'll begin to share

Weeds not a problem I'll make my own mulch
Veggies will be healthy and my heart will boast

No one's garden will be better than mine
I'll nurture and nourish it and all will be fine

The universe hails that a woman did great
Mother Earth is our essence; it's bound to our fate.

Marilyn Maddalone
Acra, NY

Autumn

My soul drifts from place to place
As my spirit flies free and high
The birds chirp from the sky
Squirrels playing at my feet
The sweet summer breeze
As it turns to fall
Watching all the leaves turn colors
As the harvest comes, and we carve the pumpkins
Before you know it, it's autumn

Heather Stephanie Lewis
Cockeysville, MD

Common Sense

To those who were born without this trait
I'll let you know, I'll set you straight
For those who rhyme without a reason
I'll let you in on this unknown season

Common sense as it is commonly called
Should not be called that at all
For though we think we all possess it
I think that we should reassess it
For this sense is quite unfound
In the most of us around
For if we knew
What we think we do
Would we be better off?

And if a shouter and a scholar
Put their wits to test
I'd think they'd find
Common sense is quite uncommon
I put my case to rest

Marcy L. Bowser
Newark, OH

I wrote this poem many years ago. My husband really likes this poem, so I thought I would share it. I am a homemaker and a mother. I worked as a secretary for many years, and now I am working as a resolution specialist. My husband and I enjoy spending time with our children and their families. We also enjoy camping among other hobbies. Writing poetry has always been a passion for me, so I appreciate this opportunity to share it.

You Are Here

Your laugh is in the rustle of leaves,
    as the wind blows through them...

Your smile is in the rays of sun,
    warming my face...

Your strength is in the rock,
    day after day withstanding the elements...

Your touch is in the wings of the butterfly,
    kissing my skin while fluttering by...

Your beauty is in the vibrant colors
    of the sunset...

Your love remains with us,
    keeping you in our hearts.

Beth A. Romano
Fitchburg, MA

[Hometown] Fitchburg, MA; [Ed] BA from Wheaton College, MA from Assumption College, CAGS from Fitchburg State University; [Occ] middle school counselor; [Hobbies] golf, cooking, kick boxing, walking the beach and reading; [GA] helping my students find success in their lives

This poem was inspired by the realization that even after our loved ones have passed from this life, we can still find that their love and spiritual presence are with us. This one is for you, EBM.

Welcome Home

A young boy trying his best to survive in a world of unrest!
He joined the army—he thought that was best.
He did himself proud—he passed the test!
From Oklahoma, Iraq he was bound. Arches he saw
from his campground!
There for a year—that's such a long time!
Dear Lord, I pray, keep him safe every day!
Home for the holidays—Thanksgiving we had.
Where to next? Africa he said.
So tall, so lean and so quiet too,
I sit and I wonder what's in your head?
A gunman, a sergeant, and a part of a team—
doing what he was trained to do—
to protect this nation and the family he loves too!
I'm so thankful to the dear Lord above.
My prayers were answered—*He* brought you home!
Now it's *our* turn to stand by *you*—
to protect, honor and listen too!
We have no idea what he's been through—
some things are kept quiet to help them endure!
Let's not forget! We're not the ones who left our homes,
who stood in harms way and did what he had to do!
Welcome home, Sergeant Rose!
We're so proud of you!

Olivia Alban
Deer Park, WA

[Hometown] Fresno, CA; [DOB] March 3, 1949; [Ed] high school; [Occ] educator: homeschool K–12 children; [Hobbies] painting and wedding consultant; [GA] birth of my two children

This is written in honor of my grandson, Brandon Rose, who served this country while in the army. His family is so proud of him and love him very much!

Family

In 1947 I met the love of my life
The following year I became his wife.
It is great to live with someone
With whom you feel loved and also have fun

From this union we had one daughter and four boys.
They made us proud and brought us many joys.
We have two granddaughters, one grandson and one step-grandson.
We also have two great-granddaughters and two great-grandsons.

At our house sports were a way of life
Sometimes it was almost strife.
The boys were very athletic
While the daughter was very scholastic.

The daughter is a retired school teacher
The oldest son is a restaurateur.
The second son is a color stylist painter
The third son is a truck driver and the youngest son is a mail carrier.

Carolyn Hurley
Thomasville, NC

[Hometown] Thomasville, NC; [DOB] September 16, 1929; [Ed] one and a half years of college; [Occ] sixteen years rural mail carrier; [Hobbies] my flowers, canning fruits and vegetables; [GA] in 2005 I went to Brazil

In school I always enjoyed English class. It was my favorite subject. In 1987 we lost my husband to renal failure. I retired from the postal service in 1988. The children are very good to me. They see that I have everything that I need. I am blessed.

Moon Over Jade Grasses

One day we shall meet in a
Place sacred to my very heart
Where giant pine trees are the
Honored gate keepers
In this forest bright and dark.

Warm white sandy beaches
Await mystical blue waters
To kiss its shoreline sweet
A morning dove sings a melody
Of her solitude and peace.

As pink and orange sunsets
Come and go silently behind
The many hills and trees
This moment of twilight hushed
In time.

Jade green are the tall grasses
Bowing in summer's tame wind
Beneath this wild crescent moon
I sit near the water's edge
Embracing memories of the precious
Loved ones I once knew.

Rebecca A. Borreson
Sparta, WI

[Hometown] New Amsterdam, WI; [DOB] July 5, 1963; [Ed] high school and home school; [Occ] bartender when I was eighteen, now I am disabled; [Hobbies] photography, writing poetry, feeding birds, bird watching; [GA] having children, a boy and a girl

I am a nature enthusiast. Also, I love to fish, plant flower gardens, and be around horses. I grew up on a hobby farm, so we had many farm animals—also two horses. I really like exploring new places while camping. Right behind my house are many beautiful places to see on a long trail in the forest. I love to walk up there to see wildlife and all the different trees. This poem was inspired by the beauty in nature, family losses and the giant pine trees in the woods just behind my home.

The Hunter

I started hunting as a young boy.
The first years had little success.
Each year thereafter brought me joy
because I listened, read and did my best.

I learned of ridges, funnels, crossings
and how to track. I learned a trophy
is in the eye of the hunter,
not in the size of the rack.

The sights and sounds of autumn guns
I thought would always be mine,
but time is clearly tracking me
and grows more and more unkind.

As I sit in my blind this season,
aware it could be my last,
I know memories will surround me
painting pictures of the past.

William E. Muehlmann
Midland, MI

[Hometown]Frankfort, MI; [DOB] July 28, 1937; [Ed] X-Ray studies NIH, two years; [Occ] registered rad. tech; [Hobbies] hunting, fishing, training retrievers; [GA] marrying my wife, Nadene

After high school, I became a merchant seaman on Lake Michigan. After four years, I was accepted at the National Institutes of Health (radiology) in Bethesda, MD. I worked in hospitals for thirty-three years. I love to carve traditional duck decoys, train my labs, golf, hunt and fish.

A Memory

He was there
at the mouth of the Nile—
Where was I?
He was there
where stairs wind upward
to nights of fire
but empty of me.
Where was I?
On the calm of the shore
down thousands of miles
Where was I?
The ibis I had seen with his mate
the Nile source's queen,
but he was alone in Africa's green.
Where was I?
With me at the spring and him
at the head—the distance meant nothing
and time went ahead to the night
where longings are heard
and dreams come awake—
Where his face and mine blended
once
on the timeless river Nile.

Monique Adam
Oakland, CA

I was born in Paris, France on July 18. I have my two French Baccalaureates, a BA from Barnard and some graduate work on organizational theory, graduate policy and literature (French and German). Presently, I am retired. I write, teach French at home, and read avidly. Books, flowers and my cat, as well as movies, are my hobbies.

Please Don't Cry for Me

Even though it was too soon for me to leave,
Please don't cry for me.
We've had good times and happy memories.
We smiled, we laughed
We played, we fought
So please don't cry for me.
Just remember one thing:
I will always be in your heart
And forever in your memories.

Elizabeth Hayes
Muncie, IN

[Hometown] Mexico, IN; [DOB] March 18, 1994; [Ed] high school; [Occ] waitress; [Hobbies] acting, writing, and crocheting; [GA] graduating high school and playing with my bandmates one last time

I wrote this poem for my Aunt Michelle. She may have been stubborn and maybe a little bit crazy, but she was my aunt. I could tell her anything and she wouldn't tell a soul if I asked her to keep it a secret. She was not only my aunt, she was my best friend, and I miss her very much. Michelle Lynn Hickling, November 13, 1973–January 1, 2014.

Halloween Night

Halloween night gave me an awful fright.
I stepped down the street to see a vicious cat fight,
Feral friends battling to the death,
Territorial boundaries determined by the winner.
Screams and howls filled the silent night.

By the light of the moon I could see the fur and claws fly into the air.
With sudden urgency did they attack.
All the commotion attracted more to the pack.
Wounded combatants rolled and tumbled just like a ball of yarn.
My how the cats of the night do rumble.

Suzanne Parker
Maryville, TN

[Hometown] Maryville, TN; [DOB] March 18, 1963; [Ed] BSN, ASN, AA in general education; [Occ] registered nurse, writer; [Hobbies] writing, running, music, reading; [GA] running 26.2 miles, my education, publishing poetry

I would have to say that Halloween is a very fun holiday. I enjoy this holiday the most and Thanksgiving second. I like Christmas, but Halloween has a magical, fun quality to it. I love to decorate with pumpkins and to see all the different costumes. I wrote "Halloween Night" this year to celebrate autumn—my favorite season of them all.

Sister by Osmosis

Bouncy, bubbly, beautiful baby sister
Explodes with energy day and night and
Can make you laugh until you hiccup uncontrollably

Animals come up and eat out of her hand
While she tumbles like tumble weed in the
Hot desert sand

Loving little lass
With long loopy hair and
Freckles, freckles, everywhere
And not a single spot to spare

The best loving little sister
Anyone could have

Kayleigh Smith
Richmond, TX

[Hometown] Richmond, TX; [Ed] high school student; [Occ] piano teacher; [Hobbies] design, art, writing, photography

Although writing is a big part of my life, my "sister" and I share interests in art and love to create together. Be it painting or photography, we do it together, and that is what matters the most. I love her with all my heart and can't wait to continue our growth together as creative partners.

Invitation to Share the Rest of My Life

Leaving our prints upon the sand
Walking along hand in hand
Luscious dreams of you and me
Embracing my mind
In the wildest of ease.

In picturing this moment
Over a thousand times before,
In my most precious dreams,
I know I couldn't love you more.

And this is why, from tonight
Through the end of time,
I give you my *love*
With the rarest of thine.

Shawndra Lyn Daniels
San Augustine, TX

[Hometown] Battle Creek, MI; [DOB] October, 1968; [Ed] Kellogg's Community College '89; [Occ] poet, retired naval wife; [Hobbies] crafting, drawing, singing, being a grandma; [GA] my family, being me, living life to the fullest

I am "Momma" to all who know me. I am a mother of three and a new grandmother, too, and a "Neothinker." I served as a naval spouse in Pearl Harbor, HI, until 2007. I had my first poem published in 2006, internationally had one published in 2007, and am still achieving writing more poetry. I have a children's book being published soon called Mother Dragon, and I am working to achieve more. This poem was written for a very special moment of my life that only continues to this day. And with each moment, I am blessed and very thankful.

The House of My Childhood Is Gone

1932 to 1946

Houses, I once read, retain the memories left behind
by the people who once lived in them.
So, on a visit to St. Louis in the 1970s I returned to 3904 Cleveland,
hoping for a chance to walk through
to see if the mirrors reflected the images of my family's faces
as they were in the 1930s and '40s,
or if I still could smell fresh flowers in vases throughout the house,
or if the sound of exploding bottles of Grandpa's home brew
or Grandma's ketchup echoed from the basement,
or if the voices in all those rooms were still audible—
the gay laughter, the hateful arguments—
but most of all the sound of my Uncle Walter and I
singing along with the Gramophone
as it played the operettas he taught me to love.
But I found the house of my childhood was gone,
burned down years before, I was told, by a careless boy
playing with candles that ignited curtains
in the room where I once slept.
All of my family who lived there are now dead,
and all that remains of the place are my memories
and a vacant lot so narrow I wonder how it could have contained
the 3-story brick building that lingers so large in my mind's eye.

Bill Cento
West St. Paul, MN

I ran across a quote that might fit this time in my life of looking back: "...with the normal aches and pains that come with moving past eighty and also the sadness of seeing more than a few friends grow ill and die, mortality is on my mind."

My Daughter

Today the earth and the skies sing in harmony
Today the sun's immensity caresses my soul
Today she looked at me for the first time
Today I cried; it was of joy
Today nothing but love is in my heart

Today she was born
Today all is love
Today I've found my God

Today her eyes and my eyes saw the eternity
Today the love divinity embraces us both
Today because of her, my life begins
Today I have smiled; it was of joy
Today I've finally found peace within me

Today she was born
Today all is love
Today God reigns in me

Pablo Hugo Penalver
Ridgewood, NY

[Hometown] New York; [DOB] January 1, 1947; [Ed] second year of pharmacology; [Occ] retired; [Hobbies] writing, painting, hand crafting; [GA] my children

My poem was inspired by the blessed gift of my daughter, Angelica Maria Birth; a God-unique and beloved life present.

What Am I?

I am insecure
I am afraid
I am broken
I am withdrawn
But
I am also a dreamer
I am a fighter
I am heart-strong
And I am a survivor.
I am who I am,
nothing can change that.
What am I?
I am my flaws,
But my flaws aren't me.

Aisha Hellman-Lohr
Austin, TX

[Hometown] Austin, TX; [Occ] student

My Help

An expression.
An impression.
I didn't.

Could you have ever?
Seen my smile?
For a while?

Disconcerted for elation;
Alive like a genius;
I lost you…

Are we stars in the sky?
Did you see?
Alone is you? Is me?

Wind my willows.
Pain counts.
Let not.

At a point!
Don't spoil it!
Are we there, yet?!
No! We are not…quite…
There, yet!

Samantha Conrique
Hemet, CA

*[Hometown] Hemet, CA; [DOB] November 6, 1966; [Ed] school and life studies; [Occ] housewife; [Hobbies]
cross stitch and other; [GA] talking to my children and family, their love*

*In my childhood, I was everywhere with only glimpses of God, but protected, then, from the cross of Christ—I
married. I bore children, four. Five years later…onto a major anxiety attack, depressionistic, bipolarism and
worse. My husband gave me a roof and food for what I was worth to him. I couldn't understand why there was
so much time lost in cereal bowls and dog poops. A widow at forty, I am still wanting to provide for my family.
They grew gracefully into adulthood. Their abilities to be apart and their wisdom bring much happiness. Good
for bad/bad for good—I am trying to choose my life, now. Whence, my husband? I don't know.*

Fire

The motion of leaping flames,
Feeding on carbon with names,
Reproducing with sparks and coals,
Breathing and taking its toll,
Energy begetting energy,
Dies and leaves a legacy.
Worshipped by Druids and sages
Igniting the millions of ages.
Is it alive? We're curious,
Does it evolve, like us?
Creation of fire by the Universe
Gave rise to this curious verse.

Camille Einoder
Chicago, IL

[Hometown] Chicago, IL; [DOB] the dark ages; [Ed] multiple degrees; [GA] thinking

It Isn't Enough

There are some sacrifices a parent has to make,
Hoping that their children will learn from their mistakes.
To love and guide them isn't enough.
So what is the answer? It must be prayers,
To keep them safe from what's out there.
We all love our children, at times it isn't enough.

Gloria Esperanza
Sun Valley, NV

Kindness Eternal

Kindness eternal—smiles radiate warmth
Inspiration leads the soul to dance
Generosity abounds joyously
Magic of man unleash creativity
Charity enlightens the dark
The heart song sings

Shannon J. Schultheis
Santa Fe, NM

[Hometown] Santa Fe, NM; [DOB] July 21, 1970; [Ed] AA in human services; [GA] getting my degree and being there for my family

My family has always been there for me. Your love is priceless!

Wind

Wind is blowing so hard, not sure if it makes it right,
Not sure of many things that come my way and willing to understand in many ways,
The stronger wind blows the harder to see which way to go or just stay still.
Wizard me in anyway and just complete my wishing well,
My guardian angels are above to complement or see my fall,
I guess it all is just to me to grant myself be free and flee,
Peaceful words coming to me just complement your inner be!

Natasha Yonker
Pearland, TX

I was born in St. Petersbourgh, Russia. I love to do everything creative. I finished art school in St. Petersbourgh and interior design school in London, England. I love to write poems too.

The Stab of Maybe

This is no home
But a sterile operating room
Under general anesthesia
Yet sensitized
We muster our bid before the razor's edge
Hoping this cut will be more precise

You are no lover
But a volunteer for the needy
Bearing capsules of benevolence
You go the rounds
Letting your heart bleed when it's necessary
Dropping the empty cup at the door

I am no man
But a white gown showing crimson stains
Constant desire for assurance
And fulfillment
Waxes and wanes while I am writhing in pain
Punctured by the stab of maybe

Jeffrey Magnuson
San Diego, CA

Parents' Legacy: Sharing

From childhood, my Pa had shown what sharing is:
He'd stop a bare-footed vendor of fruits and veggies
With paper and pencil, her dusty feet he'd trace,
With instruction to see him the following week.

He'd cut a branch of our acacia tree
Then shaped it to a pair of wooden shoes
Flapped with strips of sack-cloth to fit the toes
When given, the vendor would jump and yell with glee!

My Ma also had a way of sharing her talent
She'd buy 3 lbs of meat each market day
She'd cook adobo, calderetta, barbeque and lo mien
Come Sundays, her 4 siblings would enjoy free buffets!

With those sharings imprinted in my mind—
When married to an equally open-handed man
Gladly, we'd help and share our limited funds
With kin, neighbors, friends and deserving ones.

Now, with 50 years of married life
We can claim having helped 24 professionals
Nurses, lawyers, engineers, teachers, accountants
Who now have uplifted their own family lives.

With 1000 pairs of donated schoolkid shoes
Entrusted to us by our parish church
To six village grade schools in the Philippines
We distributed the shoes to excited and happy kids!

Francine T. Savellano
Jersey City, NJ

[Hometown] Buguey, Cagayan, Philippines; [DOB] April 26, 1936; [Ed] BS of literature in journalism, cum laude; [Occ] retired, currently a Eucharistic minister; [Hobbies] traveling, fishing, reading and serving the Lord; [GA] 1999 Grand Marshal, PDOC Parade & Festival, Passaic City, NJ; 2012 New Jersey Parents of the Year

My poem was inspired by the mercy mission my husband and I had undertaken in the Philippines— distributing one thousand pairs of shoes to bare-footed school children in six remote villages of Cagayan and Ilocos Sur, Philippines. Unfortunately, during the week of our mission, typhoons "Luis," "Mario," and "Neneng" hit the areas, saddling us with gusty winds and heavy rains. But with God's mercy, we were able to withstand the inclement weather and accomplish our mission safely and successfully.

Gone but Not Forgotten

The past has slipped away so gently I would say,
The loves we share, our hopes, our inspirations.
Our failures and despairs.
But through it all we gave it to Him to share.
And with his loving care He taught us how to bear,
So farewell to thee wherever you may be.
My loving Lord in Heaven has set me free.
So, hello there New Year's Eve!
For now, I'm ready for Thee no matter what the year may bring.
But know for sure my heart and soul will always remain free.
Because my wonderful Lord has shown me the path we all so truly need.

Gloria C. Schumacher
Chicago, IL

[Hometown] Evanston, IL; [DOB] April 20, 1931; [Ed] nursing at Evanston Hospital; [Occ] federal nurse US Navy; [Hobbies] dancing on roller skates; [GA] grammar, high school after twenty years old

I'm German, Danish, Swedish and a wee bit of Irish. Life was not easy growing up, but what is?! I learned more about others and to love and care no matter who they were. Especially those with disabilities. My oldest brother never walked a day in his life and died at the tender age of twenty. I love music and to sing it with deep feeling. I still love to dance on roller skates and in a rink with old-time, real music. I started my poetry in my twenties, and with feelings. I also write short stories and some music.

Quiet Awakening

Young sir, I am a willow
I see your mother crying at the sink
Almost every day
She will tell you it is onions
I hold cardinals and mockingbirds
on my limbs to cheer her
Sir, you are asleep, dreaming of clipper ships
and I am talking to you
Do you believe me?
That's odd, he murmurs
So real, so sad—
Something he did not know
Putting on robe and slippers
he pads to sink for glass of water
and there on cypress sill rests a cardinal
fluffed up sweetly in cool night breeze
Willows, he calls softly, and willow again
what am I to do?
Setting down glass, he wipes his eyes
Now in darkened room
there is a rustling and scent of pine
from candle lit upon the stair
Son, what's wrong? Comes the gentle voice from there
I don't know, he cries
blankly staring into the night—
I don't know.

David M. Schmidt
Panama City, FL

Beyond Words

You can see it in their eyes,
It's almost a whisper.
A visible touching, not of the hands,
A face to love, they understand.

They've been together more than years,
Can a lifetime really be measured?
They shared each other's bread and bed,
Together always everyone said.

A wife and family are very fine,
But they fade from memory in time,
But my dog's companionship is above the rest,
Will lay beside me, in my time of eternal rest.

Edward Cohen
Glen Oaks, NY

[Hometown] New York City; [DOB] September 29, 1930; [Ed] James Monroe High School; [Occ] retired;
[Hobbies] writing poems; [GA] in the making

My Heart's Deepest Desire

Like a dagger through my heart every word you said to thee,
but I still love you for it is the way you feel for me that
changed my world. Yes my heart beats for thee.
What more can you ask of me? I can't bear it be
this way, the way we were when a thousand
miles apart. I know you say it isn't that far, but I
know it is because the distance or rather I should say
the loneliness haunts me at night. I still hold on to your
desires deep in my heart. We shall love in such a way
they all shall reminisce throughout the ages just how
deep the rivers of romance flowed between
us. You are my deepest emotion. I love thee too
much. It was love, then by destinies powers this love
was banished away into the land of heartbreak.

Gohar Minassian
Los Angeles, CA

[Hometown] Hollywood, CA; [DOB] June 24, 1989; [Ed] BS in animation; [Occ] designer and painter in the animation industry; [Hobbies] fashion design, tae kwon do; [GA] Gold Medal from US Congress

The inspiration of my poem came from a very handsome young man whom I met during the summer of 2008. He will always have a special place in my heart. The awards in my life that I am most proud of are my four medals from the US Congress.

Dream, Little Girl

Welcome to my dream
The smell of fresh mountain air
It's a crisp, refreshing burst
Colors changing, leaves falling

My saddle, a well-fitted glove
My horse bears me well
My fence long, fervently ridden

My eyes bright and wide
I'm as free as the wind
As I ride, I glide through it
As though I was meant to part the air

My heart light and full of joy
I'm complete as a woman
Riding on, my completion draws me near

For there stands a man
His faith brings his shoulders wide
His love seen on the outside
His admiration holds my glance
Dream on, little girl
Dream big, little girl

Mary G. Heitman
Whitefish, MT

[Hometown] Trego; [DOB] August 29, 1981; [Ed] cosmetologist entrepreneur; [Occ] personal assistant; [Hobbies] snowboarding, camping and biking

I am a straight-up Montana girl. I love the mountains, the lakes and the freedom to experience beauty on a daily basis. I love to smell the rain, feel the snow coming, and breathe in every scent that summer and spring brings. The earth is my inspiration—the relationships, the hurt, the pain, the love. From every successful person who's written books, I've learned two basic things: Never stop moving and believe in something!

The Little White House

Going back home to live in the house
of my childhood has so many memories some
are happy, some sad.
Looking over the fields where cotton and
corn grew when I was a kid and the hard
work we did making us so tired at the
end of the day.
Then it was time for us to go to school
it was walking over the fields and through
the woods and streams for two or three miles
to the school house whether it was
sunshine, rain or snow.
But living in this house makes me happy
no matter where I have gone or have been.
My twin brother, mom and dad, who have
gone to our home beyond the river leaves
me so many memories.
As I close my eyes I can hear echoes of
running feet and laughter of voices from the
childhood we shared together.
Mom has her pots and pans to fill with
food as she calls to us saying it's supper time.
Dad is listening to the news so he can keep
up with what's happening in the world.

Jewell Roper
Cullman, AL

[Hometown] Cullman, AL; [DOB] January 13, 1928; [Ed] high school; [Occ] retired; [Hobbies] writing, poetry and stories, yardwork, flowers, sewing, traveling; [GA] retiring and enjoying my senior year

I was born in Cullman, AL on January 13, 1928, but I also have a twin brother, Euell Williams, as he lived in Cullman until his death six years ago. My parents, Leeota and Henry Williams, have passed away, but they always have been supportive of anything I wanted to do with my life. I have a daughter, Sabrina Wagmon, two grandsons, Trenton and Dalton Williams, and one great-grandson, Michael Williams. I wrote poetry in high school, but over years it was misplaced. I started writing again in 1987.

Soul Mate

This is for you my soul mate if you could have only
seen inside my heart.
Now you're gone and it's too late to tell you how much
I loved you right from the start.
You were always with me and I depended on you a lot.
Now all I have are memories and my thoughts.
You got sick and my heart went out to you.
There is nothing worse than to see
what you were going through.
We never had the time to say how we felt
about each other.
Now you're at peace with your father and mother.
No, you will never know how much I loved you so.
Goodbye my soul mate, my love.
God willing I'll see you in Heaven above.

Eileen Vigil
Walsenburg, CO

[Hometown] Walsenburg, CO; [DOB] March 22, 1943; [Ed] high school graduate; [Occ] retired; [Hobbies] writing, reading, crocheting; [GA] having my poems published

I love to write poetry and have been writing for years. I also love reading, and I keep myself busy crocheting. I go to Bible classes twice a week. I am a mother and grandmother. I had a wonderful relationship with Michael, who was diagnosed with Alzheimer's at an early age. It progressed rapidly. Before I could make sense of it, he passed on. He will always be a part of my heart, and because of him I was inspired to write this poem.

Smile

The things we hear with our very ear;
Good music, a cat's purr, "I love you, dear."
Can sometimes startle, sometimes soothe,
Can be so subtle, and that's the truth.

Do you hear the bird fly through the air,
Or the clouds drift by without a care?
Or as you talk across the miles,
Can you hear a loved one when he smiles?

I do believe you can hear a smile,
The voice takes on a certain style.
A lilt, a tremor, a soft, soothing tone.
Voila! I heard you smile across the phone!

Jamie Sutton
Bossier City, LA

*[Hometown] Bossier City, LA; [DOB] March 10, 1939; [Ed] two years college; [Occ] retired from AT&T;
[Hobbies] writing poetry; [GA] becoming one of Jehovah's Witnesses*

*I went to college for two years, but wasn't interested in the few career choices open to women in those days.
Then I got a job at Southern Bell in Shreveport, LA as a telephone operator. I later landed a "man's" job as
a switchman in the equipment room with step-by-step electromechanical switches that phone calls went
through. I loved my job. I have written poetry occasionally through the years, and it became a hobby. I like
mostly happy, funny stuff, and my poems are sort of like love letters to the readers.*

Forgiveness

A gentle ear that's full of love,
has accepted God's grace, sent from above.
A childlike soul so simple and pure,
will inherit the earth, if it can endure.

Along life's way comes a twist of fate,
ushering in dark emotions of lust, anger and hate!
We're taught so young to be good and kind,
that failure begins to play tricks with our mind!

Guilt soon becomes our very best friend
binding our heart in thorns, never letting it mend.
Sit down, relax, take a moment to breathe,
think like a child, who's happy and carefree.

An innocent soul can be ours again,
If we shed our pride and let God enter in.
"I'm sorry" are words God loves to hear,
that erases the torture we've felt through the years.

We're born into this world to be His beacon of light;
forgiveness and mercy make our heart's flame ignite!
Share your joy every day with a heartwarming smile,
Let others know they're not alone in their trials!

Vicki Griffin
Houston, TX

[Hometown] Meadville, PA; [DOB] November 19, 1951; [Ed] high school, religious studies, Carmelite Secular Order; [Occ] homemaker, Secular Carmelite; [Hobbies] writing, art, bird watching, experiencing nature; [GA] love of family, my faith

For thirty-seven years, I've been married to my best friend, Les, whose keen insight encourages me to strive harder toward perfection in all my endeavors. We are blessed with two sons, Les Jr. and Ken; a daughter-in-law, Kathleen, who is married to Les Jr.; and their eighteen-month-old son, Drake, who is a delight to us all. My family and my faith have brought me profound experiences that allow me to bring stories alive in the melodic verse of poetry. It is my desire that you find peace-filled hope within my words.

Independence Day

Oh! America, beautiful America.
'Tis the land of liberty, opportunity and prosperity.
We joyfully celebrate our birthday
On this Independence Day,
Which we didn't achieve easily.
Throughout the saga of wars,
Our valiant, honorable heroes
Shed their blood, sweat and tears
While they fought courageously on the battlefields.
We are grateful and thankful for their sacrifices.
Ultimately their triumphs and victories
With great acclaim acquired our freedom.
Incorporated too, with John Adams and his fellow patriots,
Were advocates for independence from England.
Therefore, we hold these truths of evidences to be true,
To commemorate and observe the Fourth of July
As our admirable historical Independence Day.
To acknowledge it with a national holiday, which was proclaimed,
And Old Glory proudly displayed on poles and elsewhere,
As colorful marching bands and planes demonstrated in the sky.
In the night, fireworks brilliantly lit up the celestial sky.
To suffice our enjoyment, we dine on gourmet foods with a merry heart.
Happy anniversary, America.
God bless America.

Wilbert Roberts
Port St. Lucie, FL

26 Lines or Less

Down with slight force goes the finger on the key
the lead point, the ink and the ball
A welcome home to the whispers, echoed cross that vast unseen
Here we enter with a joyful blindness
and a shameless look inward, outward, toward the hellfire of
virtue, and the blessing of sin
Another flare has risen from yet another's 'planet me'
a restless guild well dormant though perpetual at once
an enigma so simple, its puzzles never solved
the heart, the sun, dispositions of near all that creeps
its way into our notice
Twenty-six lines or less, daunting, though a mere stanza
in the long verse we inhale and exhale along this
stage of the morning
I think of all the others out there, strangers of the same
ilk, not saved or lost, or with any insight that will close
the case of any search in any place
I think on us all, poised at the top of some parchment
and I pray for our pride in the burden of our pulse,
as we embark on another march through vocabulary
to weep, or kill, or love
Down with slight force, the quill, the stick in the sand,
the finger in the wind
the nod to one another, as we endeavor,
as we be.

Daniel J. Alden
Spring Lake Heights, NJ

[Hometown] Spring Lake Heights, NJ; [DOB] March 7, 1974; [Ed] high school grad; [Occ] fence installer/ truck driver; [Hobbies] music, movies, reading, Audree (fiancée); [GA] yet to be determined

I have been actively reading and writing poetry for as long as I can remember, but it's only recently that I decided to try my hand at submitting. I think this poem will speak for itself and it's my way of saying hello to the rest of you poets out there at every level. Enjoy, and I can't wait to read your work.

Guided from Above

There are times we feel that we are
In tranquility, just to realize it's our beginnings
To our mortality. Some of us can appreciate
What life can offer, for we can stop and think
At one time that we no longer would suffer.
For there's a God that can guide us through any
Situation, as we go to a place where we can
Meditate, and are able to realize our purpose
And to go into with so much motivation. And
As we conquer our days, there he will be
Clearing our ways.

Carlos W. Rodriguez
Lancaster, CA

[Hometown] El Salvador, San Salvador; [DOB] October 15, 1961; [Ed] high school; [Occ] plumbing supply wholesale; [Hobbies] bowling, movie theaters, crafts, fishing; [GA] writing poetry

The poems I write are based on all the challenges and obstacles I go through each day that I live. With the help of my savior, our God, He and only He guides me when my life is at most troubled times—and the kindness of others as well.

Thantos vs. Eros

I believe that
one of the most powerful
movie scenes in the history
of movie making was not the
sled with the name Rosebud,
carved on it in Citizen Kane. No! I think
it was the last scene of the film,
All Quiet on the Western Front.
This was the scene
in which the main character
played by Lew Ayres who, in
the film portrays a German Soldier
in the First World War. Most
of his army buddies have been killed in the war.
In this scene, he crouches in a
mud-filled trench, surrounded
by the stink of death. He
notices a small flower that has
just blossomed in a muddy and bloody
piece of ground. So he lifts his
head slightly above the trench
and the camera focuses on his
arm and hand as it slowly reaches
for the flower. Then there is a rifle shot
and the hand and arm recoils. In this no-man's land
of senseless destruction, death
has again triumphed over life.

Allan Mohl
Ossining, NY

Allan Mohl is a licensed clinical social worker who has a private practice in Dobbs Ferry, NY. Allan has a PhD in health and human services from Columbia Pacific University. In addition, he has a master's degree from the Silver School of Social Work, which is a branch of New York University.

Eber & Wein Publishing

Comforted by the Cloth of the Mask

Reality treated the cement conduit, as if
a nice shadow in the mirror wobbled
near the lake shore. The marvel
wore a face like a fox, and
the fight, cutting across the channel,
fascinated the brother of the sapphire,
clipped blue with chipped ice,
under which the clown frowned
liking to crawl beneath the perfume
of lilacs. Shaking the basket settled
everything; the figure fell. The stream
rolled and concerned the lips,
the edges drooping; the child wailed.
A daily ritual of service interrupted
the quiet, thick lapping of waves
licking feet. The sister danced
away; a bucket fell into the well.
This employment applied to every
value. The wrecks had shattered
windows. New replaced old; some
were rolled into a corner and parked.
The others made up tunes and
dances. Engineers became musicians.

Joseph A. Uphoff
Colorado Springs, CO

[Hometown] Colorado Springs, CO; [DOB] March 15, 1950; [Ed] MPS, LittD; [Occ] surrealist (different logic); [Hobbies] gardening, collecting books (the Arjuna Library); [GA] Order of International Ambassadors (American Biographical Institute)

Walking up to take his place among the others, Dr. Baron Joseph Uphoff pulled typed pages from a pocket, unfolded them, and, with a microphone in one hand, began to read at the front doors of the Penrose Public Library, out to the street. This was in April, National Poetry Month. Later in 2014, he was awarded a Gold Certificate of Excellence by Mark Schramm (and Lavender Aurora.) He received an Editor's Choice Award from Betty Cummins Starr-Joyal, Ashland, OR. One of Dr. Uphoff's projects is to indicate the immensity of the poetry scene by documentary photography.

To Ask a Time Traveler

Why, O why, time traveler, do you want to travel?
Why, O why, do you wish to leave?
To depart this land in all its fervor?

Ah, my boy, this time does not offer me
The power I need to make a change.
I stand alone, a wretch, a pain.
I act and things do not react, I move and no movement returns.

His words, they touched me, so deep inside.
Help him, I must, before he is lost of time and self.
My mouth and the gates began to open;
My words reached his ears first.

Now is where your feet stand, now here you have your power.
Do not go leaving this time and place
For a time when you were never!

Now is where you can make a change,
Just look at the ground under your feet!
Do you see a change simply from your stance on the street?

A glance down, he took, and see he did, the imprint
On the soil from his very own feet! His eyes returned
To my face; a smile I gave, to guide his fate.
You are here now, here make a change.

Charles W. Siegel
Granby, CT

*[Hometown] Granby, CT; [DOB] May 23, 1994; [Ed] high school classes, practice and a love for poetry;
[Occ] martial arts teacher, nature photographer; [GA] working on it every day*

Reminding to Remember

Love is like a sunrise,
Forgiving to forget.
Forgiving for the wrong,
Forgetting for the right.
The eternal desire
Promises another moment.
The breathlessness of its beauty
Clings onto your heart.
Eager to wake up,
To hold onto a glance.
Giving you an excuse
To smile for no reason.
Waiting for your companion
To finally awake.
Holding on tight
With strength of gentleness.
Kissing with affection,
So soft and tender.
Cherishing each movement,
Eyes closed with passion.
Adoring each other,
Being honestly faithful.
Love is like a sunset,
Reminding to remember.

Sasha F. Riner
Gaylord, MN

[Hometown] Grand Marais, MN; [Occ] nursing

Although I spend most of my time caring for others, I have found writing to be my secret escape. It's a time for me to be me without any judgment or criticism. Writing is my escape from reality but my portal to peacefulness.

Loved Ones

When you think of family,
Loved ones come to mind
To be around them is what you look forward to!
It's hard to leave once you are there.
The day will come, you will stay
They that don't go away,
Only memories linger on
Every day you do your best to keep going,
But the help of others will see you through!
So don't be blue.

Ernest Asselin
Brigeland, WA

[Hometown] Boise, ID; [DOB] April 17, 1943; [Ed] barber school and high school; [Occ] retired, disability; [Hobbies] winning sweepstakes; [GA] home business

My hobbies are writing books and poetry, and winning sweepstakes. My home business is all-natural health care products. I have been a barber, so I cut my own hair. I have a lung condition; my kids and wife take good care of me! I love God and His word. My brother, Biff, had MS. God took him home. Thank you, Eber & Wein Publishing for asking me to see my work in poetry.

Together in Dreams

The wedding party entered with style and grandeur
We walked proudly with the bride creating many smiles
Bridesmaids wore black dresses with sprays of red roses
What a picture-perfect moment photographed in style.
A vision of radiant beauty was shown by the bride
With a dress that flowed gently as fresh melted snow.
Her long strides graceful and soft curls glistened
What a breathtaking moment with the sunset aglow.
An anticipation rose as the happy couple united
Sparkling rings tenderly placed implied a new start.
Words of love and respect spoken with deep affection
Precious is this union that warms the beating heart.
Heartfelt pleasure touched the crowd with joy
Together the couple walked down steps of roses.
Cameras flashed and families grinned with happiness
Champagne glasses in hand as toasts were proposed.
Listening to music provided an enjoyable time
Eating, dancing and speeches set a brand new tone.
These two wedded lovers now joined together
To pursue a path of loving patience but not alone.
Remembering this night with memories and tears
Still waters twinkled under the moonlight beams.
Willowy breezes brought a light mist of rain
And blessings of love created countless dreams.
On this journey of two, one is never alone.
Seek a life together with a love all your own.

Carole Ortale-Curtis
Rancho Palos Verdes, CA

[Hometown] Rancho Palos Verdes, CA; [DOB] August 15, 1944; [Ed] BA in English, graduate certificate in career counseling; [Occ] career coach and counselor; [Hobbies] photography, travel, writing poetry, going to plays and concerts, being published in a poetry anthology

Although I have been a career counselor for many years, I started writing poetry as a senior in high school. It was published in our school newspaper. About fifteen years ago, I started again to write poetry about the events in my life or my children's lives, along with the illness of my mother. I found it very helpful to release these emotions on paper. This poem was inspired during my daughter's wedding. My husband and I walked her down the aisle and what a thrill that was. The beauty of it all and the emotion of the day set the tone for this poem's theme! "Together in love but remain yourself."

A Farmer's Wife

She is a mother and a farmer's wife.
It certainly isn't an easy life!
Juggling chores between the house to the farm,
Watching the kids to keep them from harm.
Makes time for her family, the cows and dogs.
Tends to her garden, feeds the chickens and hogs.
Meals to the crew as they cut the wheat.
Her baked cookies and pies are such a treat!
Her homemade apron is very well worn,
from collecting eggs to saving kittens just born.
Her family is always properly fed,
then at nights, tucked safely into bed.
She will gladly go that extra mile,
'cause she cares to see someone smile.
She gets her strength from the Lord up above.
She is my mother, whom I dearly love!

Shirley Hoskinson
Dodge City, KS

[Hometown] Dodge City, KS; [Ed] high school; [Occ] caregiver; [Hobbies] gardening, photography, history; [GA] growing up on a farm

Growing up on a Kansas farm inspired many cherished childhood memories. We had a special love for the land and for all of God's creatures. We understood determination, teamwork and good common sense. We didn't have much money, but yet we were rich with loving family ties.

A Heart to Heart Transplant

There was a slacking
as if there was no backing
behind the face
of someone severely lacking
in the arena of heart.

But I didn't care
which was a good place to start
because it was time for me to depart.

Oh, dry severity—how dare you foul the environment
with a sourpuss;
who do you think you are staring at empty walls
afar in some lonely bar
never to see a bright star?

How some suffer so as one cries out for them to join the band
to play and play and play
in a joyous land.
but no...sayeth the damned
made miserable by their own hand.

Inject yourself with love
and you can begin to fly like a dove
soaring into the sky above—
you can fly into the horizon with gossamer wings
and bask in life's wellsprings
with a smile that bliss brings.

Get that heart transplant
and don't say you can't!

Henry F. Mende
New City, NY

This Poem, "A Heart to Heart Transplant," was inspired by an ex-boss who could have driven Gandhi to violence! Indeed, I believe even Jesus Himself would have joined in with Gandhi crying out, "I have him by the neck, Jesus, I have him by the neck!" God hath thrust me into this world to deal with difficult personalities which has served me well in developing a unique form of dry humor, like a man falling off a cliff in the full lotus position while reading the Bhagavad-Gita.

The Cup

It was in the Garden that Jesus went to pray.
He asked God, His Father, to take the cup away.
But Jesus agreed to drink it, which took away our sins.
And so His path charted toward the cross now soon begins.
The communion cup we now drink is to take away our sins.
In hopes we're forgiven a new life for us begins.
As Lent approaches let us pause to thank our Father now.
On bended knee we pray that we can change our life somehow.
With help from friends and family we go along life's way.
We realize the choice is ours to live the Christian way.
So pick a road to follow, and make it straight and true.
Your prize awaits your progress, an eternal life for you.

Blin Scatterday
Medina, OH

[Hometown] Akron, OH; [DOB] August 4, 1928; [Ed] master's degree, math and education; [Occ] teacher, professor; [Hobbies] stamp collecting, writing; [GA] professor emeritus, University of Akron

I taught mathematics for fifty years at all levels during my career. My wife, Suzanne, died in 2010 and I have two children: Dr. Mark Scatterday, conductor of Eastman Wind Ensemble, and Cindy Sabula, counselor at a junior high. During my career I was president of West Akron Kiwanis, Lt. Governor of Ohio Kiwanis, Akron Symphony Board and Education Committee, president of Summit County Teacher's Association, and president of Ohio Retired Teacher's Association. I received awards for excellent teaching, ODK, AAUP, OATYC, and Kiwanis McChesney award for community service.

The One to Cherish

You came to us by surprise
To some people you being
Here is too much to bear

You came to us stressed and lost
We told you we will take care of
You no matter the cost

You are happier, healthier, and
Such a joy to have around us
Knowing our lives without you
Would be a bust

Hearing the words I love you
Helps you a great deal
Having you here with us is
Such a steal

Lisa Bowman
Jonesboro, TN

[Hometown] Jonesboro, TN; [DOB] May 7, 1987; [Ed] AAS in office administration specializing in medical; [Occ] cashier; [Hobbies] writing, reading the Bible, going to church; [GA] being able to inspire young people with words

I am twenty-seven years old living in Jonesboro, TN. I work with my parents at the restaurant they are currently in the process of buying. I love writing poetry with inspiration from my family and friends. This poem was inspired by my cousin Kaleb Hardin. The adjustability and spirit he has shown in his life with many obstacles attacking him head-on at home really show how resilient kids can be. My life changed forever for the better on July 28, 2013, that is the day the Lord cleansed my soul when I was baptized at Strong Tower Baptist Church in Gray, TN. God has forever changed and blessed my life—that was the best decision of my life.

How?

How can I lose you?

I can lose my sanity—
Consumed in futile flights of fond imagination.
I can lose my dignity—
Renounced in pitied pleas and pure humiliation...

But how can I lose you?

If my voice were one day lost—
I'd softly speak in whispers of my love
with just my breath.
If my life would be the cost—
I'd gladly give it guarding yours,
I know no nobler death...

But how can I lose you
If you are not mine?

Eldridge Custer
Rockport, TX

[Hometown] Rockport, TX; [DOB] July 25, 1937; [Ed] BA and MA in economics, Rice University; [Occ] retired; [Hobbies] music, chess, golf, tennis

Heartaches

Have you ever wondered how the sky can be so blue
while my heart is calling out with memories of you?
Flowers still unfold in springtime, their beauty to behold.
The birds still sing, echoes still ring, as in the days of old.

Moon-made leaf patterns on my windowsill,
dancing in the breeze at night; can they not be still?
Brooks still play their music, roses waft their smell.
Children play, throughout the day with voices so shrill.

It seems that time keeps rolling on, as time is wont to do,
and yet the memories we shared were anything but new.
You were but twenty-three years old since last this Earth you trod.
Too soon to go, but yet I know, your business was with God.

Jane S. Humphrey
Keystone Heights, FL

Healing was my profession as I am a retired RN with thirty years of hospital experience. Now writing is my hobby and joy. I attended both CFCC and FSU for my nursing degree and I am a fourth generation Floridian—not many of us around! Family and friends are foremost in my life now—couldn't do without them. GO 'Noles!

Listen

There is nothing as sweet
as a beautiful child
Dirty little face with a sunshine smile
dirty little hands and a snotty nose
wet little feet with mud between the toes

Mommy, Mommy, all day long
You better listen to that sweet, sweet song
Too many children are being lost
Just stop and think of the terrible cost

So listen each minute of every day
And what you hear is what they say
Mommy, Mommy means I love you
Just listening tells them you love them too

The wonders of this life you see
Each time you see their face
And with each laugh or giggle you hear
This world is a better place

Rick Freeman
Milton, FL

[Hometown] Milton, FL; [DOB] June 11, 1949; [Ed] high school, vocational colleges; [Occ] retired; [Hobbies] music, writing; [GA] my two children and loving wife

I am a retired firefighter and retired corrections officer. I've had four heart attacks and I'm permanently disabled. But I've been blessed to be able enough to take care of my loving wife, who is now in a nursing home after she survived a heart attack, kidney cancer and leg amputation. We have been married for thirty-nine years and been through a lot together. She is my life. We have a girl, twenty-eight, and a boy, twenty-seven. They have blessed us with six beautiful grandchildren. Thank you for this chance to show my love for my children.

Untitled

From this day forward
To yesterday's back
I have never dreamed of
   Not finishing my tasks
My life for Jesus, I do live on
The calming words of Proverbs, and then again Psalms
Well thought out, they carry me through life
Into my Lord's wisdom
My wholehearted faith
That I am able to speak of this
Remembering each day
To bend on my knees
My head bowed in prayer
To count all my blessings, my heart be so true
To pass on a smile, in meaning be true
To reach out to a neighbor, a stranger or friend
There is no harm if giving my praise
    To my savior and kin
Who died on this planet, to carry out his name
So while in my time, across this great earth
Let the truth be quietly known, no peace
   In our lives
Until God takes us home
Our lives unrehearsed

Cheryl Linder
Sterling Heights, MI

This poem is dedicated to my sister Nancy Jean—friend, wife, mother, aunt, grandmother, and most important inspiration.

Music

Music, the angel that wraps her arms around me.
She calms me down when I am upset.
When I am on stage, she is in me.
Every time I sing, she is in me.
Her hands take control of my fingers when I play the piano.
She is beautiful, smooth, and connected.
Although she can be rough and loud, she is still very beautiful.
Music glides all across the room; she is graceful and patient.
She has blessed me more than I can say.
She is in my blood, running smoothly like a river in my veins.
She will never desert me; she will always be with me wherever I go.
My beautiful, beautiful angel called *music*.

Carrie Carlton
Murfreesboro, TN

[Hometown] Murfreesboro, TN; [DOB] August 11, 1985; [Ed] BS in communication disorders; [Hobbies] writing, music, reading

I have always found music to be a joy and a comfort. I was inspired to write this poem during choir practice following a lecture on the Greek Muses.

Armed Forces

someone's son or daughter, husband, father
wife, mother, or significant other,
a person in uniform, brave
defender, one to save
the principle of our lives
they freely and wholeheartedly give

they in Armed Forces, supreme
are proud to be seen
in the uniform of their country
protecting their homeland security
waving the flag of our land
red, white, and blue, our portal stand.

Mildred E. Frazier
Urbana, OH

*[Hometown] Urbana, OH; [DOB] October 9, 1935; [Ed] high school and some college;
[Hobbies] poetry, crafts and friends*

*I have always loved to read and write poetry. I find I can express myself better in my writings.
I write from the heart.*

Afterlife

I no longer will see the trees grow,
I no longer will see the waters flow,
I no longer will breathe the air,
Because my body is no longer there.
Will I pass through the light at the end of the tunnel,
Or will my spirit just wonder and wonder?
What kind of eternity will I live?
Depends on the lifestyle and the love I did give.
My remains are of no value this I know,
But my spirit must have someplace to go.
I want eternal rest and eternal peace,
So I must live a harmonious life you see,
Think of others and give true love,
And there will be a place for your spirit in Heaven above.
Don't send your spirit to eternal hell,
When all you have to do is live your life well.
Do unto others as you would have them do you,
And the light at the end of the tunnel will let
your spirit through.
So take the time while you are body and soul,
And do God's work, the reward is more precious
than gold.
Now that I have done my best and all I can,
My spirit will rest in God's promised land!

John Wesley Short Jr.
Newport News, VA

[Hometown] Chicago, IL; [DOB] September 30, 1942; [Ed] two years of college; [Occ] semi-retired airport shuttle driver; [Hobbies] bowling; [GA] staying physically fit at my age

My poetry is my serenity, it's my peace and calm! I write because I feel I have something to say! Maybe no one will read them, but when I read them, I find peace within. Someday others may read them and feel what I feel!

Her Journey

For Raegan Angela Smith Farley
July 7, 1977 to May 14, 2014

So young, so unfair to be taken away,
Losing a child, it shouldn't happen this way.
So many things she had yet to see,
But it just wasn't meant to be.

We all have a purpose when we come here,
So carefree and innocent, no trace of fear.
We have victories and struggles we all go through,
It is our path, it's what we are here to do.

Once we fulfill our purpose, our own destiny,
We must return to where we came to be.
Back to our heavenly Father up above,
No more pain or sorrow, only pure love.

Everyone will miss her but know this to be true,
You'll have your very own angel watching over you.
Take comfort in knowing she is once again free,
She finished her journey—fulfilled her destiny.

Mary J. Legue
Vassar, MI

[Hometown] Vassar, MI; [DOB] July 4, 1965; [Ed] high school graduate; [Occ] accounts payable/receivable; [Hobbies] writing poetry, photography

I began writing poems in high school as a way of expressing my feelings. I didn't write for many years but was inspired to write once again by my husband, Wayne, who is the love of my life. The love we share has truly influenced my writing. This poem, although under sad circumstances, was written for a young lady I had known since the day she was born. My hope is that her family finds peace in knowing that, although she isn't here physically, she is still with you in your memories and in your hearts.

I Have Not Yet Dreamt of Lions

Many years ago a film I enjoyed immensely
Was *The Old Man And The Sea* with Spencer Tracy
Just a young boy at the time whose mind was receptive
Now at times comes to mind while contemplative
The scene where the old man dreams of lions
So clear my mind seems filled with ions
My conception of the scene to tell the truth
Was that he was dreaming of his long lost youth
Because a future is short for those long in the tooth
Through Hemingway's genius I have come to believe
Not dreaming of lions will prevent my life to leave
We lived in a cottage by the forest until the age of two
Many happy memories flood back of the cottage by the zoo
The lions could be heard roaring both day and night
Quite an impression on a small child and quite a fright
Three times death came knocking on my door oh so near
But I had not yet dreamt of lions so nothing to fear
Wonder what the early Christians dreamt about in the Colosseum
The night before being fed to the lions surely not a mausoleum
Hemingway must have thought his end was near
Perhaps he dreamt of lions but felt no fear
Victories on the tennis court and home runs over the fence
Are now a distant memory relived only in dreams now suspense
Fills the nights wondering when the lions will make their way
To my dreams there really is no way to know or say
When they come I hope to be ready for this I pray

Rolland Johnson
Eureka, CA

[Hometown] Eureka, CA; [DOB] October 27, 1945; [Ed] high school; [Occ] retired US Postal Service; [Hobbies] fantasy sports, gardening, eating; [GA] keeping my wife satisfied for forty-two years, surviving three close calls that required an ambulance ride, two motorcycle crashes and one stabbing

I'm still alive and kicking, not quite ready for the lion's visit to my dreams yet.

Intuition

As nature would have it,
The sunshine it warms my skin.
As emotion has it,
You warm me from within.
As the stars light up in the darkness of night,
You, my dear love, fill me with wonder and delight.
As the plant shows off its precious flower,
You instill in this life strength through your loving power.
The wind has the elegance
To have trees dance in its breeze.
You till the end of time, I chose to be with.
For to all that sees.
Water flows over those giant falls,
Refreshing my thought.
This life to live it without you, rather not.
I'm saying you touch me, spiritually,
Within the heart. I thank God daily for you,
Nicole Lynn, and pray we never part.

Brendan H. Beck
Leechburg, PA

[Hometown] Vanderfrift, PA; [DOB] July 3, 1974; [Ed] GED; [Occ] laborer; [Hobbies] cycling, fishing, hunting, nature; [GA] being published, finding my niche in life

I am a person who writes to deal with life. Between ups and downs, here on paper it is so much easier to see.

The Reunion

Ethereal images
Off in the mist
Heavenly stars
Moon drenched and sun-kissed

She rests in a chair
In a world all her own
With memories of love
Since he left her alone

An old picture album
A dried-up bouquet
The dreams of the dreamer
Now all tucked away

The beautiful dress
Now tattered and torn
Packed in a trunk
Looking lost and forlorn

The reunion now closer
As angels draw near
She whispers to him softly
"It's Heaven's bells that I hear"

Slowly she drifts
Towards the light she now sees
"I know he'll be there,
Waiting for me"

The flames now flickering
Her dreams have all crashed
As the burning embers
All turn to ash

Joan R. Faulkner Sr.
Port Penn, DE

[Hometown] Philadelphia, PA; [DOB] May 25, 1942; [Ed] two years college; [Occ] everything; [Hobbies] writing, cooking, sewing, designing, remodeling, crocheting; [GA] fifty-seven years of marriage and three generations together

For my husband of fifty-seven years as of November 9, 2014, who passed away November 21, 2014, I miss you, hon.

Autumn Is Wearing Her Magnificent Gowns

Once again, autumn is appearing forever fashionable
In her designs and radiant colors of scarlet, orange,
Rust, yellow, red, purple, and golden leaves.

Her runway is free and available to all as she poses
In her continuous kaleidoscope of fall colors.
Autumn's beauty is enhanced by her patterns
As her falling leaves drift down upon us
In their wonderful array of ballet movements.

Some people seek to rearrange her graceful leaves,
Into hay-like stacks, looking like a crowded closet.
It would be wonderful if the wind could stir them up
Before hands with rake and shove could pick them up.

What would be more delightful is a child, two, or four
Could run and jump into their colorful midst.
Diving, rolling, and tossing of jewel like leaves,
Children are laughing and frolicking in glee.

All of a sudden a clap of thunder and burst of rain
Send all back into the safety and warmth of their home.
While Dad rushes to the door with gloved hands,
To discover that God and his kids are faster than him.

Idonna Tryon
Concord, CA

[Hometown] Long Beach, CA; [DOB] spring of seventy-six years ago; [Ed] bachelor of arts degree; [Occ] retired elementary school teacher; [Hobbies] reading, enjoying the company of family, and learning the merits of sports from my husband of forty-eight years; [GA] learning to let go of "stuff" and trusting in the Lord to see me through the more challenging times in my life

The joy of learning was slow in my earliest school years since I did not read, spell, or write very well until a teacher at my new school in third grade discovered I had a learning disability. Today we call this challenge dyslexia. This beloved and wonderful teacher spent one whole summer beyond the regular school year showing me the magic of words in the afternoons in her lovely home garden. She was my magic carpet to soar into learning. My life was more complicated than most of my school friends, as I was raised by two fathers and four mothers.

Life

Through Your eyes…
I will see
with sight or not
what life
will really be.
What is right
and what is wrong
it will come to me.
Like an old song
drifting through my mind…
one word at a time.
Words to follow
right or wrong
through Your eyes
I will choose…
sight or not
what life
will really be.
It will come to me.

Sheryn Scarborough
Seal Beach, CA

[Hometown] Seal Beach, CA; [DOB] November 29, 1948; [Ed] two years of college; [Occ] sales; [Hobbies] art, floral and jewelry design

It's Christmastime Again

Children singing, bells are ringing, lights are shimmering all around, joyous season, Christ the
    reason,
How I wish that we could keep this glowing calm and sleep going on all throughout the season,
    all along; care for a plum?
Oh how I love to see the Nativity, in all of its promising Divinity, we need this love so very much,
There are parties, and gatherings, celebrations many, and such, and such;
I go to the traditional Posadas, eat tamales, buñuelos, pumpkin pie, and cinnamon swirls, but my
    heart
Is heavy-laden, thinking of the sad world; lost my appetite for the last calleta de Sol, O Sofia, girls?
How I long and wish for happiness, for joy, for love, for absolutely *Everyone*…how can I truly be
Happy? People rushing all about, some very snappy, many not so preppy cheerful, as I see!
I try to flee the gloomy ones, need to keep my spirit up, it's Christmastime! Christmas once again.
The mall is bursting with excitement, decorations of silver, blue and red are all around, "Oh look,
There's Santa and his elves, and ever Mrs. Santa," looking swell, and I can smell the tasty treats,
    selling
All around, as shoppers run from store to store, I stop to hear a carol, Nat King Cole, or Elvis
    maybe
Singing, to discover Bing or Old blue Eyes crooning a childhood song, I hear, as I smear, latte
    cream from
Steaming hot chocolate, I'm holding in my hand! Need a plan, gifts for all my loved ones, oh what
a list, oh what must be amiss, if I forget someone? Think I'll go home, kick off my shoes, and
make them things, instead, they won't resist! Yes, it is Christmas, alright, I feel it in my bliss!
Ho-ho-ho, and a Merry Christmas to you too, I must insist!

Mary Alice Peña-López
San Antonio, TX

*[Hometown] San Antonio, TX; [DOB] December 20, 1947; [Ed] English degree, Texas A&I University;
[Occ] kindergarten teacher; [Hobbies] singing, acting, poetry, watching MGM musicals; [GA] meeting and
marrying Jaime, my beloved husband since 1993*

*Christmas renews my faith in hope and love for family, friends, and mankind. It reminds us that Christ is
supreme—He is our Savior and greatest gift of all! I was born in Laredo, TX, to a large family. We always made
a Nativity ourselves, celebrating Jesus and the Holy Family. We were poor money-wise, but rich in our spirits
and devotion to the true meaning of Christmas. I hope my poem will inspire you and remind you of good things.
My husband Jaime and I wish you a blessed and very merry Christmas!*

Poem of the Life of Love

Love is here, and love is there, but the love of life has flown the coop.
The love of life is floating in the air.
Where it may be I don't know.
Could it be that it is in the park on a bench, or in a tree on a branch?
Could it be that the love of life is all around,
or could it be that it is near, but with fear?
I will have to wait to see if the love of life will find me.

Gust D. Makres III
Lake Havasu City, AZ

[Hometown] Afton, OK; [DOB] February 16, 1988; [Ed] high school; [Occ] Walmart night stocker; [Hobbies] hiking, camping, writing poetry, fishing, playing pool; [GA] being able to help others whenever I come across someone in need

I wrote this poem to help me in my life at the time that I was hurt, and also to help others know that everything that happens always has a reason for happening. The poem is about a love in my life that is no longer here to see or speak to. To lose someone that you love very much can hurt your heart in a way that words will sometimes be hard to understand. There are always loved ones that are taken away from us all. We just have to understand that our loved ones are in a better and also peaceful place.

Campfire

Have you ever observed a calm fire?

Watched how the flames dance upon them coals?
How the flames seem ghostly, because they don't look like they're there, but still visible?

You want to touch it
But a warning voice reminds you of the consequence

How did we come to discover fire?
I don't know, but I'm glad we did

There is nothing as captivating as fire

JaNeli Holladay
Fremont, CA

[Hometown] Fremont, CA; [DOB] May 11, 1995; [Ed] high school; [Hobbies] reading, hoop dancing, and journaling; [GA] finally graduating high school

I dedicate this poem to my pyromaniac brothers who are now an engineering manager and an engineering student. If it wasn't for their pyromania, I wouldn't have found mine, thus inspiring me to write this poem.

Last Plea of the Sorrowful

Hello! Hello! Is someone there?
Can anyone hear my cry?
I can't find anyone anywhere,
If you hear me: answer, 'tis I!

I can't find Mother, and Father is gone
Doesn't anyone hear my plea?
It's far too long until the dawn,
Won't somebody rescue me?

My friends have all just disappeared,
My companions have flown away.
This is exactly what I feared,
Why I always pushed them away.

I have been abandoned, left all alone.
I reach my hand up to the sky,
But it seems I am on my own.
Left to be forgotten; left to die.

My child! My child! I heard you!
I have been here through it all!
Know, should your troubles begin anew,
I am always here, and I shall never let you fall!

Conner L. Sheets
Sandy Springs, GA

The Forgotten Gems

The grey and the little one
Start the day
Enjoying a past
Unconcerned with the ruby in the onyx mask
Darting around
Suspecting a fight
Over the jewels hidden last night
Rolled up in a cast
Of the first fall
A surprise in a package waiting to be found
By others arriving in the cool morning rays
As diamonds drip
From emerald tips
Not yet turned brown
Unnoticed by all
But the grey and the little one
Whom no one recalls

Helena M. Langley
Granite City, IL

Like a Blanket

Unfolding like a blanket,
Your friendship comforts me.
Your smile envelops me
Like a misty fog
Rolling in.
I welcome your arrival.
Your closeness,
Though never touching,
Warms my soul.
Your presence
Gives me pause
To be—me.

Pat Gregg
Oakland, IA

[Hometown] Oakland, IA; [DOB] March 24, 1943; [Ed] AA management; [Hobbies] reading, sewing, antiquing and church volunteer; [GA] receiving my degree in my forties while working full time and raising three children

Growing up, I was a prolific writer of prose and poetry. Everyone thought I would be a writer. I stopped writing after I married and had three children. My life was full, rewarding and busy. Previously, writing was effortless. After twenty-five to thirty years, jumpstarting verses is very difficult for me. Eber & Wein has given me the courage and vehicle needed to revive an interrupted talent. This poem emits my feelings for the friend who was a beacon for me during a sad time in my life and later became my husband.

The One True Love of My Life

There's a softness in your eyes when you
look at me. A tender smile on your lips,
happiness on your face. And when I take
you in my arms and hold you close to me,
you seem to melt against me ever so gently.
Since the very first time I saw your smiling
face I knew I had found the one true love
of my life. From the moment I took your
hand in mine I stopped searching for the love
I had been longing for. Several years now have
passed since our Lord called you home but I have
still so much sorrow and pain. It is still so hard
to take the emptiness. I so long to feel your
loving touch again. Now, with my faith in the
Lord, the one consolation that keeps me
going on is that in my mind and heart she
is still with me always at my side as the
one true love of my life, Lillian.

Stanley F. Pachniak
Oshkosh, WI

[Hometown] Oshkosh, WI; [DOB] November 18, 1940; [Ed] music, writing, art; [Occ] retired plastics manufacturing; [Hobbies] writing poetry and other forms, photography, Bible study; [GA] my marriage, being published

I was born in East Chicago, IN, also known as Harbor City. Our family moved to the north central part of Wisconsin. My paternal and maternal grandparents, along with some of our relatives, were farmers. My family moved to Milwaukee, WI in 1954. Throughout my adult life, my interests were mainly in music and writing. You might say that many things interested me and that life itself was, and is, my inspiration. That is why, at this time in my life, I write poetry, and many of my thoughts and feelings in general, which also included my late lady love, Lillian.

Love

The most tangible thing that can be used, abused, and fulfilling
Is also the thing that for any pain brings healing
Whether it is from a relative, friend, or the one you hold dearest
When it is true that bond cannot be broken
It covers a multitude of sins and the greatest form of it was given
By a man sent down from heaven and once his blood was shed we were all forgiven
Some give in vain, some blaspheme the name, and to it bring shame
Yet it is a precious token that goes beyond what is said
And how you feel when it is displayed you know it is real
No matter how much hate exists it conquers all
Without it all is meaningless because without charity nothing makes sense
And if not possessed your gain is penniless
It is patient and kind giving *all* you need so your wants are satisfied
It is not envious nor is it proud yet about its beatitudes you'll express out loud
It is not boastful and does not seek sorrow yet it gives lustrous hope for every tomorrow
It doesn't think evil or rejoice in iniquity but dances in honesty
Its passion generates from the one who first gave it for a demising humanity
Because he knew it will bear all believing all things that are true
Hoping for all and enduring eternity through—*it will never cease*
Under its reign I humbly fall, give my soul because it will cover me
Like a hand wrapped in a glove
Man can exude a tainted replica but the purest supply Elohim gives is love

Teena M. Johnson
Camden, NJ

[Hometown] Philadelphia, PA; [DOB] August 6, 1983; [Ed] majoring in business administration; [Occ] retail manager; [Hobbies] writing, singing, enjoying my family; [GA] being a mother

I began writing at the age of fourteen as a way to express my emotions lyrically. Seventeen years later, I am a composer of over four hundred pieces. From this spawns several of my poems being professionally recorded and published in and outside the United States. I never had any formal training for writing because, for me, life is my best teacher. I fell in love with poetry once I realized how effective I can be with words. Poetry is my passion that takes me to dense territories exploring the various complexities of my being. I was inspired to write this piece because of the most important gift I have in my life, which is my faith. It is because of what I believe I exist and have an obligation to be a witness of Yahweh Elohim. So while I have an audience I will share this good news.

Plight of Man

A man starts as a seed that grows into a baby
He crawls as a toddler and schools as a child
Then grows into a teen
As he becomes a man and has children
He grows older yet acts younger
As his son grows older, he becomes a teenager
Then when his son has sons
He has become a child once more
Only to revert all the way back
To a big ol' baby for sure!
In the end he becomes a seed once more
And life starts over again
What happens to the seedless
When they die, that's it
It is as if they never exist'd

Debra Jo Rogers
Germantown, OH

[Hometown] Germantown, OH; [DOB] January 9, 1959; [Ed] high school; [Occ] retired; [Hobbies] poetry, working out; [GA] having my own poetry book published

I have recently had my own poetry book published by Eber & Wein Publishing. Life: A Collection of Poems, by Debra Jo Rogers. I am very proud of that and hope you look me up in book stores soon. Monies from the sale of my book go toward my hubby's welfare. He has stage three colon cancer; he has been through chemo and is doing well, for now. This cancer has a high reoccurrence rate. He is scheduled for tests in December, so fingers crossed. I hope you buy and enjoy my poetry book. Thanks for helping us out.

Get-Up-and-Go

My get-up-and-go just got up and left
Don't know where it went, I hope it's for help
And if it comes back I'll grab on real tight
My get-up-and-go is in for a fight

As a young man I had good get-up-and-go
As the years slipped away my get-up was slow
I took many vitamins and minerals too
But then one day my get-up was through

The young ones are playing, but they don't share
Their get-up-and-go and they don't care
So I'll ease my bones into this old rocking chair
No better I guess or worse for wear

The days of our youth were Heaven sent
And I hope not all of yours are spent
But my days are numbered, this I can tell
'Cause my get-up-and-go has sure gone to hell.

Wayne Masters
Kingsport, TN

[Hometown] the entire state of Tennessee; [DOB] January 29, 1943; [Ed] high school graduate, one year college; [Occ] retired; [Hobbies] writing poetry, songs, singing, guitar; [GA] hopefully still yet to come

Most of my life has been in radio broadcasting. I've worked for stations in Virginia, Tennessee, and Kentucky. I was part owner of a radio broadcasting school in Nashville, TN, where I lived for more than forty years. I love performing, writing songs, and writing poetry. My poem, "Get-Up-and-Go," is somewhat of a parody about getting older. Sometimes it takes a good laugh to keep us going. I hope my songs and poems inspire others who may read them. I know how much I've enjoyed writing them. You may never know what you can achieve until you try. I keep trying!

The Puppies H, C, D, F

As the story goes a litter of puppies were born. These puppies were extraordinary, with excellent behavior; they were also covered in the oil of honor.

Puppy "H" represents respect; adherence to what is right and to a conventional standard of conduct.

Puppy "C" represents a territory of a nation with its own government; policies for territory, possessing its own language for the people, and culture; rural district opposed to town and cities or capital, and land of a person's birth rights or citizenship.

Puppy "D" represents moral and legal obligation; a responsibility with a binding force of what's right and—what is required of oneself—and legal recognition of documents.

Puppy "F" represents the mission in life that should never change, throughout your journey—the mission of life remains unyielding with a commitment to faith; maneuvers and demands with excellent decision making it employs the human elements of boldness, creativity, and faith.

The four pups represent honor, duty, country and the last pup is for faith. Even now the "Creator of All Things" offers you faith.

The presentation of the oil of honor is a blessing, gift, and reward; use your gift for loving, sharing and risking loving someone; be eternally grateful and exceedingly humble—and you deserve this glorious experience giving of yourself.

Curley E. Jackson
Seattle, WA

[Hometown] Galveston; [DOB] July 19, 1948; [Ed] BA, MA, PhD; [Occ] retired; [Hobbies] golf, chess; [GA] yet to be accomplished

Because Life Is a Surprise

To the life we all come and go away.
Life is like a train traveling.
It is very short, come and gone.
How we come, we go because life is a surprise.
That's why wherever we are going,
We must croop friendship, not unfriendship.
We must join to pray into a friendship's circle.
Life is a surprise, how it come it gone.
Because life is too short, and so beautiful
We must share love, caring, compassion,
Faith, hope, confidence, smiles and friendship.
Because life is like a blow, we can not go running.
We have to take easy and relax living according
To the commandments of God.
We must take care of us, patiently awaiting—
Until the end of our days.
Because life is so precious God wants us to keep awake,
Until he gives us a neat and clean paradise
With beauties and love, how in the beginning of the world,
Life comes and goes away…
Surprise comes and we all are responsible—
To live according to God and the world's laws.
We have to take care of our life and preserve it like
Flowers and roses in gardens of spring.
Because life is a surprise one day we will go away;
And we never again will not see another spring.
Because life is a surprise!

Gladys Antonia Martinez
New York, NY

I am author of more than two thousand poems. I am a teacher, painter, designer, and composer. I was a poet winner four times: Best Poet 2014 winner with the poem "Sept. 11, 2001." I was also a winner with the poem "God Is My Support." I was a winner with the poem "Anhelos de mi Patria" (1982). I have more than 1,300 poems published. I am retired and my favorite hobby is writing poems.

My Home

Listen, do you hear the cries of battle?
I walk among the fallen searching for what once was.
Love of God and Country to know of sacrifice.
Take pride in our traditions and our way of life.

Were the cries of anguish all for naught?
As a people we have forgotten
What it took to become a great nation,
What our foundation was built upon.
In God We Trust!

America is a land of beauty and of awe to be cherished.
America today is a land of constant talk yet saying nothing.
A people obsessed with self image only.
What lies within makes the person.
This too is true of what makes a nation.
Greatness lies beneath the surface.
The roar for quality that only comes with
Principles, values, morals
This is the greatness of a nation.
Let all nations take a stand for quality.
Let all nations look within for there their answer lies.
It is who we are, not what we are, that matters!

Florence Compher
Wartburg, TN

[Hometown] Wartburg, TN; [DOB] December 3, 1950; [Ed] college; [Occ] retired; [Hobbies] reading, writing, walking; [GA] singing on stage at Carnegie Hall

Where Life Leads

Wherever your life leads you, just go with the flow.
Remembering the old, embracing what's true,
Lift up your heart, and never be low,
God's grace will always carry you through.

From your past life into the new
With memories of blessings from now and then,
Forming new friendships that He brings to you,
God guides your life to a place you have never been.

God will provide in all you do
Throughout the life you give to Him,
Blessings He will give to you,
Thus filling your heart with a joyful hymn.

If His love you have within,
And following wherever God then leads,
Your light will always shine and never dim,
Encouraging others and planting His seeds.

Denise E. Bowlin
Shreveport, LA

[Hometown] Shreveport, LA; [DOB] April 26, 1952; [Ed] BA in music, history minor, MS in English; [Occ] teacher, dept. head, high school alternative diploma program; [Hobbies] fishing, carpentry, cowboy action shooting, farming, sewing; [GA] 95% yearly success rate of students receiving a high school diploma

On the last day of work before shoulder surgery, my students passed a journal around expressing their thoughts and well wishes. I was instructed to read it only after surgery. While reading and reflecting, one theme continuously ran through my mind: "Wherever life leads, go with the flow." Many graduated before I returned, but they have been constantly in contact wanting me to know how their lives have changed because of my encouragement to make a better life for themselves.

Oblivion

Lurking in the shadows of my mind
A monster waits.
Biding his time, the right moment to attack,
Attack my thoughts, feelings
Leaving me numb.
It thrives on fear,
Growing stronger and stronger.
I'm not in control.
It'll take over, pushing me into the shadows,
Where it'll have me body and soul.

Jennifer Terrell
Mahomet, IL

[Hometown] *Danville, IL;* [DOB] *May 15, 1989;* [Ed] *bachelor's in history, minor in creative writing;* [Hobbies] *reading, writing, watching old movies;* [GA] *graduating college*

All of my poems are based on my life or on hopes that interest me. This poem was inspired by a nightmare I had. It kept replaying until I wrote it down.

Come to the Circus

A multitude of children
Scampering so gay
No one has forgotten
To come to the circus today

They gasp at the glittering costumes
They laugh at the jolly clowns
And hold their breath
While the acrobats
Perform their ups and downs

A ground that's strewn with popcorn
And papers everywhere
But that's the sweepers worry
And not the children's care

See the elephant with his funny trunk
Like a vacuum cleaner it curls and twists
Sucking up the peanuts
That are clutched in tiny fists

Juicy apples on the stick
Candy cotton, pink lemonade,
Puffy popcorn, hot dogs too
Of such things is Heaven made

So forget about your troubles
In this merry atmosphere
And have a good time
At the circus
For it comes but once a year

Doris Insero
Schenectady, NY

[Hometown] Schenectady, NY; [DOB] January 10, 1934; [Ed] high school; [Occ] retired; [Hobbies] reading, writing songs; [GA] publishing my poems

I am an eighty-year-old widow and live with my sister, who is also a widow, and we have an orange cat.

A Happy Place

Twins in the womb not much room.
Sharing our space is a happy place.

Jumping up and down, turning all around,
bouncing off the wall with no fear at all.

Swimming, splashing, darting and dashing,
hands a clapping and feet a tapping.

Squirm and wiggle we start to giggle.
Sounds that rhyme begin to shine.

Tossing and turning so much learning.
As night settles in we huddle and cuddle.

Cozy in our space is the perfect place
to softly hear mom's voice beginning to rejoice.

Singing us to sleep another day to keep.

Marianne Gorman
Morrisonville, NY

[Hometown] Morrisonville, NY; [DOB] November 14, 1950; [Ed] BS and associate's in nursing; [Occ] retired staff nurse of twenty-nine years; [Hobbies] stamp collecting and metal detecting

I am inspired by God to write and represent the unborn baby in the form of poetry. Eventually I hope to write spiritually inspired cards and children's books.

Sweet Pumpkin Dreams

I didn't want to have to leave, run away
Believe it or not I wanted to stay
I didn't feel the need to go slow
We have plenty of room to grow
He didn't stop kissing me and whispering in my ear
He plans to be there

I didn't laugh off and scoot back
Stopped hiding my voice and let myself react
I didn't scream out for help and cry to stop
No rolling out of bed and finding my clothes
He didn't make me do anything I didn't want to do
Showing me it's okay to live with flashbacks and anxiety

So this is what it feels like not to cry myself to sleep at night
To not worry about the burns
The cheating or the urges
To be held, kissed, and held through
Not to be thrown away as soon as
What was wanted was dead and not alive
It's what I only thought dreams were made of
My sweet pumpkin dreams of murders and fiends

I fell asleep. I fell asleep next to him
I fell asleep. I fell asleep in his arms
I fell asleep. I fell asleep…

Jessica Freeman
Hillsborough, NJ

[Hometown] Hillsborough, NJ; [DOB] February 7, 1994; [Ed] music industry major at Ramapo; [Hobbies] lyricist, model, dancer

I started writing lyrics when I was thirteen years old. I've written over 430 songs so far. Writing has always been a great way for me to work through any problems, situations, or events that have happened throughout my life. I plan on recording some in the near future.

Eber & Wein Publishing

Shehe

A bout
Shehe
heretic deity
 hearing we're free
living to be
discovers
listening freedom dies
those mothers
trying to breach the chains
causing many pains
myself
and others
children
dads too
still believing somewhere
beneath
the titter
of con guys
the glitter
of electronic spies
the litter
from mac's and fries
Freedom lies
hiding behind storm clouds
Shehe Easter *Sonrise*
hovers
Daughters
must know about
Shehe family
Spirits
The
Earth

David Roubik
Muskego, WI

My mom started teaching me to read when I was four years old. I knew how to print before I went to grade school. I had four years of high school. I went to seminary, no ladies there. I went from retail grocer bag boy to store manager—lots of ladies I talk to. I like music. Two of my favorite songs are "Imagine My Way," and "No Heshe Know Shehe."

Photo Child

I found a picture today,
A little girl sat under a tree,
Her blue eyes swam with dreams,
Blonde hair wild in the wind,
Smile bright and daring,
A happy girl she seemed,
I knew her from somewhere,
Every time I passed a glass hanging on a wall,
Only she has grown.
Her eyes still full of dreams,
Not ones with mystical creatures,
One with possibilities of the future,
Blonde hair,
Still wild but longer,
Fitting her more now,
Smile bright as ever,
Held together with metal and rubber bands.
Now I know who she is,
She was a younger me,
One lost in dreams,
One who I have grown to be found,
Piece by piece,
The puzzle slowly comes together,
She was my child self.

Robin M. Lang
Summerton, SC

[Hometown] Summerton, SC; [DOB] March 20, 2000; [Ed] still attending; [Occ] full-time high school student; [Hobbies] writing, reading, singing; [GA] growing in to the young lady I am

My name is Robin Marie Lang. I have lived with my disabled veteran father, Jessie Lang, my whole life. My father and I have been working together through tough times. We have been through a lot. I would love to become an author of novels and poetry. I plan to go to Harvard University for business in law and to enter the air force as an officer. I really enjoyed being published and hope for more opportunities in the future. Every day I write; it is one of my many passions. I hope you will, or have, enjoyed my poem. Thank you!

Time's Incessant Moment

Solitary and defiant
Time's incessant moment
Moves swiftly upon Destiny's
Indifferent trajectory,
Continuously separating
What was from what will be,
Like a sullen self-involved youth
        aggressively approaching
        relentlessly retreating
Forever beckoning the front
To the back of life.
Curious, I flick a lighted match
To illuminate the fleeting apparition.
Instant conflagration!
Exhilarating as the moment of birth—
Separating what was
From what will be.

Ron Matros
Mesilla, NM

A good poem flows over its boundaries. A great poem transcends its boundaries.

Her Lustrous Illumination

To the window I walk, and looking up
through the blinds, I see her hanging, there, in
the clear night sky, lustrously illuminated.
A white brilliance upon my countenance, she smiles.
My mind drifts, plays back time, recalls a shapely
worn, flowered dress, white flowers on silk displayed.
My heart, at the remembrance, warms. Time now, as
time that night, passes by unkept and unnoticed.
Senses: my nose, mysteriously inhales traces of scent,
a bouquet of lavender, crafted, weaved and purchased.
A goddess's crown, for and in her hair worn until
full light of oncoming day upon her countenance shone.
Mother Moon's lustrous illumination and a sky full of
stars she veiled. Only in dark passages did she allow
their presence to be seen. Realization overcomes me.
Fact: My love alone still prevails. Left I, upon
my own resources. I alone to stand in her presence
and this stepping back, this time past recalled,
Stops! I stop, fingers against my temples pressing.
Here, there is no warmth. It has been replaced not by
a hearty yearning for a repeat of events long past,
but for a time, hopefully forthcoming, in which
she may witness, beneath the white brilliance of
her lustrous illumination, a love illuminated.

Hugo T. William
Eugene, OR

[Hometown] Eugene, Springfield, Creswell, OR; [DOB] early February; [Ed] University of Wisconsin, University of Oregon (in architecture); [Occ] writer for twenty years; [Hobbies] gardening in pots, golfing, playing cards, doing puzzles, building models; [GA] the lives I've nurtured and strengthened including three ex-wives

Novel and poetry writing have become my obsession and life. When not immersed in one, I find that I am lost—a life without purpose. Expression of your true self in all that you do—no matter what the effort—I have found to be the true meaning of life. After we've gone and left it behind, it will be all that remains of our passing in the minds of those still living.

This Flag

It flies unfurled, a signal to the world.
Its stars and stripes salute the winds of time.
When foes arose and, full of malice, hurled
Their hurtful hate, no matter place or clime,
This flag was lifted high to own the sky.
This flag, with selfless heroes dared to fly.

This flag sends out a silent hymn of hope
For all who yearn to know true freedom's song.
This flag is blessed with blood! And all who cope
With evil while it flies will right the wrong
Of tyranny, will change warfare to peace,
Will bid war cease and God's own doves release.

Charles Poole
Wesminster, CA

[Hometown] *Phoenix, AZ and Los Angeles, CA;* [DOB] *September 27, 1934;* [Ed] *MDiv, Emory University;* [Occ] *United Methodist Pastor, write novels with a pseudonym;* [Hobbies] *oil paint large landscapes*

I have lived most of my life in the Phoenix, AZ and Los Angeles, CA areas. But since age fourteen, when I discovered Prescott, AZ on a bicycling trip, I have regarded Prescott as my hometown. At last, before the end of 2014, I will have the opportunity to live there. After my novel Night of the Black Moon was published, I have been seeking publication of three other novels. I believe everyone, in their heart of hearts, is a poet.

Beautiful Girl

The beautiful girl with the emerald eyes
sat upon the ledge
Her heart was broken and her body hollow
from the burdens she had to bear
Her body shook with unearthed sobs
as tears quickly fell
"Ugly, stupid, freak"
she remembered the words from her peers
Each word stung as it punctured her heart with self hatred
The beautiful girl was breaking
her life seeping through the cracks of her beaten body
Leaning forward she pushed herself off the ledge
Falling she smiled and looked towards the sky
"I'm free" she whispered

Samantha Price
Ellington, MO

untitled

the returning wren
nesting in her private world
a new front door wreath

Sharon Whitman
Williamsburg, VA

[Hometown] Beaumont, TX; [DOB] 1949; [Ed] master's degree, BS in music education; [Occ] retired choral director; [Hobbies] traveling, lighthouses, touring historic homes, reading; [GA] teaching music to thousands of students of all ages over twenty-eight years

Joseppie

Oh Joseppie how often do you have a gift,
to find a friend that has your back
no conversation was off limit
no holding back, there was no limit.

When we were down—the way was up
often nothing said "just fill the cup"
We shared the good, the sad, and bad
A sounding board, a listening friend, I knew I had

We joked, we laughed, we cried, we understood
when down advice ended, we knew we could
He spoke, I listened, he spoke, I knew
We had that bond, every day to renew

Joseppie you were always there
advice given—always fair
sometimes gracious, sometimes dared
I hope you knew...how much I cared

We had a friendship with no holds barred
a friendship treasured—nothing charred
you spoke with honesty, pride and soul
nothing could replace it—not ever a soul

Thanks for friendship, honesty and fun
a nine hold golf course...a game won
standing in with family...playing in the sun
a friend like you...in life I won...Geno

Judith M. McKillip
Iowa City, IA

A dear cousin passed away, and in his life he had great friends. This is a peek of how he lived.

The Storm and the Sign

Dark clouds cover the sky,
a storm is coming.
The rain begins to pour
at a slow and steady pace,
then gets louder and faster.
Lightning fills the air with a
bright light, followed by a large
crackle of thunder.
The storm continues long into
the night, but then stops right
about dawn, the sun comes up and
reveals a sign that the storm is over,
a rainbow of many colors.
So whenever a storm is near just look
for the sign afterwards and it will
make all the difference.

Katie S. Neal
Little Rock, AR

[Hometown] *Little Rock, AR; [DOB] September 8, 1989; [Ed] high school, one semester of college; [Occ] student; [Hobbies] reading, writing, electronics, being with family; [GA] having my first poem published*

I love to read and write, and hang out with my family. Someday, I hope to be a professional writer. I love just about anything that is fun to do. I dream of also owning my very own inn, with either a bookshop or library in it. My poem "The Storm and the Sign" comes from my point of view of how a storm comes, and, when it ends, there is often a sign of hope to reveal that it is over. My inspiration for this poem came to me when a storm came through my hometown the other night.

A Tear Has Fallen Now and Then

It seems a century has passed since you've been gone. We were saddened to see you go. We have shed a tear or two since the day we had to say our final goodbye.

There is not a day that goes by that we don't miss you more and more. We wish you could have stayed a little longer, but we knew you were too tired and needed to rest. Your work on Earth was done and it was time for you to leave your earthly bounds behind.

You were a good Christian in your lifetime and all your good deeds, we're sure, are recorded in the Book of Life.

We hope you knew you were quite an inspiration to us, one and all. We miss you and love you very much.

What a joy it must have been to see God's Face and to hear him say, "Welcome home, my beloved child." Your work on Earth is finally done.

Mollie G. Salazar
Phoenix, AZ

[Hometown] Las Vegas, NM; [DOB] November 17, 1938; [Ed] high school, one year of college; [Occ] retired school secretary; [Hobbies] writing poetry and collecting Elvis Presley memorabilia; [GA] having my poem published by Eber & Wein Publishing and being chosen a Best Poet four years in a row

I have been writing poetry for the past four years. It has been a great experience for me. I never dreamt I could ever put words together that had much meaning. I am really pleased with how much I have accomplished in such a short time. I thank my family for all their encouragement and help, especially my son who once read one of my poems and turned to me and said, "Hey Mom, you're a poet and didn't know it." Thanks son!

I Thought I Heard You Call My Name

Today, as always, I thought I heard you, Mother, call my name.
Not loud, but softly, like gentle rain falling on my windowpane.
I listened to hear your voice again, but all I heard was the rain.
I know you are in a better place, but nothing here remains the same.

People say that in time, all is forgotten, yet this not always true.
My mother was the giver of my life, my teacher and my friend.
So when she became ill, I cared for her until the end.
She was everything good in my life, and she always saw me through.

Everyone loses loved ones, from which no one can hide.
Some people think nothing changes, always remaining the same.
They don't understand, until one day someone calls their name.
Not just anyone, but a loved one, not seen anymore, seen only inside.

Today, I thought I heard you call my name, yet no one was there.
It was not a figment of my imagination, but the voice of my mother,
In her sweet and gentle way, showing her love and her care.
One day she'll return, calling, "Come home to a place like no other."

Alice Marie Young-Lionshows
Lodge Grass, MT

[Hometown] *Lodge Grass, MT; [DOB] December 10, 1946; [Ed] BS in education; [Occ] teacher; [Hobbies] collecting porcelain dolls, growing plants, reading, writing, advocating for the right of others in Tribal Court; [GA] Who's Who among American Teachers in 2006*

My name is Alice Marie Young-Lion Shows. I am an enrolled member of the Apsaalooke (Crow) Indian Tribe of Montana. I have lived on the reservation for the entirety of my life and am a product of the culture, traditions, and heritage of the area. It is a matriarchal society where your mother is held in high esteem. I too hold my mother in high esteem, which inspired my poem, "I Thought I Heard You Call My Name." In the Crow culture it is said that you have four mothers: your natural mother, Earth, lodge, and adoptive mothers.

You Sure...

I am trying to stay pleasant
But it is harder every day,
I am trying to keep my mind about me,
But I feel like it is slipping away.

No one pulls you up,
No one will pull you down.
But where is the line?

Very dangerous lines
The other, a careful balance
Between sanity and none.

Alone only with my passion
Or will it be gone?

I am lost and lonely.

Virginia M. Richardson
Metheun, MA

I live in Methuen, MA. I am a widow; I started writing a lot more after my husband passed away.

The Power of a Wish

Build a home for the homeless
Educate a failing student
Help a single mom with a child or children

Give all seniors plus money for fun
Feed the masses peanut butter sandwiches
Put shoes on pudgy toes

Find a cure for racism
Smile a little more when you see the poor
Hug a person, just because

Or hide your power under a cloud
So no one can ask for help
Would this make your heart break

Your heart of steel, your lock of gold
Withstanding folks with blow torches
Trying to get into fields of happenstance

They say wishes come true, if you believe
But behind each wish you speak
Must be a willing hand

Are your hands open or closed?

Dorothy Ann Anderson
East Islip, NY

[Hometown] Detroit, MI; [DOB] October 20, 1931; [Ed] two years of college; [Hobbies] collecting elephants, learning and listening for wisdom; [GA] being the sister of a brother who loved me all his life

When life throws curves in my path, someone or something crosses my path that softens the blow. You sit in a doctor's office and someone sits beside you and says, "Hello." Then they proceed to give a medical history of their entire life. You listen, because where are you going to go in a crowded waiting room? When they are called into the doctor's exam room, you sigh and think, why am I here? What I came for has become a small "dot" in comparison to a stranger. So stop complaining so much. Enjoy who you are right now.

Till the Last Second

Death by fire
Would be dire
Death by ice
Would suffice

Death in sleep
Would be meek
With less pain
It is more humane

Preferring the last
Yet possibilities are vast
How one will die
Is always left on standby

April Simpson
Garland, TX

[Hometown] Garland, TX; [DOB] April 8, 1999; [Ed] attending high school; [Occ] life; [Hobbies] writing, spending time outdoors; [GA] memorizing a new part in a play, hours before show time

My poem was written shortly after I lost one of my pet parakeets. She hadn't lived for long and it got me thinking, we never really know when or why death happens. I thought about this and how I would prefer to die; thoughts spilled out on the paper.

My Pleasure

The sun is up.
The coffee is brewing.
The dog wants out.
The cats are mewing.
It's Saturday morning
We could sleep late,
But the kids are up
And playtime can't wait.
The man of the house
Wants his morning news.
She'll pour his coffee
As he slips on his shoes.
She will make their breakfast
And serve food cold or hot.
By the time she is finished
The morning is shot.
As she sits in her chair
For five minutes of rest,
She smiles and she knows
Her job is the best!

Shirley A. Zimmerman
Lebanon, PA

[Hometown] Lebanon, PA; [DOB] November 1, 1937; [Ed] bachelor's degree plus; [Occ] retired after thirty-three years of teaching; [Hobbies] reading, writing poetry, baking; [GA] elementary teacher for thirty-three years

I have always enjoyed cooking, baking, and especially reading, but my greatest interest was enjoying raising our son. We adopted him when he was almost a year old, and going camping introduced him to the beauty of the surroundings and the wildlife we saw, and the people we met.

A Dog's Tale

Detached and criminally insane,
I crawled up the wall and across
the vaulted ceiling—with near
reptilian alacrity.

The dog came too.
At woof speed, of course.
I recorded it all for prosperity,
but none came.

Gravity appeared.
We had a long affair once.
She always kept me grounded.

I landed squarely on top of the dog.
Poor Val.
All of her bodily fluids (and a few solids)
were expelled through one nostril—
at woof speed, of course—and hit
the wall quite spectacularly.
 Dali applauded.
Pollock thought there was a little
too much red, then threw up
all over the floor, creating
another masterpiece.

Stuart Allen
Coral Springs, FL

[Hometown] Brooklyn, NY; [DOB] March 4, 1941; [Ed] four-plus years of college; [Occ] retired international technical director and home repair specialist; [Hobbies] gardening (mostly orchids and bromeliads) and coin collecting; [GA] traveled to twenty-six foreign countries

Regarding "A Dog's Tale": I woke up late one morning in November and just wrote this. It appears I was dreaming about my dog Valerie, a greyhound, who is a royal pain in the ass but also totally lovable. I liked the surreal quality of the content and action. Salvador Dali and Jackson Pollock are two of my favorite artists. The whole experience reminded me of my many wild times in Greenwich Village back in the '60s. Val is in excellent health—not climbing up any walls, but definitely running at "woof" speed.

2LIV 4GV

Your license plate I read.
My heart got the message.
To live, forgive right now!
Ugly divorce pending.
I know what to do first.
I choose to forgive her.
Tears flowing, hugs for both.
A sigh and a thank you!
A free man walked away.

Bev Cull
Pewaukee, WI

[Hometown] Pewaukee, WI; [DOB] November 9, 1927; [Ed] BS in education; [Occ] teacher, elementary (3–8) and special education; [Hobbies] soul to soul conversations, reading, writing, bridge; [GA] raising four beautiful children

When I applied for personalized plates, I was asked to send more than one. I sent twelve. I received 2LIV 4GV. What a blessing it has been. My poem was inspired by a man I do not know. As I was leaving church he said, "Thanks for saving my life." I never saw him again. I am having a wonder-filled life. My joy and awe far outweigh the trials and tribulations. My days are filled with gratitude and keeping a positive attitude. Bridge table, here I come!

The Greatest Gift

Gifts of kindness make the heart glad,
Some are precious things to receive,
A new car is fine, a diamond is not bad,
Some like a fur coat, others flowers I believe.

There are many kinds of gifts, large or small,
The greatest gift is from above,
If you don't have that gift, you've missed it all,
That's Eternal life, through God's love.

This gift is free to us. It cost God His son.
It is the greatest gift we could receive,
Even through tribulations, we've already won,
If in God's only Son we did believe.

Earlene Eastes
Gordonsville, TN

[Hometown] Gordonsville, TN; [DOB] June 30, 1931; [Ed] high school; [Occ] homemaker; [Hobbies] gardening, grand- and great-grandchildren; [GA] raised five children that I'm proud of

I am a wife of sixty-four years and mother of five. I worked with the handicapped for five years, but I quit to keep my granddaughter. I live on a sixteen-acre farm. We have divided it among five children, raised to be honest, God-fearing people. This poem is my way of telling of God's love, His free gift to everyone who will repent toward Him—I did in 1988. I'm on my way Home.

A Magical World

I long to live in a magical world
Of make-believe and fairy tales,
Where rainbows come and go each day,
And unicorns roam and play all day.
Where fairy tale people come to life,
And dance a princess waltz at night.
Where superheroes are flying about,
With mystical powers to help you out.
Where fairies, gnomes, and trolls are there,
Inviting me into their whimsical world.
Where winters are mild and summers are long,
And birds and butterflies glow in the sun.
Where there's a Crystal Palace up high
And a prince to greet me as I walk by.
Where you can see through rivers and streams,
Because they are pollution free.
And magic is used in every way
To make your dreams come true each day.
What a mystical, beautiful world it would be,
This magical world of make-believe.

Jennelle L. White
Cincinnati, OH

I am a registered nurse. Also, I have a diploma as an animal care specialist, and am a wildlife and forestry conservationist, and a medical assistant. I started writing at an early age while in junior high school. I love to write, read books, and travel. I love animals. I am an author of two books, one is a children's book and the other is a self-help/business book. My children's book is a poetry picture book.

Waiting for You

Waiting for you,
waiting for you to come
and take my hand—
I will give you my heart
for in your hands
I know it will be safe.
Though it feels like forever
since I received the promise,
I have to hold on to
what I know is true—
that one day you will come
and take my hand in marriage.
For it's then you'll know
you've always had my heart,
as I've been waiting for you,
but until we are together
never to be torn apart,
I will hold on to what I
always knew was true—
that you are for me, I am for you,
and together, we are a whole—
complete in one another
finally finding a home
in one another's heart.

Hannah M. Clayson
Hemlock, NY

*[Ed] graduated from Calvary Chapel School of Ministry; [Occ] daycare worker; [Hobbies] playing guitar,
writing poetry*

*Poetry is sort of a creative outlet for me, as is playing guitar. Like many people, I have dreams, and some that
seemed to have "died"—so to speak. But recently Jesus showed me that He can bring back to life dreams I
thought were dead, and that gives me hope for the "broken" dreams, that one day they may come to pass. This
poem came out of that renewed sense of hope I received. It's all to Jesus I owe for this gift of writing poetry.*

Christmas

Christmas
Means—to some happiness—others unhappiness
Tree trimming with family—no tree or family
Gifts under tree—no gifts
Smell of cooking dinner and cookies, pies—
No food of any kind.

Christmas should be a wonderful time of the year

But to some it's the worst time of the year.
For those who have family and friends,
Thank God every day, for what you have.
Remember the ones who have nothing,
Say an extra prayer for them.

Katherine M. Lilly
Centerville, SD

[Hometown] Louisville, KY; [DOB] January 13, 1949; [Ed] GED; [Hobbies] making fancy table cloths; [GA] being able to write and have others read them

The Great Resolve of 9-11

So many souls, so many tales
Of courage through the deadly trails,
We turn to God for guidance now,
To pray and make a solemn vow

That evil will not triumph here.
Our nation's goals are ever clear:
Bring faith and freedom to us all;
Today we harken to the call.

With hope arising from despair,
A unifying love we share…
A love of God and family,
Our country's flag that all can see,

A love for justice and our land;
We know the world will understand
That our resolve is mighty now;
Through God we will fulfill our vow,

To honor thousands who were killed
Because some evil minds so willed.
We'll end the reign of ruthless hate
And show, indeed, "Our God is great."

Jim O. Berkland
Glen Ellen, CA

[Hometown] Glen Ellen, CA; [DOB] July 31, 1930; [Ed] AB, Berkely; MS, San Jose State University; [Occ] geologist; [Hobbies] garden, fishing, earthquake prediction; [GA] first county geologist in northern California to publicly predict World Series Quake of October 17, 1989

My third grade teacher, Miss Marin, liked my first poem, "Three Little Birds;" she printed it by hand, attached a baby bird picture, framed it and presented it to my mother, who was then a PTA president. What other inspiration would I need? I have since written more than one thousand poems for birthdays, graduations, retirements, science, world events, philosophy, nature, religious topics, humor, etc. Most of my poems are in traditional styles of rhyme and meter, which I find most satisfying. It helps to have inspiration, such as I had when wooing my wife to be, Jan. I was successful, judging by our forty-eight years together.

Judgement Day

It's not for me to say,
what the Lord will do on that day.
When He comes back to judge all mankind.
But in His word He tells us this,
those on His right will go into His bliss,
but those on the left will go away, nevermore to exist.

Seek the Lord's face, while He may be found.
Call upon His name and you He won't deny.
He is calling to those, who want to be made right.
'Cause He's the only way, the Truth and the Light.

Jesus is the One of whom I speak today.
All you have to do is repent and believe in His name.
He is God's only son,
the One He sent to take our place.
To bleed and die and go to hell,
and on the 3rd day be raised.

Lord, I want to be ready,
on that great and terrible day.
To be able to stand in Your presence
and not be judged and sent away.
Oh God, I'm trusting in Your Son
and I believe what Your word does say.
That all who call upon the Lord
will in that day be saved.

Susan Stark
Colfax, LA

Never Too Late

I never knew what happiness was 'til
happiness was no longer there.
    Days filled with doubt and uncertainty,
it was more than I could bear.
    I had no other place to go, no place that
I could turn.
    What I thought was long lost was
actually something I yearned.
    My family stood by me—whatever I needed
was given—no questions asked.
    But what I needed only One could give,
something that would always last.
    My heavenly Father lifted me up and
He took away my fears.
    Prayer after prayer, my heart poured out,
He heard them through the tears.
    I got the strength I needed when things
were really rough.
    If it wasn't for my faith in Him, how
different things would be.
    I finally have new hope today—a light at
end of the tunnel.
    He got me through the trials of life—His
love is truly the key.

Krista Lail
Connelly Springs, NC

[Hometown] Drexel, NC; [DOB] June 12, 1962; [Ed] high school and some college; [Occ] retired; [Hobbies] gardening, I'm a master gardener; [GA] finding my husband

I have discovered, the past two years, a strength that I never knew I had inside of me. Dealing with my husband's health issues and his losing his job, and almost losing my father due to his health issues, has shown me that I can be strong with God's help. Things are still tough financially, but we will get through this, this I truly believe. Being a master gardener and having my poetry has been my way of gaining strength to face the next day's challenges.

True Faithfulness

Gerhardt, a German lad was tending his master's sheep.
It was near the edge of a forest, away and deep.
A hunter emerged from the woods looking ill.
"How far is it to the nearest village still?"
"Six miles, sir, but the road is a sheep track."
The hunter looked at the sheep track then looked back.
"Will you leave your sheep and show me the way?
I am hungry, tired and thirsty and for you I will pay.
I lost my guide and will pay well for your trouble.
I will match your pay by double.
I'll give you more money than you can make in a year."
"I cannot for I have my master to fear."
"I'll look after your sheep while you get me some food."
"My sheep don't know your voice, it would not be good."
The boy opened his dinner pail and gave his lunch away.
The man ate the coarse food gladly and did not stay.
Later the boy learned who the hunter turned out to be.
The Grand Duke who owned all country that he could see.
The Duke was pleased with the boy's faithfulness so he
sent him to college, gave him a home, so did him bless.

God always remembers, and one's faithfulness rewards.
Remember, everything on this earth is the Lord's.
God loved us so much, His only son His life did give.
So that who is faithful will with God in Heaven live.

Virchel E. Wood
Redlands, CA

[Hometown] Leominster, MA; [DOB] February 13, 1934; [Ed] MD; [Occ] orthopaedic surgeon; [Hobbies] gem and mineral collecting

I am a retired orthopaedic surgeon and a professor of orthopaedic surgery at Loma Linda University, School of Medicine. One of my great joys has been practicing medicine, teaching, and writing. In addition to writing multiple medical journal articles and medical textbook chapters, I enjoy writing poetry and the fulfillment it brings to me personally. All my poems are religious in nature and hopefully provide food for thought.

Do It for You

He's a corpse of a man.
His own reflection disgusts him.
All around is dark and lonely.
Voices scream inside his head.
More! I need more!
He searches for it, just to make them stop.
To make the pain stop.
His body screams in excitement.
He found what his body wanted.
He is plunged into a black abyss.
Dead to the world, he lies alone.
His son cries for his father.
His mother regrets her ignorance.
"My poor baby," his mother says.
"I want my daddy," his son cries.
The black crowding his vision slowly fades away.
He sees his son,
Tears flowing down his face.
"Daddy, please stop."
His heart is touched, his mind is clear.
The dirty needle in his hand falls to the floor.
"I'll quit," he says.
"I'll quit for you."
His little boy reaches up.
"No, Daddy, quit for you."

Brandi Dunlap
Cheyenne, WY

[Hometown] Cheyenne, WY; [DOB] November 14, 1996; [Ed] high school; [Occ] Papa Johns; [Hobbies] drawing, working

This poem was inspired by someone very close to me. He knows the struggle and made the final choice.

Recollections

At an international airport:
  A young man
    alights from a plane, gets on his knees,
    kisses the ground
    In the terminal, stands in line for customs' clearance,
    looks at his passport, and recollections zoom:
      "Fascinating cultures, friendly people,
      beautiful structures, marvelous historic sites."

        More musing: "There as here, Mother Nature rules:
      tides come in, go out; rivers, streams flow; droughts
      smother; rains cleanse, bring forth life; the glorious
      sun rises, sets; the wondrous moon glows...

        But why is it that I so gladly left my travels behind
      me? Ah, I know! It was the limitations, and with that came
      smothering feelings...

        But still—why the magnetic pull to home? What
      makes my country so special? Its achievements?
      Various religions, cultures? Unlimited choices? Hopes
      not dashed, aspirations realized? Fair elections?
      Freedom galore, including the right to criticize,
      protest? Emphatic yeses! That's it!
          I'm overjoyed to be home—
            like Dorothy in Kansas!

Tillie Atkins
Stow, OH

[Hometown] Stow, OH; [DOB] October 9, 1924; [Ed] BS in journalism, BS in education, MA in sociology; [Occ] retired high school teacher; [Hobbies] reading, photography; [GA] being showered with happiness by my beautiful family—children, grandchildren, and great-grandchildren.

Returning to the US from overseas during the "Cold War," the group (a plane load) I was travelling with was overjoyed to be "home" as we landed at the Cleveland Hopkins Airport. Two young college men stepped off the plane, kneeled, and kissed the ground. I based my poem on that flashback.

A Walk in the Park

Each day I take a walk in the park
And I love to watch the children play
But every day as I'm walking I see this little boy sitting on the bench
He never gets to play
To ease my curiosity, I go over to him who sits with his little head hung down
He seems to only focus on the ground
I begin to talk to him but he never looks up or makes a sound
I finally realize the little boy can neither see or speak
From that day forward as I daily took my walk
I started fervently praying for this little boy to get to play, see and talk
A few weeks later, to my surprise, the little boy was nowhere sitting so
I stopped and looked all around
I started praising God because the little boy was playing and running all around
I went over to him and he looked up at me
He said you must be the angel whose presence I felt and heard every day but could not see
You must have talked to Jesus 'cause I can now see and talk and now they let me play
He said *thank you, angel*, and then he ran away

Anna Richard
Taylor, MI

[Hometown] Taylor, MI; [DOB] February 23, 1941; [Ed] high school and some college; [Occ] retired; [Hobbies] bowling and writing my poems; [GA] being married for fifty-six years and raising a wonderful son

I love writing my poems and never did anything like this until my mother passed away (September 24, 2012). Writing gave me comfort. My mother was a very religious person and my poems always end with something about Jesus and Heaven. I am involved in my church and taught children's Sunday school for four years and still do it occasionally. Mother was ninety-eight and seven months when she went to be with Jesus. When I write poems, they are in honor of her.

I Wish I Could Write Love Poems

I wish I could write love poems
about your curly hair
the fullness of your skin
the purr when I touch
your heart center
the deeper sounds when I caress
your garden.

Love poems
like the Brazilians
or the Chileans write
honoring your red dress
and amber-pink thighs.

The hint of breast
when you lean forward
a shadow that lights my desire
and reveals
how deep a kiss
how hot a hand can be.

Bobby Minkoff
Buffalo, NY

[DOB] April 27, 1943; [Ed] PhD; [Occ] psychologist in private practice, retired professor of psychology

My Dear Mother's Gentle Hands

In cherished remembrance of my dear mother Ruby Ann Long Hinton
September 5, 1901–August 25, 1990

My dear mother's gentle hands
always busy through the day
into late at night
always busy setting everything just right
Busy cooking, cleaning the house shiny bright
my dear mother's gentle hands washing my face
brushing my tousled hair
Teaching me to always say a prayer
my dear mother's gentle hands
her loving gentle touch
in long ago bygone yesterday
I still recall today
Therein my heart I long forevermore
for my dear mother's gentle touch
of so long ago bygone yesterday

Billie Jeanne James
Smithtown, NY

[Hometown] North Myrtle Beach; [DOB] July 5, 1931; [Ed] high school; [Occ] homemaker and poet; [Hobbies] writing, collecting, photography; [GA] raising ten children

When my dear first son, Jimmy, was killed in Vietnam in 1969, I started writing poetry in cherished remembrance of him. I have been writing poetry ever since then. I believe through poetry we can reach people on a much deeper level and help build a better world of peace.

I Think; I Arrive Instantly

Practicing, with passion and patience,
And training as outlined by our teachers,
Do Yogis unleash the brain's lush potential,
By mining mind's farthest, deepest reaches.

When every pore in the body is in frenzy,
And every nerve in your skin you recruit,
Then, through the lids your eyes will see,
Hear you will, the slightest wistful thought.

Why, what surrounds you, you cannot see;
Whether you feel or sense is all up to you.
When we imbibe, we experience ecstasy,
And our seventh sense will come on cue.

Then,
I think, I arrive instantly,
I feel, I experience intently,
I touch, I perceive intricately,
I look, I reach all interiors,
I pen, I affect intimately,
I wish, I am granted inevitably.

What Indians mustered through meditation and Yoga,
Now the world in new Millennium is going all gaga;
How without drugs you experience joy and bliss,
And the infinite power of your mind you harness.

Puthalath K. Raghuprasad
Odessa, TX

[Hometown] Vadakara, Kerala, India; [DOB] May 3, 1943; [Ed] MD, MRCP (UK), ABIM, ABA; [Occ] physician; [Hobbies] painting, writing, inventing, astronomy, martial arts; [GA] seventeen US patents

Powers That Be

Tits worn as weapons ready,
Balls still in cavity,
Brassy women, smooth-skinned men
Preen and prate absurdity.

To war, they say.
Surgical strikes, they say.
Incredibly limited, they say.
International norms, they cite.

Your sons, your
Daughters, not ours,
Must go, must fight,
Be maimed, must die.

Now, let us wage justly
Just one more
Teeny-weeny
Little war,

They say.

Mike Welsh
Sioux City, IA

[Hometown] Sioux City, IA; [DOB] February 7, 1946; [Ed] MS in business administration; [Occ] retired US Air Force colonel; [Hobbies] all sports a field; [GA] being a husband and a dad

Memories

Memories can be good or bad,
They can make you very glad!
Memories can come and they can go,
What else about memories should we know?!

Memories can play tricks on you,
Sometimes memories don't know what to do!
Memories can come from the heart,
Your memories can play a big part!

Memories are like a great big book,
Is there any need that we should look?!
Memories can come in the day or at night,
They can have a lot of power and light!

Memories are something we don't want to lose,
Sometimes it's hard for us to choose!
Memories can be great or small,
We hope we remember our memories after all!

Memories are like a game,
They aren't always the same!
Memories can put you to a test,
Sometimes your memories are the best!

Carol Gough
Collinsville, MS

[Hometown] Collinsville, MS; [DOB] January 11, 1958; [Ed] some college; [Occ] assembly worker; [Hobbies] sewing by hand, painting animal magnets; [GA] being a poet

I have been working for thirty years, and I love what I do! I love writing, reading, and creating new poems. I also love reading poems from other authors. My poem was inspired by my best friend whom I admire, love and care for. We spend as much time together as we can at work. I also want to dedicate my poem to my friends whom I will always love and admire!

Eber & Wein Publishing

The Very Best There Is

Truth is, we haven't known each other a very long time
It also didn't take long to realize we were partners in crime.

You've impacted my life in so many ways,
There are just a couple things I would like to say.

Thank you for giving me a friendship I can believe
Not those which lie, cheat, and deceive.

A genuine person is quite hard to find
A special and true one of a kind.

I will forever be grateful to you these past few years
Always having my back, the laughter, and tears.

You've always picked me up and pushed to do better,
I thank you, my lovely volleyball competitor.

I hope we will always be in each other's lives
As we grow older and become mothers and wives.

Teaching our kids a thing or two,
Of love, sports, and the crazy times we've gone through.

This distance thing could never get in the way
For I miss and love you more and more each day!

Heather Ingram
Susanville, CA

My dearest Kaleigh, thank you for everything—everything you are, everything you do. I am truly blessed to have such a wonderful person as part of my life. I am grateful for you every day.

 146

Lingering Love

One summer afternoon
you said hello to me
informally;
I did the same;
but when you walked away
I couldn't help but take
a second look at you.

One summer afternoon
You smiled at me
like you'd do to any
passing stranger.
But why am I awake
at night remembering
the fleeting candor
of your eyes?

One summer afternoon
I held you for a moment
in my arms so tenderly;
and while you're gone
I feel foreboding sounds
that our embrace was more
than just for friends.

It's been so many summer afternoons,
and soon the leaves will fall.
Why do I keep on missing you?

Fidel B. del Rosario
New Britain, CT

Ever since I was a kid, I've always loved singing. I was raised by my grandmother since I was eight months old. She was always humming if not singing while doing her chores. Growing up in a tiny rural town in the Pacific Islands, there wasn't much in entertainment; we didn't even have a radio. But there was always singing. Fast forward to my high school days when I was introduced to poetry by my English teacher. She chose me to recite Joyce Kilmer's "Trees" on stage in a poetry reading contest. Since then poetry has been a loving friend. Let's say I got hooked on poetry. Isn't reading poetry singing?

Cold Echoes

Cold echoes shatter the silent night
Metalic noises drift over stone walls.
The iron gate slams shut with such demonic force,
The sound thunders down through darkened halls.

Winter winds howl within the barren trees,
Branches bend and tear violently at the hardened ground.
Vibrations on old shutters send shivers down my spine.
The bitter cold on the floor has spread all around.

The windows are covered with a blistering white frost.
While frozen icicles hang outside the upstairs loft.
Long, jagged edges that could cut like a knife, vivid and bold,
Present a haunting chill that picks at your soul.

It's a winter like I've never seen,
Bitter and long, merciless and mean.
Relentless in its madness, relief yet to be dreamed.
I stare at the horizon, waiting for the dawn
To break through the darkness and bring the light of day on.

Judy A. Alford
Dunbar, WV

[Hometown] Dunbar, WV; [DOB] February 1, 1948; [Ed] associate's degree in accounting/business management; [Occ] retired secretary, TMH (hospital); [Hobbies] art, poetry, gardening; [GA] my children, my poetry

After my family, life has no blessing greater than that of the written word and the love of a good poem.

Songs of Solitude

Sitting all alone,
Listening to the sounds
Of night,
Dreaming of the future
And the love
We share,

The songs of solitude
Can be
So soothing to hear,
Especially when I'm
Thinking of you,

Soothing sounds,
Listening to the rain
Falling against the pane,
And dreaming
Of my love
For you.

Songs of solitude
Are much more special,
Dreaming of the future,
And love
We will
Always share.

Sharon A. Birmingham
Glen Burnie, MD

The Millennia Star

A savior was born that holy night,
borne of a woman bathed in heavenly light.
At His rising the star shone bright above,
heralding victory, bringing peace and love.
The earth's very core even felt God near.
And evil had everything to fear.
For here came one who would lead the fight
for all people to partake of the light.
And after all these millennia do pass away,
God still will be here to stay.
Then we shall live in God's very city,
promised to us for infinity.
Earth is our footstool.
Moon is our crown.
Son holds us fast,
borne of the light.
The universe, as God, scatters all followers,
more numerous than the stars at night,
all to bring the universe the light.

Darlene M. Dann
Milwaukee, WI

[Hometown] Milwaukee, WI; [DOB] July 18, 1957; [Ed] BS in secondary education, BA in broadcasting, MA in theology; [Hobbies] photography, stamp and elephant collecting, art, piano; [GA] only female graduate among eleven men that became priests and being one out of five winners in University of Wisconsin–Milwaukee alumni art show

This poem, as most, "wrote itself" in my mind. It accompanied my artwork, becoming my Christmas card, with rave reviews! The format connotes images: head, lightbulb. My love of art and writing drive my spirit, making me happiest when creating. I write and create art to inspire people to look beyond the immediate, to evoke something inside that opens their heart and mind anew. I also write and speak French fluently. With bills, no money, nor employment, especially as professor or in lay ministry, my publishing dreams aren't possible. I truly need a miracle for work, art and home!

The War on Peace

"Peace on Earth, good will toward men"
is suffering from dual attacks again
by foes without and foes within.
Religious zealots are the foes without
whose violent beheadings leave no doubt
they aim to drive all peacemakers out!
Peace foes within seek war for gain
as long as arms sales do not wane.
"War on terror!" is their refrain.
"War of error!" a more honest way
to name the folly that every day
adds to the debts our kids will pay!
This war on peace goes on and on
with these two foes from dawn to dawn
perhaps until they both are gone.

Philip N. Martin
Tulsa, OK

[Hometown] Tulsa, OK; [DOB] December 27, 1924; [Ed] University of Missouri–Columbia, AB/BJ 1953; [Occ] seismic exploration, business owner; [Hobbies] reading, writing, gardening; [GA] patent holder, still working, learning at age ninety

Fascination with poetry began in kindergarten with A Child's Garden of Verses received as a birthday gift. Crafting words with rhythm and rhyme to state a stark or subtle thought is akin to the magic of notes arranged for shocking or subtle music. I enjoy both, poetry and music, shocking and subtle.

Eber & Wein Publishing

Old Dogs Give So Much Love

She was faithful, loving, caring,
Even though she was hurting.
She listened to your voice, let you pet her
And call her your silly nicknames!

It was my morning routine.
Get up, fill the water bowl,
Tip the dog feeder, so food would be ready.
She would come to the door, maybe bark to get you up.

When she heard your car, she was at the gate,
Watching you leave and return.
She loved to follow you, back and forth, back and forth
As you puttered in the yard or garden

Loved her kids, playing, chasing, splashing in the pool
Running in the house for the boy,
And letting him put a funny Santa hat
On her head

Her big old head could never get enough petting,
And nudged you for more.
She was part of the family.
Friend, comfort, love, peace.

Mary J. Wakefield
Minden, NE

[Hometown] Minden, NE; [DOB] July 6, 1950; [Ed] BS in education; [Occ] elementary teacher; [Hobbies] reading, crafts, golfing, writing poetry; [GA] marriage, three children, love of career

The Mask

Too scared to reveal
what's deep inside
Your makeup covers
what you try to hide
You know deep down
if the truth should surface
you're scared to death
they would deem you worthless
The mask you hide behind
became your shield
You're no coward
but the enemy real
You know I love you
but it's such a task
I never know
who's behind the mask

Darrell Heath Sr.
Prosperity, SC

[Hometown] Fort Pierce, FL; [DOB] August 15, 1959; [Ed] high school diploma; [Occ]
carpenter; [Hobbies] archery, fishing, oil painting

God's Marvelous Works

I experienced the sun's fiery splendor
As it sets on Caribbean sands.
I surveyed the moon's glorious glistening
On rugged Andean Peaks.
I viewed Michelangelo's elegant art
High above the walls of Sistine.
I raced down the virgin white playland,
Of snow-covered Swiss Alps.

As the candle grows dim on these past memories,
Your image stands out sublime.
For nothing compares to God's marvelous work,
As you do to my heart and eyes.
Your brilliant blue eyes and radiant face,
The touch of your hand in mine.
For the love that we share eternal is etched,
Deep in my subconscious mind.

Kerry Moffett
Layton, UT

[Hometown] Layton, UT; [DOB] January 26, 1962; [Ed] MBA; [Occ] business manager; [Hobbies] golfing, skiing, traveling; [GA] married for twenty-seven years with three wonderful children

English was never a fond subject of mine, but over the years I have found great joy by expressing my feelings through poetry. After traveling the world in my youth, I met my eternal companion and married her twenty-seven years ago. This poem is my tribute to her as God's greatest gift to me. Her radiant smile and stunning beauty brings greater joy to me than any of God's countless and amazing creations.

Dear Lord

I know that I have sinned
I have tried to believe and to forgive
I truly do want to give and live
but everything just goes so bad
for once I wish something would go right
These things make me feel so sad
They say don't worry everything will be all right
Just believe God will take care of everything
He always does things right
You just have to believe
everything will be just right
I guess that's a relief
So I'll just have to believe

Betty Levesque
Cola, SC

[Hometown] Lewiston, MA; [DOB] March 10, 1962; [Ed] high school; [Hobbies] writing poetry, doing crafts; [GA] becoming a mother and nana

I started writing poetry in 1996 when I was going through a rough time—been writing ever since then. I am a mother of three boys: Paul, John and Reggie, and a nana of one grandson, Christian, who is the light of my life. My greatest achievement is getting some of my poetry published. My goal is to someday to get a book of all my poems published.

Lost

Things are said that we don't mean
Hope is found and power filled
All from that one little lie
Deep inside, the spirit's killed

Know the pain that lies inside
Hide it all from prying eyes
Hold it close, keep it still
Piece by piece, the spirit dies

One can live with a broken heart
Carry on no matter the cost
But once the spirit breaks and fades
Everything else is surely lost

Feel the fear and sense of loss
When trust is broken, what's the cost
Betrayed and shattered and left to die
Beyond redemption, a soul is lost

Sydney Chilson
Junction City, KS

[Hometown] Rapid City, SD; [Occ] soldier; [Hobbies] cross-stitch, writing, reading, hiking, skiing; [GA] participating in Bataan Memorial Death March

Most of my poetry is written following some instance of happiness or loss. I have always expressed myself better with words. I find that my greatest inspiration has come from my experiences as a soldier. I have had the benefit of learning from many people I would have never known otherwise. This poem was inspired by a close friend's suffering in a time of loss. In 2012, I had the opportunity to participate in the Bataan Memorial Death March. Though I was unable to complete the course, it was a humbling experience, and I'm planning on participating again.

A Few Good Men

One day a man walking down a street
Started dancing with the trees
As the wind blew the leaves
The man thought of being a thief

Thief of love and truth
Love for the one that made him blue
Truth to reach in his path of life
To find her right to be his pride

He can tell the wounds and aches
Healing upon the scars it takes
Restless nights sharing alone
With moon and stars under the sun

Lonely road he used to go
A few good men walked by the road
Gathering with the hood
They were all as well good

Stepping up and stealing time
To bring you the best of these rhymes

Ilsa E. Garcia González
Aibonito, PR

I Met the Son

I met the son
One day not long ago
I met a man you all know
He turned water into wine
And walked the earth at
That time
He walked on water and
Raised the dead
I saw the heavens open and
I heard a voice say this is
My beloved son
This all happened when I met the son

Ronald Leroy Grayson
Fayetteville, NC

[Hometown] Johnstown, PA; [DOB] October 11, 1954; [Occ] retired military; [Hobbies] collecting coins

The poem is dedicated to the one I love, the love of my life, Gloria Grayson.

God's Creation

Isn't it amazing what was created by the hand
Of our Father, God who made all the heavens and the land?
If there's anyone who has a doubt
About our world, what life's about
Just look around, see the wonder
The lightning flash, the roar of thunder
The trees their boughs reaching for the sky
The graceful birds we see on high
The stars and moon that brighten our night
The shining sun He gave for light
The changing of the seasons, and the colors thereof
The beautiful hues of rainbows that's God's covenant of love
He made the majestic mountains, He made the deep blue sea
He's got a mansion waiting that He's made for you and me
So let's continue with our faith, and continue with our love
And continue to praise our Lord up above.

Doris Parker
Marion, NC

[Hometown] Marion, NC; [DOB] June 17, 1945; [Ed] high school, CNA II training; [Occ] retired nurse; [Hobbies] reading, writing, drawing; [GA] having poems and story published

I am a retired nurse, having worked in the health care field for many years—including nursing home, hospital, and home health. This past November, my husband and I celebrated our fiftieth anniversary. We have two children and five grandchildren. I guess my writing ability, and inspiration, came from my mother. She was a wonderful writer, who could weave pictures with words. She also had some writing published. I have many of her journals. I've written poems for years, usually for family or friends. I also draw pictures occasionally to give as gifts.

Yesterday, Today, Tomorrow

When our tomorrow becomes today
We know not how many more tomorrows
Will come our way

As our yesterday was also today
Tomorrow will now become today

Our yesterday was today yesterday, and
Our tomorrow will become today, tomorrow

So enjoy today, today, and don't worry
About what happened yesterday
Or what might happen tomorrow

So when yesterday was, and tomorrow will be today
Give each yesterday, tomorrow and today
Your very utmost best, as each

Yesterday, tomorrow and today
Will slowly turn into another 24-hour day put to rest

Here's hoping you have pleasant memories of your

Yesterdays, todays, and tomorrows

Harold Stephenson
Center Point, IA

[Hometown] Center Point, IA; [DOB] May 31, 1934; [Ed] high school; [Occ] farming; [Hobbies] carving, writing; [GA] making a 3' x 4' map of the US out of wood and buying a farm

I'm an eighty-year-young, semi-retired farmer. My wife of fifty-eight years, Donna, and I spend our winters in Texas after the crops are harvested. I milked Holstien cows for thirty-five years, and we raised market hogs for fifty years. I did home construction with a neighbor for about ten years after I quit milking. Donna and I enjoy playing mini golf, potluck dinners, musical jam sessions at our rec hall, and games. We have two sons, one daughter, seven grandchildren and three great-grandchildren. We have had a good life.

Observations of the Day

Have you ever?

Sitting out in a parking lot of the hospital,
The day is bright, sunny, and cool.
Perfect day ever!

So why is the parking lot so full?
Why are there a lot of people going in?
And others coming out?

I sit here and see people struggle to go in
And slowly coming out.

What people don't see
Is a 300-lb-plus person barely getting to the
door.
He stops and hides behind a pillar at the door.
And scarfs down a big old candy bar.
In four bites and 9 chews.

Wipes his mouth on his sleeve,
Picks up his bag,
And struggles to get to the door.

And we wonder why the parking lot is
so full.

Lana Tipps
Cedar Lane, TX

I am sixty-four years old and live in a small community in Texas. I've always observed people everywhere I go. That's my entertainment. But now at this age, I'm able to put observations into poem, short story form. That's also my entertainment. I have a lot of people from all walks of life as friends, so I'm in contact with people daily. I raised three daughters by myself, and I am very proud of each one of them. They have raised their children to be good and caring independently.

His Masterpiece

Creation of the world, a masterpiece so fine
Given from His loving heart, to yours and to mine.
Different animals, different weather, even a different race
Extreme changes worldwide, going from place to place.
Different religions each giving out their call
Different powers rising, we can only hope will fall
So much to take in now, it's easy to get lost
But we must get it together or pay the cost.
It's not only financially that we are involved,
But loss of life from differences never resolved.
In this world there is so much dissension
It's time we all give it our undivided attention
Diplomacy certainly hasn't been the way to go,
Answers haven't come till now, so!
God made the world and it should be
A more perfect place than what we see!
We must remember our Creator, beg Him in prayer
"Please dear God Almighty, please I beg be there!
Let's get down on our knees, beg our Father please
Save this world we love so much
Save us with Your loving touch.
Let's all join together, faithful in this race,
His world surely can be such a better place.
With prayers and love it can all be done
In the end *we all have won.*

Constance Floreske
Bath, MI

[Hometown] Detroit, MI; [DOB] November 27, 1939; [Ed] high school; [Hobbies] *writing poems,
playing cards and living*

I am a seventy-five-year-old mother of four, grandmother of five, and great-grandmother of one. I am
retired now, and my life and body have slowed down since the working years. I was always a happy-go-
lucky kind of person—loved to sing, write poems, and just enjoy life with my children who truly were my
life. I give thanks to God for pulling me through some tough situations. I strongly believe he answers our
prayers, and I definitely see the need, so I decided to write about it in a poem. We are his masterpiece!

Dreams

Dedicated to Mom and Dad

As the sun is setting upon my face
It brings a tear to my eye.
I can remember many moments
That could make you laugh or make you cry.

When you stubbornly cannot or will not
Absorb all the beauty surrounding you,
Take a step back and make a wish
Then, possibly, all your dreams will come true!

Life you live to the best that you can
As the sun lowers down upon your head.
Remember this, you are always loved!
Let the moon hold your dreams 'til they be read!

Joan E. Campeau
Clarksville, TN

[Hometown] Clarksville, TN; [DOB] February 28, 1969; [Ed] Gonzaga University—English, science, forensic science; [Occ] medical disability; [Hobbies] writing, science; [GA] my faith and three of my own books being published; also being included in This Time Around

I have a wonderful husband, son, parents, two brothers, a sister, three brilliant aunts, amazing childhood friends, my faith and my therapist! They help me stay grounded while still allowing me to fly free.

My Best Friend

To my best friend Ryleigh Dobson

Moving is very hard.
Last time I moved, my friend sent me a card.
She tells me how much she misses me,
I think of her when I hear the song "Rather Be."

We always laugh at each other's jokes,
Then we would always share a Coke.
She and I always loved to read,
One of my favorites is the one with a boy and a seed.

In the summer we would swim at her house in the pool,
Then her mom would bring us some lemonade to cool.
She said she was stuck on a part in a game,
It was always the same.

We had our ups and downs,
Sometimes it would even get out to the town.
I hope these memories don't fade away,
I hope they are in my mind to stay...

Joey Shears
Middletown, DE

[Hometown] Westerville, OH; [DOB] August 11, 2002; [Ed] seventh grade student at Redding Middle School; [Hobbies] hanging out with the people I love and playing outside; [GA] winning $1000 from a contest about Mark Twain

My name is Joeseph Isaac Shears. I was one of the finalists from last year's contest. I have a wonderful family, Timeka (mom), Mark (dad), Kaitlynn (sister), Zach (brother), Halia (sister), and Tony (brother). And if it wasn't for my grandparents that got me started in poetry, I wouldn't be doing this right now. I have dedicated this poem to my best friend, Ryleigh Dobson. Even though we are a thousand miles apart, nothing will break our friendship.

Untitled

My soul and God keep company
By the winding river that leads to the sea.
As long as I live I shan't forget
The graceful tern or the white egret;
Or the vast expanse of marsh and sky
As the silvery river drifts slowly by
The moss-draped oak and cedar, bent
With scars that wind and time have lent
Or murmuring fronds of tall palm trees
Kissed by a soothing deep sea breeze.
I hear the marsh hen's mating call
And watch the tide's sure rise and fall.
No artist's hand could ever capture
This view which fills my soul with rapture.
So, if you seek tranquility
Go to the river that leads to the sea.
It's there I find a perfect peace
Where heartaches ease and find release.
My soul and God keep company
By the winding river that leads to the sea.

Carol L. Sikes
Hinesville, GA

[Hometown] Brunswick and St. Simon's Island; [DOB] August 9, 1928; [Ed]LPN, RN, PA; [Occ] retired RN and PA, certified interior decorator, ballet teacher; [Hobbies] painting, writing poetry or verse; [GA] opening a daycare stroke center in Savannah

I've done a number of things—I've taught school, ballet, flower arranging —I've been an RN and physician's assistant. I've skied in the Alps and Colorado. My husband was a sheriff for thirty years. He had part of I-95 named for him in May of this year. The legislature also commemorated our sixty-seventh anniversary the day the highway sign was put up. My middle son is now sheriff of our county, Liberty.

Divine Revelation

The grass is green
And 'tis all so serene
With blooms lingering, endearing each scene
Dear smiles springing, enamoring as can be seen
And to the flowing river that doubles its stride
With mission of love to which I give a glad eye
Then on Earth those pictures vault up to the sky
Unveiling heavens so gently as they pass me by
Through those leaps of faith that so disguise
In precise sense, where every meaning belies
Afar those church bells in distance ring
Silent slumber from heaven down they bring
Such beauty in measure I wish to call
With themes of pleasure in view for all
O my! What charms arrest my soul
For every inch of eloquence they gently stole
And to the things created in revelation serene
A stature arises in majestic supreme
He stands in fervor 'midst full orbed gleam
Immortal, unchanged, innocent within
To whose magic these eyes get glued in awe
'Tis that glance that pleaded me to pause
O! Will you not wait nor listen to me for a while
Say not those adieus which take you away for miles
For, in you, lie those chords to my life
Aimed at my heart, chasing me to alight
And now my heart forever stays beguiled
Waking gloriously to each usurping delight

Madhu Goteti
Sugarland, TX

I'm an avid lover of art, culture, psychology and philosophy. The thrums in strums and delights in the humdrums of life have always fascinated me. It is to that feast of reason and flow of soul, all that I see and parts your eyes shall behold! This poem has a Gnostic appeal and its verse portrays spiritual awakening. The supplication to the deity during meditation made me indite this poem. An urge to express divinity in unusual form led me into this rhetoric excursion. Assuredly, you will connect to the intents of my soul if you sink deep to a thousand folds. Happy journey! Hope you enjoy this trip which I refer to as "A hermetic voyage of blissful retreat."

The Artist Is Painting Night

The artist is painting night.
Black—the 'absence of light'
The only color he ever uses,
Once his shades were vivid and bright.

His moons were orange crescents in royal-blue skies,
His colors dazzled my eager eyes.
Portraits elegant masterpieces,
Always sensuous scenes.
His models wore gowns of emerald green,
The sunsets he painted were violent dreams.

His paintings crowned museum walls,
Now they hang in empty halls.
The artist is bitter and old,
Tarnished his canvas of gold.

He said: 'There's nothing to create,
No students left to educate.
No oils to prepare and blend,
I hate these modern fads and trends.'

'Black is the only shade that's pure,
The only color to endure,
All the others fade away
Like love and hope in the light of day.'

Marian Hallet
Los Angeles, CA

[Hometown] Rochester, NY; [DOB] March 16, 1952; [Ed] private high school, one semester at Manhattanville College; [Occ] homemaker, aspiring writer, wife, mother, new grandmother; [Hobbies] writing, reading— mostly fiction and poetry by Victorian poets; [GA] winning Editor's Choice awards for poetry, National Library of Poetry, publication in minor poetry magazines, finally becoming the grandmother of a beautiful baby girl, Fiona

Timeless

The door is locked.
Let me out
My behavior is not like yours
My name is Alzheimer's
I remember the fun times
Loneliness and depression is my middle name
The door is locked
Visit me
I cry out where are my friends?
Unlock the door
Do you remember me?
I am your sister
See you in eternity with Jesus
I remember you.

Monica Sherlock
Carpinteria, CA

[Hometown] Fort Lauderdale, FL; [DOB] July 15, 1949; [Ed] AA in multimedia, AA in general studies, also studied at UCSB and achieved a certificate in alcohol and drug counseling; [Occ] florist, hairstylist; [Hobbies] sculpting, printmaking, creative writing; [GA] accepting Jesus Christ as my savior

I dedicate my poem "Timeless" to my brother, Frank, who is in an Alzheimer's ward in Pompano Beach, FL.

Because I Prayed for You

My little four-year-old came slipping into my room
He said Momma, you'll get better because I prayed for you

I know my Jesus loves me—and He can do things we can't do—
and, Momma, you'll get better because I prayed for you

The tears filled my eyes, I didn't know what to do
when I saw the faith in that little child when he said, Momma, I prayed for you

The doctor had given up, and I guess I had to
until that little four-year-old said, Momma, I prayed for you

He said, Momma, you'll feel better, and we'll be here with you
because my Jesus heard me when I said a prayer for you

Etta L. Bailey
Loudonville, OH

[Hometown] Dickenso Co, VA; [DOB] February 20, 1934; [Ed] twelve years; [Occ] retiree; [Hobbies] writing, trapshooting; [GA] writing songs, poems

I love writing words that can be used in songs, poetry and short stories. I would like to say thanks to Eber & Wein Publishing for doing a good job.

Creation of Love

I am
Creation of love
I am you first
I am me second
I am you second
I am eyes of love
I am as you are
You are as I am
Love of you
Love of me
I am full of love
As you first
As I second
Creation of love
Within me
Created to give
To give it first
The more to give
The more to fill
To love you as I love me
Love one another
Love as I love you
I am the greatest love of all
I am creation of love

Sunny Managan
Miami Beach, FL

[Hometown] Miami Beach, FL; [DOB] June 23, 1952; [Ed] college; [Occ] business administration; [Hobbies] writing, drama, music; [GA] motherhood, being a wife

My inspiration to write this poem came from the love of the holy Trinity, God, Jesus and the Holy Spirit, after all the tribulations in my life. I feel loved by my loved ones, especially my late husband and grandchild who were killed unnecessarily by human beings who have no love for anybody, not even themselves. As a little girl, my mom taught me the greatest love that we have as children of God is that we are saved by Jesus our Lord— His love in the cross saves us. Too many people walk on the blind, dark side of life, in the shadow of death. The people who walk in darkness believe they own this world and do not believe in love, the greatest commandment is what Jesus our savior commands the world: Love one another as I love you. The greatest of all is love.

It Was the Night Before Christmas

And all through the house
Not a mouse was sittin' in his house
Mom and Dad and the kids were all tucked in their beds
And not a word was said until the mouse
Fell out and landed on his head
It was Christmas Eve the milk and cookies were by the tree
Santa rode in on his sleigh that night
And landed on the roof and on his belly,
He laughed like a bowl full of jelly.
He said, I tried to be quiet so it would not wake up Mom and Dad and kids
But it was pretty funny I landed the way I did
I tried to eat the cookies and drink the milk
They left for me I ended up fallin' on
My face and now I can't see I have to find my glasses
So I can go out to the sled and bring in the
Present to put under the tree and if I'm quiet I won't
Wake the kids you see so here I go up the chimney
And I get in my sleigh and ride off into the
Night and say Merry Christmas to all and
To all a good night

Brinda M. Granger
Portland, OR

Garden Swing

As I settle into my garden swing,
a family of quail gingerly cross the edge of a path.
It's peaceful here at my secluded lookout,
capturing what nature has to offer.
As I listen I can hear the calling of two hummingbirds,
bestowing their performance.
Crickets in the distance harmonize their song,
with cautious notes, not to be found.
The sky is captivating, holding all the colors of an
artist's pallet, ever changing, never still.
The hives have slowed their tireless duty,
getting cozy for the cool night.
As the breeze picks up, the windmill follows
its direction keeping up the pace.
Leaves quiver with the descent of winter,
falling softly without a sound.
Time has a different pace on my side of the bluff.
Slowing down, taking a breath, easy and calm.
Quite often I find myself in reflection here,
and sometimes the swing starts without me.

Joann C. Martinez
Concord, CA

Prairie Grasses

Well rested all winter beneath ice and snow,
Now ready to burst forth as only grass will,
Bright green and en masse; determined and upright,
All summer to be the welcome reprieve; carefree and cooling
oases of greenery and freshness and shade.
Move in the breeze as fans would with blades,
Although not rhythmic, but wild; as if directed by whimsy.
A surprise they withhold 'til the appointed time,
When their shoots topped with plumage appear, and opening,
proudly announce a new season!
Then come their seeds.
Not to be bettered, the leaves change shades.
No more the lush green but warm gold, sun-burned brown,
festive red, plum and bronze. Such depth to behold! Spared
in the early autumn clean-up from machete and pruner and sheers.
I come again to cut them down but the sound of dry stalks
as they are blown, with the gusting wind now carrying
a nip from the north, soon to be here... Not just yet.
Let them stand and bend and move a bit more.
I shall come back when the pines are being sold.
And with that familiar, fresh scent in the air,
it will be their time!
Let me then take a blade to them, and a flame to them.
Rake up the remaining strands and let those who pass by here—
past their three season home—long for their return!
Prairie grasses asleep now 'til spring.

Sandra Cervenka
Ingleside, IL

"All human beings are like grass, and all their glory is like wild flowers. The grass withers, and the flowers fall, but the word of the Lord remains forever" (1 Peter 1:24–25).

A Very Special Christmas

At the end of the day, when the sun goes down;
I sit alone and look around.

I think about the day's events,
did I do good, was it well spent?

I think about the blessings God gives,
and I thank Him that my mother still lives.

For late at night when I try to sleep,
the memory haunts me in the thoughts I keep.

I close me eyes and I see her face,
I toss and I turn, and I try to erase.

But I cannot get those pictures to leave,
I can still feel the fear, and the disbelief.

I wonder each day, what I would do
had she gone, and not pulled through?

My heart gets heavy, and I want to cry,
I begin to pray and ask Him why?

Then I remember it's all okay,
God carefully placed me there that day.

He gave us more time to go forth in grace,
may this blessing strengthen our family's faith.

Let us give thanks this special Christmas season,
for we have been blessed far beyond reason.

Lynne M. LeBow
Henderson, TX

[Hometown] Henderson, TX; [DOB] January 26, 1960; [Ed] some college; [Occ] wife, mother, grandmother; [Hobbies] animals, crafts; [GA] my family, children and grandchildren

I wrote this poem as I have written others, to help me heal and to help me express my sadness or grief. This poem is about my mother, who had a near-fatal heart attack while at my home, and I was the only one trying to help her before the EMS arrived. Although there was no heartbeat when they arrived, she was revived and she survived. I had haunting thoughts as a result of the trauma I went through for a long time. I turned to writing to help me be able to vent and therefore heal.

Bloom Where You Are Planted

As I was looking at the different trees
I was so amazed at what I'd seen
They were in one long row, side by side
Each treetop touching to make a wall of green
It reminded me of each of us below
We should flourish just like a tree
And produce our fruit and weather storms
And be a tree of righteousness to those we see.

Our brothers and our sisters need some shade
When the heat of the day comes around
Or when the winter cold wind blows
We need to help them stay warm, safe and sound
We are the children of the most High
He gives us the chance to be a seed
In blooming and producing love
And helping others in their need.

So bloom where you are planted
And watch your blessings flow today
One day you will hear someone say
Thank you for helping me see the way
The joy that will be within you
Words cannot describe
Because you bloomed where you were planted
And the love of God in you abides.

Helen Weaver
Albany, KY

[Hometown] Albany, KY; [DOB] January 23, 1937; [Ed] two years of college; [Occ] cosmetologist; [Hobbies] writing, reading, creating; [GA] my career, my faith

I was born and raised in Albany, KY, and I always loved to read and write. I got married at eighteen and had three girls and one boy. We moved to Brandon, FL in 1967. I attended Tampa Cosmetology School, and I love being creative, working with my hands, sewing, crocheting, and quilting. I love my poetry that my father's family was very talented in writing. We moved back to KY in 1974 and I got my KY hairdresser's license. I attended Lindsey Wilson College for two years and got a degree in business administration. I love poetry. I wrote this poem to give encouragement to people who have the gifts that our Lord has given them.

When You Think You're Walking Alone

When you think you're walking alone
I feel your cold and wearier
heart the strangest trails of the unknown
flooding rivers which turn into a storm
without having any words, I
hear the tunes of hope missing
from your soul in the darkest of
your night, when you think you're walking
alone, I'm like a honeybee stuck to
a bed of roses. When you think you're
walking alone you'll hear those evening
bells ring. You will understand there's
still hope as we go in to pray. Do believe
you're not walking alone. I'm in the midst
of all your brittle steps. I will carry all
your burdens and do believe in Him.
He is the tree of life who possesses all
the heavenly doors. When you think
you're walking alone, look up!

Adgie S. Garrett
Marianna, FL

[Hometown] Marianna, FL; [DOB] March 21, 1957; [Ed] high school and some college; [Hobbies] time with family, writing poetry, cooking, going to church, fishing, reading; [GA] getting the knowledge of God, my kids, having my poem published

I'm a mother of five girls and two boys. My poem inspired me. When I'm to myself and all my memories start flowing in my thought, I just started writing what I feel on paper. It brings a clear picture of my past into understanding for me. It got more intense when my oldest son was murdered, that feeling of him being closer to me in the poems I write.

The Day We've Waited For

The day has arrived
The dream is coming true
Rainbow-colored tables
Fill the space
The cool breeze
On my face
The turquoise feathers
Parade by awaiting guests
Exotic creatures we see
Fluttering wings pass
Us by
Aromas fill the air
The dream is here
Life is complete
Let the celebration begin

Ann Marie Petrizzo
Hazlet, NJ

[Hometown] Hazlet, NJ; [DOB] July 1, 1983; [Ed] BA in English, AA in creative writing; [Occ] office worker; [Hobbies] writing, music, hanging out with friends; [GA] being published

Writing has always been a passion of mine. My mother would always say I was writing the great American novel. I hope to one day accomplish that and be a famous poet and author. I love the works of Poe and Shakespeare. They truly were amazing.

Present

Eyes lock, tips touch, fingers caress.
Knowing that things don't always happen for a reason.
Souls simply need to breathe.
And now... it is just two.
Past wiped clean.
Future white.
All that is... is now.
Bodies entwined, light breeze caressing, candlelight bathing.
There are no expectations here.
For this moment only... no baggage.
Right now it is we.
Us two on the crossroad.
Presence is all that really counts.
Past wiped clean.
Future white.
Exposed just enough.

Becki Barabas
Woodland Hills, CA

[Hometown] Los Angeles, CA; [DOB] December 30; [Occ] music marketing; [GA] my son, Jake Lennon

On the Back Side of a Tear

I saw the cross from the back side of a tear.
No hate could I see, and I saw His face so clear.
Only love and compassion, not the first sign of fear.
I saw my salvation from the back side of a tear.

The stripes upon his back were pressed against the tree.
Stripes His word does say, healing for you and me.
The devils were laughing, all around I could hear.
But I saw my salvation from the back side of a tear.

Oh how they mocked Him, when they thought he would die…
They didn't know He was giving eternal life to you and I.
Heeleei Bohamba, translate when you hear.
I saw life eternal from the back side of a tear.

You may say that it's blurry, and truth is hard to tell.
But looking through tears of repentance won't send you to hell.
You will sure know the difference when you clasp that hand so dear.
You can see your home eternal from the back side of a tear.

Timothy Dinkins
Melissa, TX

[Hometown] Texarkana, TX; [DOB] September 2, 1927; [Ed] eighth grade; [Hobbies] singing, composing songs and poems; [GA] 1969 tribute to the astronauts, Christmas on the Moon

I moved to Glendale, CA, where I was known as the Texas Cut-up. I moved from there to Lapunte, CA and put in a studio named Cartwheel Records. Then I moved back to Texarkana. There, the International Society of Poets published two of my poems: "A Witness to Your Crown" and "God's an Antique." I was elected into the International Poetry Hall of Fame.

Love

Polka-Dot Polly
From East By-Golly
Never met a man
Who could not
Make her smile
As this blue world
Kept right on turning

She awoke one morning
To wind and rain
In a house with hardly a roof
Most of the windows—minus a pane
But with six children
And a slew-root horse
She kept on smiling
Of course!

Donald Ransom
Detroit, MI

[Hometown] Detroit, MI; [DOB] December 11, 1927; [Ed] BA, Wayne State University; [Occ] retired social worker; [Hobbies] travel, landscape, photography; [GA] grandson's high school graduation

I spent nine years in the military, which took me to Italy, the Far East, and France. My inspiration is the weather and historical diversity.

To My Mother Who Was Like No Other

Mother, you remind me of so many things.
Of porcelain dolls, urns, locks, and butterfly wings.
You always loved to be out-of-doors;
Planting roses, lilies, tomatoes and gourds.
The smell I remember when I was growing up
Was baby powder and Eau de Toilette of Lilac
on your sleeve cuff.
Also, on Sundays and special occasions,
You adorned your head with hats, your hands with
white gloves, and your long hair in a bun.
Presents were always wrapped in silver
fashioned with a silk bow.
Where you hid these delights, to this day I don't know.
We always sat down, every day at three.
Good china was gotten out for afternoon tea.
Of all the things I remember when I think of you,
Is your teaching me Bible Verses, each day at two.
Then at bedtime you would always ask and say,
"Tell me, my love, what words of God did you learn today?"
So, it's no special occasion, but I just wanted to relay,
"Mother, I loved you in each and every way.
I miss you terribly, to this very day."

Jeri D. Walker-Boone
Laurens, SC

I have been penning poems for over fifty years—since I was in high school. My poems have been published in over thirty anthologies. Although medicine was my vocation, now that I have retired, poetry is now my primary career goal.

Unforgiving Winter

The wind whispers curses into the trees,
As I look out the windows of my room.
Snow keeps falling through the relentless breeze,
And the sky's a prison of darkened gloom.
Thin ice has now covered much of the earth,
With our lakes getting frozen all around.
Harsh winds work at delaying spring's rebirth,
Causing the trees to sway above the ground.
Sensing the cold air surging up my spine,
My body shutters from the chilling blast.
I see animals scurry up a pine,
As another day flees into the past.
I've found myself trapped right in the center
Of this cruel and unforgiving winter.

Thomas Koron
Grand Rapids, MI

[Hometown] Grand Rapids, MI; [DOB] May 19, 1977; [Ed] Western Michigan University—MM; [Occ] guitar instructor; [Hobbies] music, poetry, literature; [GA] my daughter, Rayana

I have always had a strong passion for poetry. I am particularly fond of the works of Edgar Allan Poe, William Shakespeare, John Keats, Robert Browning, Christina Rossetti, William Wordsworth, Samuel Taylor Coleridge, Percy Bysshe Shelley and Lord Byron. All of their poetry is powerfully written in their own unique voices. Reading their work has definitely had a profound impact on me as a writer. My favorite poetic forms include the sonnet, the villanelle and the dramatic monologue. This poem is my poetic depiction of the harsh weather that we experience in Michigan, and the scenery that goes with it.

Broken Apart

The world in the state in which it is
Reminds me of how it should be.
There is no color code, if we can see
Not the things others teach.
All minds come from one, which means in
Mind, we should all be of one.
As there is no reason to point those fingers,
Everyone passes on, have we not seen this?
Over and over, the call has been for love,
Yet where do we start to put back the hearts
Of those caught up and torn apart?

Gregory Bangs
Lake View Terrace, CA

[Hometown] Lakeview Terrace, CA; [DOB] February 26, 1957; [Ed] some post college; [Occ] security; [Hobbies] music, writing poetry, old movies; [GA] making Best Poems and Poets of the 20th Century

I was inspired by what I have learned and seen—years of watching the same thing over and over again! I've been published four times in the National Library of Poetry; nine times in the International Library of Poetry; four times by Noble House; seven times by Eber & Wein; self-published eight of my own books of poetry; was awarded eight awards and met the king and queen of Rawanda; am on the wall of tolerance in Montgomery, AL; and am a distinguished member of the International Society of Poets.

Tiger Tracks

A hunting we will go,
trailing repeat patterns in the snow
down to the river &
                                   farther below
where its current runs deep through the ice
with a black undertow....

Has our quarry eluded us
by stealing the show?

Dividing, conquering,
turning friend into foe?

Take care, be aware
of an uncertain time:

Look within, walk slow;
unseen things
could become what you know....

Suddenly—
so much depends on the call of a crow.

James W. Stonehouse
Delray Beach, FL

[Hometown] Delray Beach, FL; [DOB] May 5, 1956; [Ed] liberal arts program, Tulane University; [Occ] currently sidelined by a health concern; [Hobbies] photography, astrology; [GA] learning to fly

A poem can be the epicenter of many things coming together all at once, and I felt this especially to be true after having encountered the story, The Tiger: A True Story of Vengeance and Survival *by John Vaillane (ISBN 978-0-30738-904-6). What struck me most vividly was the theme of marginalization and its effect both in the Primorye Territory of Far Eastern Russia and here at home in overly urbanized tri-county Florida. Despite very different appearances, the life dramas being played out on a daily basis are exactly the same.*

Snow Days

For the last couple of days
adults and kids all have
been playing in the snow.
Snow men were made.
Rides and rides and rides
down snow-covered hills
on sleds and sleds made of
lids, cardboard boxes, and even
an air mattress.
Doggies ran and bit at
the falling snow.
A horse was saddled and ridden.
What a sight.
Neighbors enjoying
visiting while playing.
No mail, or going to work
or school.
Pictures sent promptly
of this fun.
And hearing of willing
help given to those in need.
Some preferred to enjoy the
beauty from the inside.
A brief slow-down pace.
These are snow days in the South.

Judith E. Tarbox
Charlotte, NC

Grandma's Tresses

I remember Grandma's hair
All rolled up in a bun
Same old 'do', no matter where
It never came undone
Matchless gray big hairpins
Held the strands together
Extra pins lay in a tin
Upon her big brown dresser
Us grandkids gawked and pondered
Does she ever let it down?
Let's sneak a peak when Grandma's asleep
Would her hair touch the ground?
Our creeping awoke Grandma—she bounced right up and sneezed
Rising tall, her hair did fall—it barely touched her knees

Carleen Bunde
Wallace, ID

[Hometown] Wallace, ID; [DOB] December 4, 1938; [Ed] college; [Occ] retired graphic designer; [Hobbies] writing; [GA] mother to my sons

The memory of us grandkids gathered around our sweet grandma inspired me to write "Grandma's Tresses." We'd watch her chubby fingers quickly move while she sat in the over-stuffed easy chair, darning a pair of our socks or mending our britches, and we'd point and snicker at her gray hair all rolled up on top her head and whisper to one another, "How long do you think Grandma's hair would be if we saw it hanging down?"

A Hidden Place

To find a place to think on things
Is best I know in autumn time,
From mist-blue hills of the northern world
A regal panoply descends
And clothes pale summer in scarlet dress.

Pressed by an urging wind
One golden leaf in timid flight
Whirls to a muffled tune
Then drifts in weariness to the waiting earth.

Hurry now before the snows of winter come
And savor deep the ageless season's change;
This place apart, a hidden wood
Where time in reverent stillness slows
And shadowed twilight dulls
The flaming forest-side
Then joins the end of day.

Bruce Mancevice
Marblehead, MA

[Hometown] Gloucester, MA; [DOB] July 27, 1945; [Ed] high school; [Hobbies] writing

Remembering Vince

Your pleasant voice
Your heart of gold
You never gave up when the doctor told
We prayed for you and wished you the best
God had chosen to do the rest
He took you so young we don't know why
You suffer no more He's taken your pain
You've touched our hearts with love and care
We cry at night wishing you here, knowing
Someday we know we will be there
To see your face, touch your hand remembering why we all began
The memories of life, laughter and love will be held close to our hearts from a glow above
Without you here our hearts will ache
But happy memories is what it takes
To heal the sadness, never forget, the blessings in life we all get
A husband, father, friend is gone
His memory and love will always live on

Judy Novak
Nazareth, PA

We love you, Vince! June 22, 1962–June 27, 2014

If

If I never see another sunrise
I have savored so much
Family, friends and loved ones
The hand of God's gentle touch

He is my comforter, my Savior
My very best friend
He will be with me even to the end
God is the Holy one on whom I can always depend

When unexpected changes in my life
Turn for the worse Don't worry, I'm fine!
Only through the word of God
I put all of my trust

Often times I felt like I was walking in despair
I prayed silently to God for I knew he would always be there
I pray my living for God was always shown
For His many blessings will forever be known

Jearlene Sanders
Maysville, NC

[Hometown] Maysville, NC; [Occ] nurse's assistant; [Hobbies] writing, reading, having poems published

I was born November 3, 1947 to the late Thomas and Florena Canady. I was a 1966 Graduate of JHS. I have three children: Kellie, Christopher, and Nevalyn (FeFe). I have thirteen grandchildren. Through poetry I can express my true feelings. Poetry inspires me, it motivates me, it encourages me. It touches my inner soul. I'd like to dedicate this poem to Van Earl Baker in loving memory of his wife Katie Mattocks Baker (March 2, 1954–September 12, 2014). Katie saw many things in her life. When she opens her eyes again, she will see Jesus. Gone but never forgotten.

Little Things

Even a smoldering ember's presence can fill a room.
Just like the lightest touch of air on wings can ignite flight.
One dewdrop can feed a hummingbird.
In the end it's the little things that get us through.
Just as it's little things that shadow the strength of tomorrow's hand.

Derek Walsh
Millis, MA

When I wrote this poem, I wanted to express how even one soft word can brighten a day, how even if one good deed finds its breath in the world it will help us all to breathe. See, it's the little things that can sustain hope and bring rise to even bigger hopes. To my nieces Jaden, Falyn, and Virginia, and all young children born of light, don't let the shadows come in and weigh down your dreams. Instead, let the shadows lead you past your troubles to rise.

A Handwritten Letter

An e-mail or text can be clicked away
A handwritten letter lasts forever and a day
A letter on screen with keyboard at hand
Can quickly cross oceans or miles of land
But a handwritten letter is a gift from the heart
Kept forever as memories until life here departs

Marcia Keck Cline
Defiance, OH

[Hometown] Defiance, OH; [DOB] September 25, 1951; [Ed] bachelor of science in nursing; [Occ] registered nurse in intensive care; [Hobbies] art, poetry, antiques; [GA] taking care of people in need

I wanted to go into art but have worked in some aspect of nursing since I was age seventeen. I feel God steers us in the direction he wants us to take. I received my critical care and cardiac medicine certification after college and have utilized my education to help others. Art and poetry are avenues I utilize for my spiritual and physical wellbeing along with the love of my family, husband, and four beautiful Yorkshire terriers.

The Sea Beckons

It isn't just the pull you feel
When you approach the shore.
It isn't the tide coming in—
No, it's much, much more!

There's an overwhelming pull
To be ever so near…
And to watch those breakers
Without any fear.

The crash of the waves
Can make your heart throb.
And lift your spirits
Till you want to thank God.

Diving through the breakers
At an early age of five,
We learned a valuable lesson—
That we really could survive!

It's always felt at the ocean,
And at times near the river or bay.
Whenever the waves are small and rhythmic
They steal your soul away!

Virginia D. Wells
Danbury, CT

[Hometown] Danbury, CT; [DOB] March 9, 1925; [Ed] BA degree plus thirty hours, Western MD College; [Occ] elementary teacher; [Hobbies] making scrapbooks, music; [GA] my two sons: Harry and Thomas

I was born on Long Island, NY, very near the Atlantic Ocean, and the Peconic Bay. We spent many nights camping at the ocean beach. We learned to dive through the breakers and swim at both beaches, cutting our feet on the sharp sea grasses. Since my mother died when I was three years old, my four sisters and I crossed Long Island Sound on many summer trips to relatives. We enjoyed the ferry rides, and they surely fostered my love of the water.

Skysong

With brightest shocking blue I'm girt,
Declare God's glory to the earth.
And sometimes whipped white clouds appear
To paint the music of the spheres.
Sometimes I'm empty, solid gray
And more subdued my song of praise.
When dawning breaks with rosy glow,
His glorious handiwork I show.
With freshest shades of morning blue,
I tell His mercies, ever true.
When heavy, low clouds stripe my face,
I sing His steady, constant grace,
And wispy cirrus clouds employ,
To sing His never-ending joy!
With sunset's fiery flaming flood,
I shout the glories of our God!
Cool lavender twilight shades abound,
And with His majesty resound.
Then with the lustrous star-flung night,
I sing the songs of His delight.
My vaulted starry heavens ring,
To praise, adore my wondrous King,
Yet though my colors shift and change,
Eternally, I sing His praise,
His marv'lous wonders tell abroad;
Behold, and praise your matchless God!

Joyce Keedy
Towson, MD

[Hometown] Towson, MD; [DOB] July 23, 1957; [Ed] BA in music; [Occ] private music teacher, former church organist 1981–2010, substitute church organist; [Hobbies] writing, music, drawing, painting, reading, walking, history, geography; [GA] using the gifts God gave me in music and writing to glorify His name

Lord Jesus is my Savior, I write to His glory. My first poem was written at age ten. I have taught over nine hundred children and adults to play musical instruments. I was a church organist 1981–2010, now I am a substitute organist. My fifth poetry book, Little Blond Child, was published in 2014. I enjoy nature and love to look at the sky, both day and night. The beautiful vaulted heavens declare God's glory! When I look at a bright blue sky with beautiful clouds, I marvel to think it will never look exactly the same way twice. I wrote "Skysong" to celebrate the beautiful, ever-changing sky declaring God's glory.

To the Less Ability Office

I'm working past the prime of life with clicking joints that freeze,
And headaches cutting like a knife that drop me to my knees.
The asthma reigning in my lungs attacks and disobeys,
now allergies take hold my tongue, with neither being okay!
Sometimes when I awake at night, being called (again) by nature,
An eye is blind, the left or right, just hope it's nothing major!
A 'C-pap' is offensively for treating me in bed,
For now there's strong propensity to fall asleep where led!
My thyroid's lumpy, (sets of two) but test prove all are fine,
Still, ultrasound being more than few, might screw up down the line!
My goiter's showing (to my shame. I'll wear high collars often!)
The nodules on my kidneys, which remain, are not forgotten!
I'm on a mild-sedating pill I'll see is worth a try,
And if it "chills," my pressure will jump hurdles to the sky!
So here's the spiel:
Are cliente at all the likes of me,
Whose health is frail—which works out well
With less ability?

Penelope H. White
New Kensington, PA

[Hometown] New Kensington, PA; [DOB] June 27, 1949; [Ed] AA in specialized business; [Occ] medical secretarial assistant (retired); [Hobbies] singing, reading, poetry; [GA] raised a good son alone

I wrote this poem "to the less ability office" as sort of poking fun at myself before I finally retired (early and now on disability retirement). I was feeling a bit overwhelmed with pains, tests, and needing to schedule doctor visits around work schedules. Looking back on this, I created this poem to poke fun at the frustrations I was feeling (and living) at that time. I really have these ailments, but life could be a lot worse! (Thank God)

Parents

We are your parents,
You can see and count on us,
For all the years we've had your trust,
Through good times and bad we've had your trust,
And have traveled far, and always looked for that falling star.
Now as parents we don't always agree,
But in this life of ours, isn't that the way it should be
The day will come and you too will be parents like us
You too will see.
Now you, you've seen the things we have had to see,
and parents you'll too have become, like us have one
Parents too, you see.

Marian Feness
Depew, NY

[Hometown] Depew, NY; [DOB] April 18, 1924; [Ed] first through twelfth grade; [Occ] homemaker; [Hobbies] sewing, writing; [GA] publishing four poems, my work teaching ballroom dancing, modeling, sewing, upholstering, writing poetry, decorating my home, teaching my six children the facts of life

The Journey

When we first met it was an instant connection
It was a shy glance, then the first smile
A nervous laugh at something silly we said
Then the touch of our hands as we walked together
The gentle kisses stolen at red lights or movie theaters
Slowly our true love bloomed as we looked to the future
First it was the diamond ring, then the wedding ceremony
Our first kiss as husband and wife
The first apartment so lovingly decorated
The plans for our future family
And our love grew stronger
It was our first house, the excitement of each day together
Then our little girl came with her golden curls
And the joy she brought us was unending
Again our love grew
Then came our little boy, his smile so sweet and shy
With his love and determination in all that he does
All of their accomplishments were ours too
Our love grew on the strength we got from each other
Because our love still grows today

Camille Copicotto
Stony Point, NY

The poems I write are from feelings I have deep inside me. This poem was written about ten years ago, and I never had it in a poetry contest. When I read it again, I thought it would be a good poem to send in.

Hold My Hand

If I hold my hand
I'm walking alone
If I hold your hand
I'm not alone
So hold my hand
Old friend I'm alone
I'm not alone
When you hold my hand
I'm happy when you hold my hand
So I'm not alone
I so can walk with you
So I won't be alone
So when I die
Put my hands together
Then I will be alone
So give me kiss goodbye
Then hold your hands
You will be alone

David R. Wayne
Kellogg, MN

[Hometown] Kellogg, MN; [Ed] high school; [Occ] retired; [Hobbies] reading books, hiking; [GA] writing stories

I have two sons. I'm over seventy years old and have four grandchildren. I have two great-grandchildren. I like to tell stories to the kids. I take care of my mother. She is in her nineties. I like to play cards and I'm working on a book. The I.D. Four Hold Your Hand From My Best Friend. We lay in bed and talk. I would rub his feet, they would hurt. He would hold his hands. His name is Jamie Derry. I call him Snicelfritz, my best friend.

Space Shuttle

In the year nineteen eighty-six, the United States tried launching a shuttle into space.
That shuttle blew up all over the place.
For weeks they went over the head and tail sections of that thing,
the problem was one of those big rings.
Made calls to Washington, some who wrote letters
said if the president would come up with six or eight billion,
the next one would be a darn sight better.
Reagan was excited, said he would get the money somehow,
even if he had to go to his ranch and sell off a few of his cows.
September twenty-nine, nineteen eighty-nine, a couple hours before noon,
they made a successful trip out there toward the moon.
Had a little trouble right at the start.
If things kept going like they had been that shuttle would have come apart.
Engine started icing up antenna coming loose,
if they would have had a couple fifths aboard, the whole crew would have been juiced.
The ground crew said they were real pleased.
But then they weren't the ones out, you see.
Making real good progress and there was no more confusion,
a few more trips around they would have caught the Soviet Union.

James B. Brown
Saxton, PA

[Hometown] Saxton, PA; [DOB] August 1, 1940; [Ed] twelve years; [Occ] laborer; [Hobbies] painting, gardening, poetry; [GA] raising my children

I am a husband and father of three: two sons, one daughter. I am grandfather to six and great-grandfather of three.

Come Walk with Me

Come walk with me
   along a country road,
   in the spring.
See the golden butter cups
   stretch and yawn
   to the call of the wind.
Hear the jays gossiping
   wonder what
   they have to say?
Listen to the whispering
   and mumbling of the wind
   through the trees;
Catch the symphony of the birds
   performing to
   the nodding daffodils;
Breathe all the wonderness
   aroma of spring,
Feel the magic of
   a spring day—
   Come walk with me.

Betty Jo Stewart
Crawford, CO

[Hometown] Crawford, CO; [DOB] August 16, 1931; [Ed] BA in English; [Occ] retired; [Hobbies] writing, sewing, some guilding

I am a mother of a wonderful family, a grandmother of twelve, a great-grandmother of five. I have a BA in English, which I achieved when I was fifty-five years old. This poem came to me one day when I was walking home across a field. I began writing poetry in college and continue today. I enjoy writing and reading poetry. I enjoy living in this small town. It is a real "home" town.

Thanksgiving

This day is a genuine American holiday
When families gather at their parents' house
And thank one another for life of great quality,
Especially parents, grandparents, and spouse.

This started at times when first settlers had landed here
From old British Isles, the whole ocean across;
The local tribes treated them finely and dandily
With bonfire, turkey and cranberry sauce.

The settlers were grateful for kind generosity,
And they have established the Thanksgiving Day
When thanking becomes an act of reciprocity
For kind things and words people do and say.

This day is observed now for over four centuries
With happy reunions abundant with joy,
With lots of exchanges of presents and pleasantries,
With thanking each other for life they enjoy.

November's fourth Thursday evinces with clarity
That kindness and selflessness play a key role
In helping the stranded to raise their vitality
In tough situations beyond their control.

Americans thank friends and relatives graciously,
They give thanks to those who had helped in their lives;
The Thanksgiving Day was established sagaciously,
It is celebrated through years and it thrives!

Paul R. Friedman
Reston, VA

I was born in Moscow, Russia, to both American parents. My father was a poet, and I apparently inherited his poetic skills, but I wrote my first poem only at twenty-seven. My new poem, "Thanksgiving," reflects my views about this, one of the greatest American holidays, celebrated for over four hundred years after local American tribes helped the first settlers by keeping them warm and feeding them with fried wild turkeys under cranberry sauce.

Cloaked in Time

Cloaked in time,
    the yesterdays stir
    from under their disguises;
        tip-toeing featherlike
        from knowing to dreaming...
Carried in light
on star-touched rivers,
    my love strays past
    our connecting points —
        unable to hold the moments
        seen so clearly
        in these half-illuminated shadows.
Emptying themselves
into an ocean of days-gone,
    the liquid hours
    bend and shift the light;
        reflecting the myriad
        images of all the touching
            that has slipped away
            between us...

Judy-Suzanne Sadler
Cortez, CO

[Hometown] Cortez, CO; [DOB] October 13, 1944; [Ed] BA in English, PE, vocal music, and health, master's in counseling, gifted certificate, ESL certificate; [Occ] retired teacher/counselor; [Hobbies] singing, writing, painting, stained glass, sports, animals; [GA] seeing my students succeed

I've been lucky enough to have lived in some of the most beautiful parts of this country and have a strong affinity for both oceans! In addition to the degrees I listed above, I maintain and update my interests in space science and earth science. I've taught/counseled for forty-three years, both in public schools and on the Ute Mountain Ute and Navajo reservations, developing a gifted program for Native American students on the latter sites. Love and loss are themes common to all people, and often appear in my poetry.

Africanized Killer Bees

They stung me again—my friend.
The murdering Africanized killer bees—please—
Buzzing around my porch light at night
They caused me a terrible fright alright.
They stung me on my big toe—it puffed up bloated
And hurt me so—you know.
I squished the bee with my tennis shoe you fool.
And fed it to my black widow spider.
She ate the killer bee—it's inside her.
The Africanized killer queen lives in my attic.
The bees fly down and make me panic and
Frantic and when they sting me they make
Me sick and swell up and puff up
Like a baboon or a full yellow moon
I feel like a goon or a loony loon.
Or a big buffoon playing a bassoon.
Africanized killer bees—
They are going to be the death of me—
If you please?

Marc B. Stein
San Diego, CA

Untitled

Move over!
I'm not yet finished!
You came to devour me
tooth and nail

I stood up gallantly refusing to fall
The fight is not yet finished!
For in the end it is I
that will be Queen of the Ball!

Joayne Baruta
Stewartsville, NJ

I'm a New Jersey-born girl! My grandfather was born in Ferror Coruna, Spain. He actually had the same name as the noble Spanish explorer, Francisco Vasquez! Story has it that my grandfather loved to decorate the patio with lights of brilliant hues. With this, I believe my artistic side/writing was borne as well as love of artist Vincent Van Gogh. My grandmother, born in Ukraine, came with great gifts of uniqueness, determination, and a jovial sense of humor, which reflects in my writings as well! And so, I attribute much of who I am to my ancestry!

Girl's Night

Girl's night we are three of a kind
looking for a club to rock our mind
Karaoke singing with a smile,
nine until two lasted a long while
Guitar playing getting down dropping
to the floor without a frown,
at the club across town.
Drinks in a fishbowl will rock your soul
one of them you will hit your goal.
Jell-O shots red, blue, and green
just two of them will make you mean
Fun and laughter at the bar,
keys hanging on the rack from our cars
Food good and plenty,
hot wings on platters ten or more just for pennies
Draft beef from a mug,
counting from one to three from club to club
Girl's night we are three of a kind
looking for a club to rock our mind
Go across the street found a club with lots of heat,
"crabcakes stuffed" extra meat!
Gasping line dancing on the floor
"packed," too full can't close the door
Girl's day throughout the year,
fun and happiness without any fear
come and join Saturday night cheer
"This night is for each its own"
We do know we are not alone

Patricia A. Allen
Baltimore, MD

[Hometown] Baltimore, MD; [DOB] April 23, 1948; [Ed] GED; [Occ] medical assistant; [Hobbies] writing, singing and dancing; [GA] being a good mother, poet writer at best

I'm married to Eugene E. Allen, a mother of six children, three boys and three girls. I also have a dog named New Whitesock. I have a host of grandchildren, great-grandchildren, family and friends who keep me very happy. The reason I wrote "Girl's Night" is because of the good times my daughters, Dreamia, Tanyell and I have every Saturday night, a very fun night, just the three of us—mother and daughters "three of a kind like to rock our mind."

Who Would Have Thought?

Maple tree branches in our yard reach toward the sky.
Bark is a squirrel's place to run to his home up high.
I found an acorn under the tree that he thought he hid.
Maple trees don't drop acorns. So I think he did.
I saw him running with something red. That was a clue.
He robbed my tomato plants, strange, but true.
I watched a choice tomato grow and ripen day by day.
The bandit angrily growled when I came and took it away.
I planted the tomatoes. How dare he challenge me?
Just because they grow near his home—the maple tree.
Attack by a vicious squirrel? No, I don't think so.
Run home, you little rascal. Goodbye. Shoo. Now go.

Janeene Versfelt
Raritan, NJ

[Hometown] Raritan, NJ; [DOB] December 10, 1936; [Ed] high school, two years college, vocational school, adult education classes on subjects of interest; [Occ] nurse; [Hobbies] music, writing, reading; [GA] raising a family

I was born in Alabama to parents who loved each other dearly. They taught by example that care and love are a way of life. I thought about writing a poem about the stately maple tree, bird nests, leaves changing colors in the fall, and physical fitness from raking the leaves. We have all read this poetry in various forms over the years—I zeroed in on an incident frozen in time in "Who Would Have Thought?"

The Plan

Dressed in a tightly wrapped bath towel of white
Keeping darkened plots hidden close and well beneath
Where depth and shallowness can easily co-exist
When the glass is half empty and when the glass is half full

It never makes sense when there isn't any sense
And the lack of it in common
Only fuels the deficiency that grows like a mold
With anxious desire to flee this ongoing loss

Patience can only be a virtue
Until I skip the next in line
For a table that isn't mine
And I haven't even been waiting until now

The choice had to be made yesterday
Yeah, I think it was last night
Wasting time wandering has to run out today
Or else it is my mystery that will

I'll send that note along tomorrow
To be read aloud in surround sound stereo
As I bite off a huge piece of this vanity
That is far much more than I can possibly chew

Patricia Richter
New Berlin, WI

[Hometown] Eagle, WI; [DOB] October 12, 1974; [Ed] AD in fashion marketing; [Occ] retail merchandising; [Hobbies] Barbie collecting, couponing, dancing; [GA] overcoming my severe shyness

Keeping a daily journal and writing poetry have always been therapeutic and enjoyable ways of expressing myself. I have also kept diaries for several years of all the dreams I have been able to remember. I find it fun to analyze them with a dream dictionary even though they are usually bad omens. As a troubled sleeper, most of my dreams are quite strange, yet a lot of them have inspired the creativity in my writing and my artwork. My passion for all genres of music has also led me down the path to songwriting. Stay tuned!

sacred

he said
she said
down gossip street
uhhhhh ohhhhh
officer on his beat
vipers up for a treat
officer cleaning the streets
vipers heading out
to a jail cell
celebrate victory
he said
she said

Marguerite Ortega
Albuquerque, NM

[Hometown] Albuquerque, NM; [DOB] May 20, 1957; [Ed] bachelor of university studies; [Hobbies] religion, helping people, learning; [GA] looking after my mamá and papá

People fascinate me! I get caught up in everything about them. I find every poem, every story is about someone in an abstract way. Writing about a bird is hard to do. God opened up creation for us. As God's children, we live on His great earth! As Americans, we live in this great country!

A Portuguese Lullaby

My bright companion, darling doll
My treasure, she's silent, ah but
She loves me, she's the Finian Queen, Renata Zoey
She tells me her secrets with her clear brown eyes
And our days together are peaceful and full
We spread out a blanket for cookies and tea
While Nature composes Her symphony
Then beside the lake in the park
Into our small boat we slowly embark
I clutch her tightly, she cannot swim
And I push away from earth and into the wind
Into a world of to and fro
As if forever we'll drift and dream, yet we know,
As shadows fall on our golden pleasures,
Our special time together will point us to the end of day
With a million nighttime points of light on display
Their beauty above silences us, our eyes heavy with sleep
Our thoughts and dreams ever peaceful and deep
And softly I whisper in her ear in the hush
"Shush, my little Zoey, shush."

Carol M. Heineman
Lehigh Acres, FL

[Hometown] Louisville, KY; [DOB] March 3, 1951; [Ed] BA in French, Spanish minor, University of Georgia; [Occ] retired; [Hobbies] languages, poems, writing; [GA] I speak French, Spanish, and German. I am studying Russian, American sign language, Arabic, Chinese, Portuguese, and Ojibwe.

Words are the powerful, noble steeds of every language on Earth upon which humanity rides with dignity and purpose into the light, we hope. That said, you may read my poem for the whimsical picture of a little girl and her favorite doll, or you may read it for the reason I wrote it, or both. I made it up as a tool to memorize the Portuguese consonants. It was fun. So, if you desire, get a book on Portuguese, work on a new language, and locate the English sounds in lines one through five and fourteen through twenty.

Our Beloved Sister

God came to me the other night in a vision. He said
"I'm taking your sister home to help seek her wisdom.

You see I need a master gardener she is the best one
for our heaven. She will tend to the beautiful flowers
and help nurture all the children."

I reached out to God with my tiny hand trembling. I
told him how we all loved her and how much we will
miss her.

He took my trembling hand and not a word needed
spoken. We sat there together as I cried my heart was
broken!

When I awoke the next morning and remembered my
vision, I thanked God for his love and eternal wisdom.

Then I whispered to God, "Thank you for letting me
see her as an Angel, we will all dearly miss her. She is
our beloved sister."

Clifford Carl LaRue
Davenport, WA

*[Hometown] Spokane, WA; [DOB] October 26, 1952; [Ed] BA in liberal arts; [Occ] author of Three
Little Alaskan Princesses Find Gold; [Hobbies] fishing, hiking, writing; [GA] twenty-five years
living an Alaskan adventure*

*Our sister, Charlotte (Sherry) Faye LaRue (McDonald), went to be with the Lord on October 14,
2014. I believe that God Almighty took her home because she was needed in Heaven. Sherry came to
me one night in a vision all dressed in white and glowing. I believe God showed her to me to let me
know she was now an angel in Heaven. Sherry left behind a husband and two sons—also two brothers,
five sisters and her mother and father. We will all dearly miss our beloved sister.*

Leap of Love

Startled awake, I need balance!
(Love has come quietly,
Caresses surround me.
The source a fountain—
Steadfast & unchanging)

Love like this scares me!
(Reaching a depth I thought was dead.
Attentive love: as if I am all there is.)

Immersed in cozy warmth,
I am blanketed with broad shoulders.
(I am so exposed:
The one who pined in a cave.)

Sighing peacefully, finally I trust.
(I pour out reciprocal love—
Dancing on bubbles of light)
We are joyfully twined—
Oh my!

Karen Zurawski
Albany, NY

[Hometown] Liberty, NY; [DOB] February, 1953; [Ed] bachelor of arts; [Occ] teacher, philosopher, poet; [Hobbies] herbology, science, literature, handicrafts; [GA] using my talents to help others

This poem juxtaposes the bitter and the sweet of realizing a love that has waited for me to conquer old fears and wounds.

Eber & Wein Publishing

Golden Years

Golden years; upon retirement, I was promised.
Thirty years, I've been searching.
Please, someone, anyone, help me.
So far, mine consists of:
Hair so thin, eyesight so dim;
Can't hear, got to go get a hearing aid,
Can't eat what I want; gastric reflux
Heart palpitations, high blood pressure.
Arthritis has made residence in every bone.
Hiatal hernia, umbilical hernia, can't lift my groceries.
Can't walk without a cane or walker,
Restless legs, fallen arches, hammer toes
Going out means going to a doctor.
Seems like a different one every day.
They all order pills for everything.
Can't remember which is for head, heart or feet,
I'll settle that, I'll take one of each every morning.
Short-term memory gone, long-term good.
Wanna hear about the good ol' days?
That, my friend, is the story of my golden years!
What's yours?
Show me where the good is, I'll take care of it.

Oh my! Poet's sudden inspiration!
The gold is when we reach God's golden realm of glory.
Amen.

Emma R. Baker
Salisbury, MD

[Hometown] Salisbury, MD; [DOB] January 10, 1927; [Ed] high school graduate; [Occ] thirty-two years nursing department; [Hobbies] collecting angels, reading, writing; [GA] seeing my first poem published at age eighty-six

Upon retirement, I moved to Florida for five years. I was homesick and wanted to come back to Maryland to be with my children, grandchildren, and great-grandchildren. There is nothing like the love of children—sure beats living in Florida without them. As far as my poem, I first wrote one to send to a friend on her birthday. She said her golden years were the same as mine. She called hers "my tin years." At age eighty-eight, maybe there will be just a little gold for me. Thanks, Eber & Wein.

A Marriage Made in Heaven

A marriage made in Heaven
is a very precious thing.
It's all the joys and blessing
that a life of love can bring.

It's living for each other,
and always being there
to offer sweet encouragement—
to understand and care.

It's sharing disappointments,
and making time for fun.
It's kindness and compassion—
two hearts that beat as one.

A marriage made in Heaven
is a blessing from above.
It's what you'll find together
through a lifetime filled with love.

Ruth E. Wilkening
Northridge, CA

[Hometown] Northridge, CA; [DOB] November 25, 1926; [Ed] BS; [Occ] retired kindergarten primary teacher; [Hobbies] writing poetry, wood sculpture, playing guitar, singing country classics; [GA] performing at retirement homes, having a country band called True Blue Country

I graduated from Newark State Teachers College, NJ. I taught kindergarten primary for six and a half years in Scotch Plains and met my husband at Audobon Nature Camp in Maine. We moved to California for my husband's computer engineer job and raised five children. I am of Swedish descent through my Stockholm-born parents. While visiting relatives for eight summers, I became a country-western, guitar-playing street musician. Now I have my own band called True Blue Country playing classic country with my guitar-playing friend, Greg Romera. We played three years every Friday night at a Mexican restaurant in Woodland Hills, CA.

Trying to Remember

Soon I'll be ninety-two,
remembering things I used to do.
My family farmed by trade,
but very little money my dad made.
They worked very hard to make ends meet,
but still no running water to wash our dirty feet.
Our old oil lamps were hard to spare,
we had to move them around and share.
We made fires in our old iron heater,
trying to keep our bodies warm in the winter.
We parched the coffee in the heat of the day,
and then we would grind it and drink it away.
I remember hoeing weeds out of the corn,
stepping in the bull nettles with thorns.
We all went to church on Sunday,
but got up, got ready for school on Monday.
Sometimes our principal would give us a ride.
Nice, didn't have to wait for the bus outside.
I remember my mom would bake a cake for a sick person
and Dad would hurry and take it to them for certain.
O yes, when my shoes got holes,
my mom cut out card board and put in the soles.
She ordered some of my clothes from Sears,
I think they lasted for years.
After all we were blessed, "We loved our neighbor as our self!"
Thank the Lord I can remember!

Lucille Tyler
Liberty, TX

[Hometown] *Liberty, TX;* [DOB] *November 29, 1922;* [Ed] *high school;* [Occ] *homemaker;* [Hobbies] *writing;* [GA] *my poems*

My nephew, David Hylton, put me on Facebook with my poem, "Trying to Remember." Great for me!

Him

His warm smile. His deep, brown eyes.
His hugs so tight. His sweet "Goodnights."
His caring heart, and thoughtfulness too,
Making my worst days better through and through

He's my best friend. I can count on him till the end.
When I'm sick, he takes care of me until I'm better again.
We get together whenever we can,
Always making new memories, enjoying our time spent.

Weekend get-togethers are always a blast.
But the time goes by too fast,
Missing him each day we are apart,
Waiting till the next time, as each day gets dark.

He is mine. I am his.
He's the one I put my trust in.
He cares and listens, and is kind-hearted too.
Whatever life throws, we get through.

I'm so thankful for him,
each and every day.
Because he is part of the reason I am who I am today.

Micayla McKinney
Spencer, IN

[Hometown] Spencer, IN; [DOB] July 2, 1997; [Ed] still in high school; [Hobbies] cooking, writing; [GA] being Chapter FCCLA president and district officer

When I was younger, I used to always write poetry. Now that I have grown and matured, I appreciate it so much more. I write about the things that come to my mind. Most of my poems tend to be deep, but sometimes I'll write a happy one. This poem was inspired by my best friend, who is also my boyfriend. We have been through so much together and I am so thankful for him.

Saying Goodbye

(Shadow of a Spirit)

I knew that something was wrong, I felt alone for the first time in my life. I walk into the rain to relieve the feelings that I was having, all I could think about was my mother. She always came to me when something was wrong. I could feel her pain, and the sorrow in side me, leaving me with a helpless feeling. Then I knew the truth that she would no longer be with me on this plane of life much longer.

She always told me never make a promise or give your word, if you could not keep it. I was told that if you break your promise or word that you must be dying or dead.

Early on this day we were doing an exercise, my mind could only see the darkness that surrounded me. Then slowly a door opened letting in such a beautiful bright light. As the door opened more I could see a shadow of my mother standing there.

She was coming to say goodbye, she came a long way to tell me that she could not keep her promise that she made to me. Never breaking her promise to me and making sure that I understand the reason why. Fulfilling the promise was not broken. She came to say goodbye before making her journey home.

I already knew that she was on her way home when the news came to me. I couldn't cry when I read the letter. Never cry in front of anyone, let them not see the hurt, nor the weakness that the letter left within me. She had left me alone, but she never broke her promise to me.

Today I can still feel her watching over me, always showing that the love she had shared had never left me, a love so strong it will always be there, an unconditional love that could never tarnish nor be forgotten in my heart, mind, and soul; for I am one.

Consuelo Giron
Denver, CO

Heartbroken

Sitting, lonely in the dark,
    tearful thoughts about to start,
        children, grands, and husband afar,
        seems a dream of confusion
            only God knows your heart.

A mother always has plans and goals,
    her generous position
        attentive roles to family needs,
        to be matured and complete,
            through thick and thin,
            never to fall backward,
                but fall forward, you'll get up and run.

One day sobbing and farewell the hardest,
    saddened, letting them go with
        blessings and good wishes,
        to face reality and destiny,
            grands will be greatly missed
            on birthdays and holidays
                occasions and celebrations.

May the seed in their hearts bloom beautifully
    towards sunshine and sunset each day,
        for we all stumble in many ways,
            but the Bible says, cast all your anxiety
            upon Him, for He cares for us all.
                Not to worry, God is in control.

Aveolela I. Tafau-Reupena
Long Beach, CA

To my lovely family, I love you all. I have a wonderful husband, Dr. Maatusi A. Reupena, and my dear children, Easter, Reuben, Fou, Johnny, Diana, Annavalentine, and Annalina (deceased). I also have beautiful grandchildren: Jacob, Luke, and Grace (Easter and Eric); Emma and Eziah (Fou and Carlos); and Kyrie (Johnny and Lenta). They are the light of my life.

Bent, Not Broken

I might be bent, but I'm not broken.
I may have a long way to go, but God knows where I'm going.

Criticism, judgement and mean people have caused me pain.
Strength, faithfulness and special friends helped me learn to dance in the rain.

Life took me places I thought I could never handle.
God gave me strength and helped me win every battle.

Experiences have made me independent, but there is nothing else to be.
I've learned there is no one in the world I can depend on but me.

I might be bent, but I'll never be broken.
One day God will lead me to where I have always been going.

Sheila Durden
Demopolis, AL

[Hometown] Demopolis, AL; [DOB] February 6, 1971; [Ed] AS degree in radiology; [Occ] radiologic technologist; [Hobbies] hunting, AL football (Roll Tide), cooking; [GA] raising two beautiful daughters, Makayla and McKenzie

I have always loved poetry. To me it is a way to express my feelings. It may be hard for me to say the words. Writing them just comes naturally. My poem was inspired by many difficult experiences as a single mom raising my two wonderful daughters. Life can be full of challenges, especially if my will is not God's plan. I am trusting God and being thankful for what I have every day. When it is God's will, He will make sure I find my way.

Have You Come?

Have you come,
Come to God's Son?
Have you seen His light?
Heavenly light
Have you heard His voice?
His tender voice
Calling out to you to come
Into the presence
Of the holy one
Have you come, come to God's Son?
Have you asked Him to forgive
The sinful life that you have lived?
Oh have you come?
Have you fallen on your knees?
Have you claimed the blood He shed
So that you can come and be
In the presence of the holy one?
Oh seek ye the Lord while His Spirit is around
And call upon His holy name
While He's near and can be found
Oh time is running out and if He appeared today
Would He say to you, well done my child
Or would He turn you away
From the presence of the holy one?
Oh, won't you come,
Come to the holy one?

LeAnn Jeannine Pisar
Bakersfield, CA

[Hometown] Corcoran, CA; [DOB] June 21, 1960; [Ed] high school; [Occ] worked as a geophysical/ geological technician; [Hobbies] poetry, songwriting, jewelry making, research; [GA] being a mother, wife, and homemaker, teaching the word of God

Who's Who? That is an important question and each of us is going to have to answer it before we die. Jesus asked that same question to Simon Peter, one of his disciples, and Peter answered with this reply, "You are the Christ, the Son of the living God." I have met a lot of people who have done a lot of really great things, who have had great opportunities and have built a mighty fine life for themselves. I've watched men live and I've watched men die, but at the end of everyone's life, the only thing that really matters is based on this one question. Who do you say He is? That one decision is so important that it will decide where your soul will spend eternity.

217

Will You Save Her?

Do you trust God or the government?
I for one love and trust my God with
All of my might, and I know He will make things right.
I have little trust for the government now.
I feel that it has lost its way and let us down.
The people we elected and trusted
To go to Washington, working hard to make
Things right for the American people seem to have
suffered memory loss when they arrive in town.
God is very unhappy with the way things are going on.
Sometimes it's like a circus, and I wonder
What planet they are on!
Americans are not stupid as Washington would
Have others to believe.
For the leadership we have had the last six years
Has tried to totally deceive us and take our
America down as if we are naïve.
Patriotic Americans will never let this happen.
For we are ready to fight, to take our beloved
Country back with vigor and laughter. America
Needs a lot of TLC, for her soldiers and veterans
And our flag. They have been cheated, forgotten
And scorned. This should go on no more.
So I am asking, pleading, with all Americans,
To help our great country return to the way
Our Forefathers and God meant for her to be.
So I am asking, pleading, with all Americans,
To help our great country return to the way
Our Forefathers and God meant for her to be.

Frances Ann McCarthy
High Point, NC

[Hometown] High Point, NC; [DOB] March 25, 1949; [Ed] computer high school; [Occ] retired; [Hobbies] writing poetry, reading, relaxing at the beach; [GA] having two of my poems published

My inspiration for my poems seem to be about this great country and our freedoms. The older I get, everything about America, I sit up and take notice. It is my opinion that our young people do not want to take the time to learn all about it. If we are not careful, and the schools do not teach this, America will lose the shining light she was always meant to have. That will be a very sad day, and I pray that it will not come. I love this great and wonderful country.

Keep On Going Anyway

Stay courageous, and keep on going anyway,
Whatever hits you from day to day.
Pray and ask God to help you find a way.
But keep on going anyway,
The road may be rough
And your burdens hard to bear.
   God please! Give me strength
   To go through this;
For my heart is aching
It seems like I am getting weak.
   Take your eyes off of your problems;
Put them on Jesus and you will make it.
   Yes! You can, say I can survive this.
Keep on repeating it and you'll
see yourself getting stronger and stronger.
   Go on you can make it.
For with God all things are possible.
   Only believe it and you will
Be surprised how far you have come.

Bernice Stewart
Middlebrook, VA

Christmas Treasures

A baby doll whose hair is gone, its body not so clean
Whose beauty isn't obvious and only can be seen
By the little girl who to this doll has given her whole heart
And nothing or nobody from it can make her part

And then there is the toy train...its tracks are not all here
But in the mind of this small boy who doesn't "give a care"
He'll play with it and make believe he's on a long, long trip
He'd rather ride the railroad than be on a giant ship

The baby really loves the top. He spins it round and round
He loves the way it whirls and loves the whirring sound
It doesn't spin so well today and baby isn't small
He's grown into a fine young man, so handsome and so tall

The tea set made of china fine brings many hours of fun
The Kool-Aid tea, the table set out underneath the sun
The little cups and saucers in the hands so tiny then
Are but a precious memory now; a just "remember when"

There are many Christmas treasures we keep from year to year
Some will bring to us a smile and some will bring a tear
They remind us of the days gone by, the years of simple joy
The years when they were just a kid, a little girl or boy

Rosalie Chastain
Grifton, NC

[Hometown] Grifton, NC; [DOB] September 20, 1933; [Ed] some college; [Occ] retired Salvation Army officer; [Hobbies] reading, scrapbooking

Watching my great-grandchildren play reminded me of the years gone by. My great-grandchildren, my grandchildren, and my children all enjoyed playing with the same age-old toys. Of course, the children now also want all the modern electronic items on the market. Somehow, though, I don't think iPods, smartphones, etc., will ever have the same sentimental value as the Christmas treasures I have written about.

Betsey Boot Hill

Out of the ground the gray stones poke
Off the leaves the light reflects
Lying there beneath the oak

The fog that lifts like smoke
Like a vision one detects
Out of the ground the gray stones poke

Color blends like paintbrush strokes
Not the pattern one expects
Lying there beneath the oak

Light shines through the trees like spokes
Guarding the graves the grass protects
Out of the ground the gray stones poke

Above the chirp a bullfrog croaks
Here lie remains of those rejects
Lying there beneath the oak

Not a trick and not a joke
But not a truer word was spoke
Out of the ground the gray stones poke
Lying there beneath the oak

Kenneth Hinkle
Winchester, VA

[Hometown] Winchester, VA; [DOB] October 28, 1950; [Ed] GED and basic electronics and computer repair; [Occ] janitor; [Hobbies] stamp collecting, gardening, pets; [GA] books, beyond all understanding and others

I survived many years in state hospitals and institutions in the sixties, seventies, and eighties, where I read many books and learned to write from a teacher from Mary Baldwin. This poem is about the cemetery where they buried the mental patients whom nobody claimed. Much of my writing is based on many experiences.

An Excuse for My Father

I never meant to let you down.
I swore I'd always be around.
I loved you then like I love you now.
Sweetly,
You're perfect…
Please don't frown.
I know I left without a trace.
But you're the spot in my heart I can't replace.
I understand if you want me to go…
But it was on my mind,
I had to let you know.
I never meant to make you cry…
I'm sorry I ever said goodbye.
You're my daughter…
But she's my wife…
I ignored my judgment,
I didn't think twice…
Just know I love you.
I always will.
Oh how I wish these words were real.
An excuse for my father that I made in
My head…
To make me feel better,
You know a little less dead.
But I know—I'll never hear these words
Because he left for a while…
And never returned.

Krystal Barlow
Rogersville, TN

[Hometown] Rogersville, TN: [DOB] June 15, 1997; [Ed] high school; [Occ] Burger King; [Hobbies] writing, singing, reading; [GA] getting published

A Crime Against Humanity

Our future is threatened because we choose to remain ignorant.
Regardless, we find it quite easy to be smug and arrogant.
Although ignorance prevails, most human beings are not stupid.
But growing up ignorant leads to a life not fully lucid.
How do we live wisely in a milieu of pseudo sanity?
It appears that our ignorance flows from a shameless vanity.
Our children are indoctrinated with fabricated knowledge.
We shun science because when it is applied facts cannot be hedged.
We are duped by propaganda in our churches and in our schools.
This results in mental abuse, yet there are no restrictive rules.
Ancient beliefs go unchallenged because we stifle all our doubts.
Earnest people raise wisdom above doubt, but have no social clout.
Credulity poses a danger to all, especially our youth.
We embrace what gives us comfort and brazenly avoid harsh truths.
So we create a shroud of darkness through foolish machinations.
Then we bitterly cry about the lack of illumination.
We need to resist the conclusion, "I believe, therefore, I know."
Against truth and wisdom that attitude levels a knockout blow.
Do not tell our children what to think, only teach them how to think.
It is because of careless thinking that hope continues to shrink.
Keeping children ignorant is a crime against humanity.
It is calamitous because we can't be both ignorant and free.
Gross ignorance is the ugly root from which human chaos grows.
Do we not know that ultimately we must reap that which we sow?
Ignorance is like the deceptive calm before a deadly storm.
When the storm hits many people will wish they had never been born.

LeRoy F. Thielman
Oshkosh, WI

[Hometown] Oshkosh, WI; [DOB] February 6, 1946; [Ed] MA in economics; [Occ] retired teacher; [Hobbies] reading, writing

Before children are capable of critical thinking, adults tell them what to think and what to believe. This is a cross-cultural phenomenon that is inconsistent with our professed goal of developing a peaceful, sustainable world civilization. Powerful "authorities" protect their earthly interests by attesting to the verisimilitude of all sorts of insidious and pernicious myths, lies and superstitions. Most of those "authorities" suffer from emotional, psychological and intellectual atrophy. Yet they are the ones who rule and support the abuse of innocent children for the sake of God and country. This undeniable truth inspired me to write the poem above.

A Blank Canvas

A blank canvas can be anything,
A mountain scene, ocean scene, a flower, some fruit in a bowl or even a naked person.
So many possibilities, so many ideas
A very talented artist can combine them into a beautiful picture.
We should all look at each day as a blank canvas,
We can make it a good or a bad day
There are many possibilities to explore.
You can do something that brings joy to others; like volunteering in a hospital or nursing home.
You can save a life donating blood.
You can clean your house and donate gently used clothing to a local charity.
Adopt a pet from the local shelter and get a new loyal friend.
Visit an old friend or make a new friend.
Go on a shopping spree, if you have to money, (Otherwise you will have a bad day when you
get the bills)
Get lost in a good book.
So just think tomorrow is a blank canvas, what are you going to do?
Walk on the head of the Sphinx?
Stand in the middle of Stonehedge?
Visit Easter Island and see those giant stone heads?
Go to a football game and root on your favorite team? (Go Steelers!)
Doesn't matter what you do.
Just remember that each day is a blank canvas for you to create the best day you can.

Kellie Frey
Saint Marys, PA

[Hometown] Saint Mary's, PA; [DOB] May 1, 1973; [Ed] high school, cosmetologist, EMT; [Occ] resident aide in an assisted living facility; [Hobbies] reading and writing; [GA] my two wonderful children

My name is Kellie Frey. I was born and raised in Slippery Rock, PA. My best friend Dee Dee Burdick introduced me to my husband Dean (now of twenty years), and we make our home in Saint Mary's, PA. I work as a resident aide in an assisted living facility and have for the past seventeen years. In my spare time, when I'm not spending time with my two wonderful children, Maggie and Hunter, I love to read novels and write poetry.

Banda Ache

Sun on a sandy beach
Most beautiful to explore
So sacred, so pure
Watering holes
Ocean currents flow deep below
You have it all

Nighttime spooks
Think positive
Think surrender
Think sleep

Then so quick
Earthquake hits
Many losses, many tears
No—not there
You were my beautiful friend
A place to remember
You made me feel like a nature lover

Nighttime spooks
Think positive
Think surrender
Think sleep

Lynn K. Martin
Middletown, NY

[Hometown] *Middletown, NY;* [DOB] *November 14, 1954;* [Ed] *AAS in art, BBA in business administration;* [Occ] *retired;* [Hobbies] *art, reading, travel;* [GA] *living life with all its good, bad and ugly*

I was raised overseas from 1960 to 1972. I continued to return due to family. My poem was inspired by the Indian Ocean in Banda Ache, Indonesia, camping on a little hill under coconut trees with the ocean a few feet away. This tranquil beach had not been touched by any Western influences—not a soul in sight. In one swim, I was in an area with strong under currents another died from. It was a moment to test my skills. The epic center hit. Thirty years before, I feared the same.

I Jump

With heart, soul and breath held boldly tight
I jump and prayed that I would be all right

I was lost within my own private self
And the answer I seek was there put on a shelf

I had no time for regrets and self-pity doubts
So I jump and felt the world spread out

I had to own that which was brewing within
And conquer the fear to let life begin

I wanted to live and feel every second of every day
So I jump and life joy came abundantly my way

The stem of life was out there waiting for me
And my heart was jumping for what my mind's eye could see

Within my higher self I knew life gave exceedingly more
I could feel the pull from the very bottom of my core

The key was to follow my heart and build my own circle of joy,
And settle for nothing I could not imagine as a toy

So I jump for the love of life I had to live
And I live for the love of life I had to give

Mary F. Peeples
Winona, MS

[Hometown] Kilmichael, MS; [DOB] May 8, 1951; [Ed] high school; [Occ] education field, preschool; [Hobbies] bowling, playing tennis, photography; [GA] being there for my mom when she needed me

My sister Catherine inspired me to write this poem, for she and I share the love of reading and writing poetry. In my life as in hers we both had to jump in order to achieve what we wanted. We both enjoy an early Saturday morning sitting by the fire with a hot cup of coffee reading poetry. Together she and I would see who could write the best poem from a single word title—those were some of the best times. To this day we still share that love of poetry.

Breeze

freshman tone
from breath
of hills

blink in blue
morning star
finding I
in my eye

landing in
oat seed breeze
of green wind
in shadow black boughs

urging moon's edge
from end
to no end
with poet's piano

drifting in
polyphonic lift
painting autumn bright
with my daughter's hello

Michael Kirby Smith
Baltimore, MD

Michael K. Smith, registered land surveyor

Loss

The night she left, I didn't know
She'd be forever gone.
I always thought that she'd come back
One day in some sweet dawn.

Then came a time, after long sad years,
I learned she was no more.
And finally I knew I'd lost
The one I did adore.

She's now been gone for many years
And though I feel her still,
I longed to kiss her one last time,
And now I never will.

Richard L. Albeen
Leonia, NJ

Love is the greatest adventure of them all. And unrequited love is the greatest tragedy.

Who Am I?

Who am I? Why am I here? And what's more,
Where am I going? Where is the door
To the answers I seek and the questions I ask?
Does it lie in my future, or deep in my past?
Does it lie in the heavens, the stars or the sea?
Does it lie in the wind, or maybe in me?
Whom do I query? Where do I look?
Does the answer lie hidden in some obscure book?
Perhaps there will come a day when I see;
And then, from my quest, at last, I'll be free.

Lois E. Van Mun
Kamiah, ID

[Hometown] *Kamiah, ID;* [DOB] *November 8, 1937;* [Ed] *twelfth grade;* [Occ] *retired;* [Hobbies] *collecting angels;* [GA] *three sons, one little girl angel*

Most of my works come from actual events in my life and the lives of others. My final poem arises out of a lifetime of multiple near-death experiences and the struggle to survive in situations including, but not limited to, life-threatening illnesses, a fractured neck, and finding myself engulfed in a burning house fire. The only question remaining is why?

Experiment

I Question:
  What should be the ramifications if the Son of Man will
  continue to negate his promise to come again?

II Hypothesis:
  By his myopic window sits Engr. Popoy scanning the sky
  with his binocular, looking for the sign of the Lord's
  coming from heaven: Love, peace and joy abound
  in his heart, he jots down…

III Variable:
  Sinners: Hard drinking and pot smoking are practiced
  everywhere, with dirty-punk dancing; man's care-free
  outburst and violence filled the earth.

IV Observation:
  The human race is carnally minded—the enmity against
  God. Satan has conquered their heart for they have
  chosen sinful living. They have surrendered the light
  of life to the darkness of death and evil.

V Conclusion:
  If the Savior will not return soon, people will keep on
  sinning and Satan would purloin their soul; mankind
  will miss the grace of salvation… the marriage supper
  of the Lamb of God won't be celebrated.

VI Errata:
  My dear Engr. Popoy, you should fix your gaze atop
  the belfry of the church to glimpse the glorious cross
  of the Lord who has always existed everlasting!

Edmundo C. Lozada
Staten Island, NY

[Hometown] Staten Island, NYC; [DOB] May 6, 1938; [Ed] BS in mechanical engineering; [Hobbies] chess, fishing, poetry; [GA] premier member of Poetry Nation, 2014

Although I have finished a purely technical engineering degree in college, oddly enough I have always been writing a more literal poetry—but only as a hobby. I simply chose poetry as a medium of self-expression to share my personal creativity with others. My poem was inspired by my wife, Mrs. Marietta Lozada nee Duray, who helped me with the daily reflection of scripture verses that touched us. She guided me to believe with faith in the One: "the Word became flesh and lived among us…"

Thanks Very Much, Earl

Earl, I hope your life will be very long full of fun,
Before the rest of its very long course has fully run,
I hope for you a great new chapter of life has begun
And if you want to you can spend time in the sun
For to know you and work with you is a pleasure
That there is no way anyone can now even measure
Also your knowledge of accounting was very great
A point you liked to often very proudly reiterate
When everyone's name in a place you did know
It seemed to fill your face with quite a large glow
For you what you thought then was very, very true
A point with others which you often liked to argue
Now I hope some wonderful hobbies you will find
In which you are able to make full use of your mind
I hope that someday soon you get much better eyesight
So playing with your grandkids will be a great delight
Fate wasn't good when you lost your beloved wife
But somehow with other family you've led a good life
You liked to do so many things in your own certain way
As it's the best way to do it was to others you did say
I wish you much longer with us you could now stay
However, I hope now every day for you is a good day
Earl, we now want to give you very, very much thanks
For being a wonderful part of the Western Region ranks
Well now has come what seems the appropriate time
To end this "Thanks Very Much, Earl" poem of rhyme

Robert C. Magill
Pittsburgh, PA

[Hometown] Pittsburgh, PA; [DOB] March 10, 1952; [Ed] BS in accounting from Duquesne University; [Occ] retired health care audit supervisor; [Hobbies] genealogy, all types of music, dancing, cultural events, gardening, walking, rhyming poetry; [GA] having fourteen poems published, five internationally

I was born at West Penn Hospital in Pittsburgh, PA. I have a BS degree in accounting from Duquesne University. I have been retired since July 2011, after being employed in health care auditing by the PA Department of Public Welfare for almost thirty-five years. I also enjoy dining, all types of soft music and dancing, spectator sports, genealogy and writing rhyming poetry. I am single.

Untitled

My father had no sons to keep his line.
His trip to synagogue that winter day
Was it with regret? Did his babe disappoint
As he saw his priestly mark slip away?

Viola donned doublet and hose and sang
Pretty songs to keep her heart intact.
She played at courtship, fought duels, laughed at fools.
She learned the script that changed react to act.

I am more mundane. On Monday I forgot
To shave my legs, and besides, the day was cold.
I wore slacks and defied the Talmudic code.
Did Jehovah mind? The Rabbis think me bold.

Viola's clothes and my father's love belie
Priests who chant prayers that God's hymns deny.

Eileen Z. Cohen
Haverford, PA

[Hometown] Haverford, PA; [DOB] December 15, 1931; [Ed] PhD; [Occ] professor emerita; [Hobbies] reading, painting; [GA] writing a poem, especially a sonnet

Close the Door Softly

Close the door softly
On what used to be
Leave no trace
If you don't love me
You say you are unhappy
I didn't know
So close the door softly
If you feel you must go
I'll love you until
Love's light fades away
It's how it must be
If you feel you can't stay
You say you want "out"
You want to be free
To be your own person
To live without me
I know I'm not perfect
And share in the blame
But what did I do
To put out the flame
We won't grow old
Holding hands in the night
So close the door softly
As you turn from our life

Lorelei M. Palmer
St. Peter, MN

[Hometown] Chicago, IL; [DOB] August 10, 1945; [Ed] master's degree; [Occ] in-home family therapist; [Hobbies] make jewelry, paint, draw; [GA] raised four wonderful children

I wrote my first poem when my uncle was killed in Korea. I was eight years old. I was fortunate to earn a master's degree after the age of forty. I worked in the field of psychology for sixteen years, working with troubled teens, parents, couples, etc. I was able to use my love for writing in the reports I had to write for each client. I started college at the age of forty and went to school full time for six years. I painted my first painting during my fortieth year. You might say that was my year to bloom.

In My Hands

In my hands the heart that bleeds
Wallowing in the carnage of discarded emotion
The war is in the house that feeds
Running in circles, nowhere to go, never letting go
The madness of the memories
Grieving so deeply, the loss of the sweet
Grabbing each piece, the memories of past and what should be
Each piece finding its way into the loving hands that may
Slowly putting together the heartfelt memories
Piece by piece held together by threads of gold
Knowing the beauty this quilt holds, despite the angst that came
The beauty that came was not meant to be held, but to be sold
Remembered once as my breath
Full of love, hope and connected energy
Fallen into the madness of life's way
Forever is this day

Lillian Strom
Huntington Beach, CA

[Hometown] San Diego, CA; [DOB] June, 1973; [Ed] MS in clinical psychology; [Occ] MFTI

I was raised in a home with substance abuse, unacknowledged and unmanaged mental illness, and domestic violence. The trials and tribulations I experienced in my childhood and adolescence, and the birth of my son, gave me strength to change the direction of my life. My focus has been on my healing and growth—providing the best home and parenting I am capable of for my son. I have recently graduated with my master's of science degree in clinical psychology, and I am pursuing a career as a marriage family therapist to help others overcome their life hurdles.

Until

We've been friends so many years. I thank our God for you.
No one could ever take your place. I hope you know that's true.

We share our lives, our loves, our fears, talk each issue through.
Side by side we share our tears; now, I shed tears for you.

We thought that it was just a bug; we thought it'd go away.
So sure of life, we laughed and smiled; Was that just yesterday?

Now, I live in constant fear, always by the phone—
Waiting for the latest news, and feeling so alone.

I love you more than you could know; without you I'd be lost.
What they say is true, I guess—no love without a cost.

You've always been within my heart; a hole no one could fill.
We'll smile again in better days; I'll just wait until....

Toni O'Kennon Shumate
North Chesterfield, VA

*[Hometown] North Chesterfield, VA; [Ed] BA in English, BA in psychology; [Occ] retired; [Hobbies]
reading, writing, painting, photography, gardening, fitness; [GA] having my poetry published*

*I wrote this poem after my best friend of forty years was diagnosed with cancer. We prayed for a cure, but her
prognosis was grim. In the poem, I look forward to the time when she is well and we will smile again, but I'm
also afraid. I ended it with the word "until" to portray hope, but also fear of an uncertain future. Sadly, she
lost her battle last year, so I'll wait, to smile with her again, "until" I see her in Heaven. I will always miss her.*

Letting Go

Falling helpless in a dream,
Life passing in front of me,
Bitter ire and memories I seethe.
It's difficult… just to breathe.
Falling faster towards the ground,
The waves, they crash below.
When I'm lifted without a sound,
On Eagles wing I go.
Acrimonious memories wash to the sea,
Like pieces of time, pieces of me,
Flying, flying oh so high,
Now resentment free.
The Eagle tips his wing goodbye.
And I am happy, just to be.

Cheryl A. Flores
Oceanside, CA

[Hometown] San Diego, CA; [DOB] August 13, 1960; [Ed] high school GED; [Occ] owner of housecleaning business for twenty years; [Hobbies] painting, wakeboarding, jetski riding; [GA] running a half marathon

Closer

Closer and closer yet so far away
I hear all the words not what you say
The world sinks down deeper into social decay
Is the end upon us, maybe today

Closer and closer the sounds of war
Not all that new just like before
Ship off your sons and then they're gone
Politicians just say it doesn't matter how long

Closer and closer the web that we weave
Escape becomes futile I can't even conceive
Things become different than what we believe
It's time to go still you can't leave

Closer and closer the light at the end
Maybe there's hope up around the bend
Traveling full circle the end becomes the start
The light begins to flicker gives way to the dark

Closer and closer we are still not there yet
The things that you wish for are not what you get
Better use caution because things can come true
The closer you get and then closer won't do

Mark Russell
Gardner, MA

[DOB] *September 16, 1957; [Ed] fourteen years; [Occ] cabinet designer and builder; [GA] poetry fellowship*

We are the brief chroniclers of our times. These are the days of my life.

The Zoo

I really like it here at the zoo
   There is so much to see
      There is so much to do.

There are animals that go swinging
   There are some that crawl around on all fours
      There are even some that go winging.

There are some animals you can hold
   There are some you would not
      There are some very friendly and some very bold.

There are some that are very small
   There are some very very large
      There are some that are hard to see at all.

There are some that have feathers
   There are some that have fur
      There are some whose skin is like leather.

Someday I would like to live at a zoo
   The animals and I
      You could come and stay too!

Irene McFadden
Conway, AR

[Hometown] Conway, AR; [DOB] September 14, 1947; [Ed] high school; [Occ] bee keeper; [Hobbies] sewing, cooking, writing, traveling; [GA] ham radio license in 1978

The zoo was always a favorite of mine. I like animals, and we had many different ones on the farm. We went to many across the US, when my children were young. I now go to zoos with my grandchildren. They like animals too, and I wrote this for them. Someday they can read it to their children. I hope it makes them smile. I like it when they smile!

Never Gone, So Not Forgotten

What tears fall for the departed, who merge with the sun's glory? They become able to warm the faces of the living with an eternally comforting touch.

What sorrow follows the deceased who converge with the flowing freedom of the wind? They become constantly able to embrace their family and dance from ground to cloud.

What withers in the passing of those who join Mother Earth? In each of her seasons blooms scores of flowers which blanket the planet with their fragrant beauty.

What legacy fades in a soul's ascension to starlight? For countless generations, friends and lovers alike need only look upward to the night sky and revel in the splendor of their constellate artwork.

So in the absence of body, a presence remains,
With a beauty of touch simply altered not strained.

Richard F. Keene Jr.
North Smithfield, RI

[Hometown] North Smithfield, RI; [DOB] February 4, 1983; [Occ] restaurant manager; [GA] too soon to say (I hope...)

I was born and raised in a small town in Rhode Island, from a large and widely known family within the community. My sister and I were given every luxury and opportunity that our parents were happy to provide. Their hard work and dedication were not always rewarded with matching results, as I often decided to rebel against the life expected of me: a life that always bored and baffled me. Writing has always been my one meaningful tool of expressing my unconventional feelings of love, regret and the praise I would often find difficult to convey with the spoken word.

Whatever Happened?

Whatever happened to the "good old"
days, when things were simpler? There
were trolleys, phonograph records, dial
telephones, and beautiful gardens...

Whatever happened to the days when we
had family get-togethers, playing cards
and popping corn over the fireplace embers?

Whatever happened to the days when Sunday
was a day of rest, and closeness of friends
was the best?

Whatever happened to the days when we could
sit on the floor, in front of a radio, to
listen to a "scary story"?

If we could only turn back time, when life
was easier, bread sold for a dime, now realizing
that the "past is gone" and retirement is
slow and long...

What will our children's future be?

Oleta P. Braley
Rochester, NY

[Hometown] Rochester, NY; [DOB] July 19, 1944; [Ed] high school graduate; [Occ] retired from healthcare; [Hobbies] artist, song writer, music; [GA] majestic record contract—"Our Vet"

I've been very blessed in my life. I have two sons and daughters-in-law, five grandchildren, nieces and nephews, and one brother. I've received many awards from International Society of Poetry. My poetry was read at Capitol 2003 and in Disneyland, FL 2004. I wrote the poem and sent it to Pope John Paul II and received a letter from the Vatican and Pope John Paul II. I also wrote a poem about the tragedy of Oklahoma City in 1995 and sent it to the mayor. I received a letter thanking me. I wrote a poem about our American vets in 2005, and Majestic Records gave me a contract and a CD was produced, but nothing yet. Country Wine picked up the CD and did sheet music for it. I love to design greeting cards, mostly comical, for anyone who likes something different. I also did a children's book called Tommy Tooth Tells The Truth. *It's all about our veggies and their values, and I did all art work too! So, all in all, my writing poetry has opened many opportunities for me, but I would still would like to publish my own poetry book in the future.*

Our Father

Our blessed Father which are in Heaven bless us all,
no matter how busy you always hear our many calls.

Some times we think He hasn't answered our prayer,
we should be a little patient we know He's there.

So many times our asking of Him is when we're down,
it should be at least a daily thing going-round.

He died for our sins so we'll have eternal life evermore,
available twenty-four/seven just knock on his door.

He's healed the sick, the deaf, the blind and more,
and His second coming will be more than a roar.

What a wonderful sight to see our loved ones and friends,
and to meet Peter, Moses, Matthew and John, Amen.

A golden city our future home with twelve gates of pearl,
jeweled walls golden streets for us and the Duke of Earl.

Bible tells of wearing white robes of "fine linen" wear,
and the angels will be under our authority while there.

Yes animals and children will surely be there God tells,
and those who reject Him will face the gates of Hell.

Written in stone, God names us long before we were born,
like Saul became Paul and Simon became Peter all adored.

All's well and He's waiting, arms wide open for us all,
no more pain, sickness or sorrow who answers his call.

Christ is the same yesterday, today and forevermore,
He has prepared a place for us, Bible tells don't ignore.

Larry L. Schroll
Spring Grove, PA

Born and growing up in a Christian home, I realized the importance of family values and respect at a very early age. I had confidence that relying through prayer and faith on the Lord our Savior, He will give us peace and blessings in return. Right choices do make our existence much easier and better because of understanding and having faith. To believe and live the word is the essence of the beginning of a lifelong experience. In the world we live in today, we must pray for peace more than ever before. God Bless.

Whatever Floats Your Boat

Whatever floats your boat
    As you sail through the seasons
    Are the reasons others may not see
        That
Whatever floats your boat
    On this sensational sea of life
    With its strife is alright with me
        And
Whatever floats your boat
    And brings you the easiness
    Of happiness is no mystery
        Because
Whatever floats your boat
    The right way
    Enhancing your day... fiddle-de-dee
        Forever
Whatever floats your boat
    For what reason through seasons
    Through the strifes in life
    With easiness bringing happiness
    Is alright with me

Bozana Belokosa
Pasadena, CA

[Hometown] *Detroit, MI;* [Occ] *freelance writer and teacher;* [Hobbies] *listening to jazz and R&B music;* [GA] *my book entitled* What Happened to Rudolph's Nose? *being permanently housed in the Burton's Historical Collection for Michigan Authors*

Exploding, Is My Business

Fireworks, fireworks a display spectacular,
beware these explosives conjure the supernatural.
Firecrackers, firecrackers an explosive noise maker,
long or short fuses, definitely not a faker.
Sparklers, sparklers are you into glitter?
burns off slowly, but watch the glintier.
Rockets, rockets who's bringing up the rear?
light my fuse and run in fear.
Duds, duds that one didn't detonate!
stay away it might activate.
Explosions, explosions the violent burst of ugly,
you'll see colors so brilliantly.
Beauty, beauty the eyes have it,
Putting it all together, it will fit.

Gordon L. Wilcox
Kapolei, HI

[Hometown] Honolulu, Oahu, HI; [DOB] August 12, 1929; [Ed] high school and business college; [Occ] retired accounts receivable; [Hobbies] writing, being a collector of world events; [GA] come what may!

My grandmother was a composer of Hawaiian songs and I guess I got the "mana" (spiritual) to do poems, besides being a "Princess of Hawaii."

Prelude to Acceptance

Loss of capacity, different choices,
So suddenly, our hair turns to snow.
Lost function, body wracked with pain,
Fire gone, embers remain,
Thrust into shifting focus and letting go.

Time passed, ripples over rocks,
Memory loss, potential diminished,
Too many tasks sadly left unfinished.
Disconnection, natural progression,
Forging a legacy for future generations.

Dianne Kaye
Roseburg, OR

Dianne Kaye retired after twenty years in human services work and found the inspiration to write from the many courageous people she met as youth worker, addictions counselor, family therapist, and HIV case manager. Aspiring to be a writer, Kaye enjoyed reading from romance-suspense, psychological thriller, and spy intrigue genres. Using published authors as silent mentors, she developed a unique writing style of weaving reality into fiction and poetry. "Prelude to Acceptance" is one of three poems Eber & Wein has published. Kaye lives in the beautiful Pacific Northwest with two cats and is working on her first novel.

Letting Go

I have not an idea
How to gather myself to you,
Your world,
Now surrounded by letting go.
Resounding in the wind language
Of ancient, giant burr oaks,
Their world as well overwhelmed
In letting go.
Oncoming Autumn's naked times
Clinging to me,
Does not allow me
Any shade beneath the limbs of your love.
Your hurt is my sorrow,
Your sorrow echoes in my heart,
Like a stone in an empty can
Kicked down the street,
When I was a kid,
Lonely, wandering,
With no place to go,
Not even home.

Greg L. Bass
Pleasant Prairie, WI

[Hometown] Waukesha, WI; [Ed] complete degrees: MSHCA, BS in English; incomplete degrees: MFA—Vermont, master's of theology—Trinity; certifications: RHU, REBC ; [Occ] health care consultant, writer and photographer (Photo Poems, LL, www.fotopoems.com)

I've been a writer and poet for over forty years. My books include Down on All Fours *and* A Day with Omarill—African adventures.

Light

Light from light
Pure and bright,
Be my guide,
Protector tonight.

Lead me safe
Across the valley,
For I am tired
And cannot rally.

The darkness comes,
Its crushing weight
Does pin me down,
A silent fate.

Yet one small star
Can lead me home,
I stumble and fall
But never walk alone.

And so like a hand
That light I'll hold,
Lead forever onward
Till my story's all told.

Mary Schneider
New York, NY

[DOB] May 1, 1988; [Ed] Parsons the New School of Art and Design; [Occ] art director; [Hobbies] poet, novelist, photographer, artist and traveler

The past few years have been extremely tough—job loss, sickness, deaths. As a result, I suffer from pretty constant insomnia. During these long nights, I've taken to walks along the harbor and watching the stars and airplanes rise over Manhattan. This poem was written as a hopeful plea for sleep and strength on a particularly difficult night. May it bring you hope and comfort, as it did for me.

Untitled

Quick! Call the authorities! Someone's stolen my identity!
I wish that meant they were responsible for my
Mistakes,
Embarrassments and errors,
Screw-ups, and
SNAFUs, or better yet—

Cleaning my toilet, disposing of my junk mail, or
Paying off my student loans.

I'm glad they can't take all the bird songs I ever heard,
The memory of my children's laughter,
The feeling (rare) of snow on my face,
Embraces of a friend,
The explosion of chocolate on my tongue,
The aroma of love and holiday happiness,
The wrinkles around your eyes when I made you laugh.

But if they stole the tears from years of pain,
Would they also stand to gain the tears of joy?
They might try to take the award I won—
Blank of the Year—you fill in the blank.
But probably I will just end up on the phone
Countless hours reading numbers to call center guys
In Mumbai off a two-by-three-inch plastic card.

Phyllis B. Walker
Athens, TX

[Hometown] Athens, TX; [DOB] August 25; [Ed] BS in education; [Occ] educator; [Hobbies] writing, speaking, traveling; [GA] 2015 Athens ISD Teacher of the Year

I never learned to swim, but I can tread water. Teaching's like dog paddling. Don't panic, you won't sink. I have helped some students to find their voices, improve writing, connect to resources for future success, discover the satisfaction of achievement, and be interested in life and school. I show them that I am interested in them. I hope to continue my journey by taking one day at a time. I will need my mentors and family for support. I refuse to panic. In my classroom, I use humor, honesty, and all the practical advice I can get. Sink, I won't!

45 Seconds (My Time Was Up)

45 seconds it's all that I truly had
I lived it up and I lived it fast
45 seconds I had a real blast
Because life on Earth is not meant to last

So instead of feeling sorrow for me
I want my family and friends to celebrate my 45 seconds of life
By raining down tears of elation
That cover the deep blue seas

Because my Eternal Father already knew
That this plan for me would come to be
When my time was up from this ailing body
My spirit God did release
So I will have eternal joy and everlasting
Heavenly Peace

My earthly life has now come to an end
But until we reunite in Heaven and dance again
Please remember all the fun that we had

Because the time we'll spend in eternity
With the Lord Jesus will always be
And it won't ever pass

LaTonya A. Seabrooks
Sacramento, CA

In loving memory of my cousin Tracie Ann Dawson-Edmonson (6-23-69– 12-24-14)

Finding Your Voice

Do we ever have a voice
Or do we just make a lot of noise
Some people speak loudly
But they're still never heard
Others make quiet noises
They're heard the most
One's true voice is heard
By their presence alone
You shouldn't ever let anybody silence you
Because we all have a right to be heard
We all need to find our own voice
No matter how long it takes
Finding your voice means finding yourself

Lakisha Todd
Pearl, MS

I've had a long, rough journey. I was lost so many times, but I've finally found myself, as well as my voice. It's a wonderful feeling. It has been a long time coming.

Rescue

Waves crashing had always been a welcome sound but on this night
the thunderous pounding was simply too much to bear. My normal
ease at navigating the vast ocean before me seemed to abandon me.
I began to struggle as the warm, murky water engulfed me and tried
to swallow me whole. I was losing the battle as the water I always
considered my friend overcame me and my body became further and
further immersed in the depths of darkness. My mind flooded with
broken pieces of thoughts and memories drifting further and further
away. The salt water was suffocating and the unbearable pressure
that was building in my lungs was choking the life from me. I tried
again to reach the water's surface but my movements were cemented
in slow motion and my last thought before I couldn't think anymore
was that I was going to drown… just before the darkness was
complete, a small pinpoint of light shone through. The murkiness
began to gradually lighten and I could feel myself being slowly lifted—
guided to the surface. I started to slip but an invisible strength kept
me from sinking. Steadily, I continued to be raised upward. Hope
began to return when I didn't think there was any left to be had. The
surface of the water was broken and I gulped for air as I painfully
began to breathe again. I searched the horizon hoping to find the
familiar but all seemed lost as I drifted without an anchor to hold me
in place. I grabbed at a life preserver to keep me afloat and the
kindest of hands gently reached out and wiped the salty, stinging
tears from my eyes. It was in that simple moment that I knew it was
not my fate to drown that night but instead to swim as if one with the
waves toward the shore and find the power to endure.

Brenda Steger
Glen Burnie, MD

New Beginning

Once we know
where to go
it's easy to follow the flow.

If the situation needs clarification,
it's better to make a decision
and cooperation with communication,
some love, and compassion.

We can create space for new beginnings,
with deeper meaning
and plenty of unselfish feelings.

The sooner we take action,
the sooner we can get out of frustration
and move on in a better direction.

This brings the peace and satisfaction
that removes the chain reactions
and resonates with wisdom's fluctuations.

We are all here to learn how to get a quick,
positive return and at least feel equal without being burned.

It's time to wake up
because the light is shining brighter
and people think they are each day smarter.

We can support all manifestations
in different directions
that have simple approaches
and are without illusionary projections.

Viviana Siddhi
San Rafael, CA

Viviana lives in California. Her hobbies are swimming, singing, dancing, hiking, riding a bike or a horse, skiing, skating, writing poetry and creating art work. Siddhi works directly with those who are open to improving and transforming their lives through a healthy and synergistic lifestyle based on the wisdom derived from the cross-cultural exchange of traditional knowledge that include many types of approaches to healing, including some that are currently considered highly metaphysical in nature. Viviana received several selected awards for her poetry and for her work as MTC Global leader.

I Miss Laughter

I miss laughter! I miss it so much!
You know the kind I mean:

Thigh-slapping,
Side-splitting,
Tears streaming,
Breath-robbing,
Pants-peeing—

Laughter! The best (maybe only) medicine for grief.

The kind my daughter brought with her wherever she went
And shared with family and strangers alike.

I'm trying to accept her loss. So far, I've managed to smile and
even laugh out loud, but it isn't the same—it will never be the same.

Damn! I miss Karen and laughter!
For me—and so many others—they were one and the same.

Melanie Ruscio
Louisville, CO

[Hometown] Dayton, OH (Denver and Lakewood, CO since age two); [Occ]: retired executive secretary; [Hobbies] cross-stitching, reading (which are mutually exclusive, so I listen to talking books)

I just spent my tenth Christmas without my only child, whom I lost to cancer in August 2005. This is the most difficult time of year for me because we were Christmas "idiots" together—shopping, decorating, baking favorite foods, making candy—all the wonderful things from her childhood. Christmas 2014 is the first year I didn't put up a tree. My favorite poets are Shakespeare and Robert Frost.

Winter Dreams

Something in the air,
Beautiful and fair.

A chill is added to the breeze,
Icicles added to the trees.

And even though the warmth is over,
A caught snowflake is as lucky as any four-leaf clover.

A fire glowing in the hearthstone,
Making a house feel more like a home.

Holidays,
Snowy craze.

Winter makes the heart grow warmer,
The earth speaks to us in a soft murmur.

Freshly fallen snow shimmers all around,
A different snowflake on every different piece of ground.

Sipping cocoa by the fire,
Listening to the music made by the choir.

Winter may come and go,
With its heavy hearts full of snow.

But the feeling that it leaves,
Happiness, love, and long forgotten grieves,

Will keep with us forever,
As long as we keep winter in our hearts as our everlasting treasure.

Aileen Rene Romsburg
Thurmont, MD

[Hometown] Thurmont, MD; [DOB] January 18, 2000; [Ed] high school freshman; [Occ] student; [Hobbies] biking, reading, writing; [GA] having my poem published by Eber & Wein Publishing

My name is Aileen Romsburg, and, even though I am only a freshman in high school, I have always enjoyed both reading and writing. I have written several poems and am currently working on a series of short stories; I hope to one day see them published. The poem that I am submitting was inspired by my love of winter, and most importantly snow, I have so many fond memories of past winters and the joyous feelings that have gone along with them. However, I love to write about anything and everything. So that's me, Aileen, in one hundred words.

Life as a Simple Shell

Sand all around,
Covering my shell,
Buried all around
Where I last fell.

Here I lie,
Stuck in the sand,
Waves drop by,
The timing always grand.

Swirls are pink,
But barely seen,
The peachy ink
Made for a queen.

Endless meetings,
Of sand and water,
Gentle greetings
Or sad slaughters.

The salty ocean
Brushes over me,
Except when frozen,
It leaves me be.

Monika J. Marsh
Centennial, CO

[Hometown] Denver, CO; [DOB] January 6, 1994; [Hobbies] reading, writing, being with my best friend; [GA] becoming a college student

To me, poetry is something special and beautiful. I wrote this poem in high school while in a poetry club my best friend Kristen Vargas and I had started. We passed out sea shells and wrote about what we were holding. Mine was swirly and pink. I thought about where this shell had been before it came to be in my hand, and this poem was born. Poetry is sacred and brings me to a place that is all my own. That is why I love poetry.

With Him We May Belong

With the glorious Christmas season coming so near,
    We realize deep within our hearts
That to us, what is ever so dear,
    Is love of family and friends together all in part.

Let us be thankful that we are blessed
    As we ask our dear Lord above
To watch over those with so much less
    So they may also know His divine love.

For what is important in all the seasons,
    Is to always help one another,
To share His love and make it the reason
    We often say, "He ain't heavy, he's my brother."

By living our lives helping one another, we believe,
    It will help us prepare for our journey beyond.
By giving inspiration to others, we pray to receive
    His gift of love, so with Him we may belong.

Our lives on this great earthly bond
    Are not even a fleeting glance
Of the beauty that lies in the spectrum beyond
    Where our dear Jesus awaits us, our spiritual lives forever enhanced.

Christine E. Antall
Dewey, AZ

[Hometown] Middleboro, MA; [DOB] June 21, 1933; [Ed] business college; [Occ] secretary, receptionist, insurance clerk; [Hobbies] music, photography, gardening, going out with friends; [GA] my family

Writing poetry is a blessing my Lord bestowed upon me along with the ability to sing. My love of music and first solo began at age six. Being an amateur photographer, making and selling cards and photos, is all part of the creativity I was blessed with. My love of our Lord carried me through the losses of my mom, two husbands and my beloved son. I am truly thankful for my wonderful family, my beloved daughter, grandchildren, great-grandchildren, many relatives, and great friends. Also, I enjoy being involved with many ministries in my church. Thank You, dear Jesus.

Don't Close the Door to Your Heart

You walked out and closed the door,
You said, you think you love another, but what about our love?
Do you really want to throw that away?

We fell in love a long time ago; then we drifted apart,
We've been together so long and I know the love is still there.

Don't close the door to your heart,
We can fall in love again.

We can do this,
You are still you and I am still me,
Give me tomorrow and the tomorrow after that,
And then give me all of your tomorrows.

Just don't close the door to your heart.

Carolyn Isgrig
Las Vegas, NV

[Hometown] Okeene, OK; [Ed] accounting degree from the College of Southern Nevada and took classes from Robert Cawley; [Occ] retired accountant; [Hobbies] crocheting, playing Sims, writing short stories and poetry

I am seventy-six years old and I have lived most of my life in Las Vegas, NV. My husband and I have been married for thirty-three years and between us we have five children, six grandchildren and one great-grandchild. I have two kitty cats and one little gray bunny. I am a cancer survivor.

Love Is a Two-way Street

The phone is like
A two-way street
The caller sends
The receiver greets

Both must speak
On a two-way street
Or the listener sends
And the caller ends

As for caller
And listener
Both must talk
Else lose the walk
On a two-way street

When they meet
On a two-way street
Both hearts leap
And often repeat

Therese Jacques Gamache
Chepachet, RI

[Hometown] Chepachet, RI; [DOB] October 13, 1933; [Ed] high school; [Occ] elderly, retired; [Hobbies] writing letters, poems, reading, praying; [GA] time for prayer during the day to relax

I wrote this poem in 2012 after my son called from Florida. Sometimes it seems he does most of the talking or sometimes I do. So I wrote this poem for lovers and often repeat what lovers know, I love you.

Friends

A friend is one, who is always there,
The good times and the bad,
A friend is always near you
When you're happy or you're sad.
A friend will stand beside you,
When there is no one else in sight.
A friend will always be there,
To help you win the fight.
You see, friends are very special,
They are those in which you confide.
They give you strength and good advice,
While standing closely by your side.
So, if you wish and you desire
To have many friends around,
Share what you have
With those in need
And many friends abound.

Bonnie Ramos
Sierra Madre, CA

[Hometown] Sierra Madre, CA; [Ed] high school graduate (with honors), two years college; [Occ] retired salesperson; [GA] being blessed with two sons who have grown up to be exceptional individuals (my youngest blessed me with my one and only grandson); they are my delight

I consider myself to be a very fortunate person because I have many good friends. This poem is dedicated to Judy Sugiyama whom I consider to be a best friend of mine. We have been the best of friends for the last fifty years. When I face a challenging situation or have a problem, I call upon Judy, knowing that she will give me another perspective to consider. We might not agree on everything, but, in the end, all is well, and this is why I trust, admire, and regard her as my best friend.

True Friends

In the beginning when we met
I never knew it would end up this way.
With the first phrase,
"Hi, how are you?"
"I'm doing fine. Thank you."
As we talk day after day,
Our friendship is growing in every way.
When the days become tough for me or you,
We'll have each other to complain about our blues.
Laughing, crying, or whatever
We're true friends from the beginning to forever.
We grew up in each other's eyes,
Knowing the memories between us would never die.
Year after year, we'll help each other out.
We'll give each other goals and ideas throughout.
True friends, that's what we are,
All I have to sincerely say,
Thanks for being a true friend every day.

Bryan Ketola
Olympia, WA

A Round of Golf

With sixty years of living and loving life,
a round of golf will help relieve the strife!
A beautiful golf course is what I want to see,
so, I walk the path to reach the first tee.

As I tee up my ball and line up my shot,
I just hope my drive finds the right spot!
My routine is the same as I address the ball,
with my limited power I give it my all!

I hit it with style and with all my might,
I keep my head down then enjoy the flight!
The walk is great as I reach my ball,
I size up my approach, what is the call?

The course is so beautiful, a sight to be seen,
I can barely see the flag let alone the green!
I hit a five wood fade and my shot does fly,
to the right of the flag, it lands pin high!

I size up a twenty-footer that will break slight left,
I read it all wrong it broke four feet to the left.
I struggled to two put and make my par,
another seventeen holes doesn't seem too far!

Richard D. Bowerman
Frederick, MD

[Hometown] Frederick, MD; [DOB] 1950; [Ed] architectural technology, Montgomery Jr. College; facilities management, George Mason University; [Occ] retired US Air Force and federal government; [Hobbies] golfing, traveling, writing poetry, volunteering; [GA] Presidential Meritorious Service Medal (US Air Force), Presidential Unit Citation (US Coast Guard), Maryland Governor's Citation (Air National Guard)

Wild Grapes

I did not invite them, nor they me
Their vines have labored amongst
Those wild roses, hiding in infancy amongst blooms
Then to thorns
Twisting and entangling
As some mystical snake
Like an evasive intruder
To hang off my trees
With their now-purple fruit. Glistening to the sky
The September sun has kissed them
Sending an aroma, as if wine would be made
Like Eve, they have come to tempt me
As if to dream of another time
Or something that would never be
To heights no ladder could reach
A contest, no athlete could compete
The birds will make their own wine
All in their due time.

Mark S. Haynes
Laconia, NH

[Hometown] Laconia, NH; [DOB] December 15, 1949; [Ed] BA in liberal arts; [Occ] facilities manager; [Hobbies] gardening, cooking

While I have a liberal arts degree in English, I have been involved in facilities management in both the private and public sectors. My studies to obtain my degree exposed me to all genres of literature. Having graduated from Plymouth State College, now a university, I had the opportunity to extensively study Robert Frost who actually taught there. His art of capturing the beauty and simplicity of New England life has always been my inspiration. "Wild Grapes" mirrors that beauty and simplicity. My greatest achievement was to succeed my mother, being elected to same local political office (which she held for fifty-five years).

Used to Be

Used to be parties, clubs and racing cars on Saturday nights
Used to hang out with my friends all night long
Used to not worry about a thing
Used to not care at all

Then you came along and changed it all

Now it's home and in bed by nine and up for school
    by eight
Now it's homework and cartoons and don't be late
Now it's how was your day and I'm hungry, Mom

Oh how that little voice and one little word changed
    everything one day

I miss how it used to be but love to hear you
    say I love you, Mom

Sandra K. Watson
Oxford, NC

[Hometown] Roxboro, NC; [DOB] September 8, 1975; [Ed] high school graduate and some college; [Occ] cashier; [Hobbies] racing, writing, computer, baseball; [GA] getting five poems published so far

I'm from Roxboro, NC but now live in Oxford, NC. I have one daughter, Kayla, to whom I am a single mother. I work as a cashier at the local convenience store. I love racing, and I am a diehard Brad Keselowski fan. I am a diehard UNC College basketball fan. I love baseball also. I don't write poetry on a regular basis, just when it comes to me and I feel the need to put it on paper. This is my fifth poem being published. I studied medical office administration in college but didn't finish.

Dialogue of Music

Vivid hues awaken the brain
Vertical strokes accent the artist's clarity for detail
Tangible tranquility

Senses and images display visual poetry hidden within
Musical notes and lyrical quotes abound
Endless discussion possibilities
Positive eye candy mobility
Interpretation open
Dialogue of music

Sandra Glassman
Oceanside, NY

I am a poet and musician. Emerald Records records my CDs and my videos on YouTube. I have been writing poetry for twenty years and have received many awards. Poetry and music are entwined together. Poetry can lift spirits as also can a conductor's baton.

Downward Spiral

Loveless despair, unity to be broken, a life of lies, no liberty.
Fear, fleeing for freedom.
Friendly relations no more, real life, countries at war.
Sympathy is dying; control takes its aim,
Down the good ones fall to hatred, living in hell,
A stab in the back, burned by the flame.
Away into infinity, the world goes on in pain, the good people hide in agony, holding,
Trying to stay sane.

Caitlin M. Conrad
Cape Coral, FL

When I Needed Love, Falling Gentle Autumn Leaves Sounded Melancholy

Iridescent tapestries blossoming of roses, forsythias, inca lilies,
Carnations glowing vivid colors so romantic, lovely and passionate,
We amorously strolled together along their paths holding our warm
Tender hands. Now, I lonely drifted with a cold bleeding heart,
Yearning for your elusive sweetheart. The depth of our intimate
Relationship aspired, was forbidden that better not sustained to hurt.

Falling gentle autumn leaves sounded melancholy, cascaded from
My eyes, imprinted our yesteryear's esplanade, waiting for you to be
Nearby. But more hurtful than not. Oh! How throbbingly hurtful your
Love departed me? I lived on this beautiful memory, tormenting it's.

Be with me Amor, so we could live our yesteryear's romance.
Lonely drifting through the empty esplanade, yearning for your
Sweetheart. Reaching out my hands to hold you in my arms in vain.
Halloo! How throbbingly hurtful the revival of our romance was?

Remembered the candlelight, wine, fragrant flowers in a delightful
Atmosphere at night playing the piano. How heartrendingly you left
Me? With the bleeding heart without you, I sang that romantic song
Playing a piano in a night club. Let us relive our yesteryear's tender
Passion; our divided hearts now be together, never be distant again.

I caressed you, holding you in my arms, kissing you passionately.
Falling gentle autumn leaves sounded melancholy, nostalgic for you
Near by my side. Would you be there with me as my sweetheart?

Keith Tran
San Jose, CA

[Hometown] San Jose, CA; [Ed] health science and business administration

Beauty

Real beauty comes from the inside
You can't mimic it
Although many have tried
Beauty is like a rose
One that God sews
With age it gracefully grows

Beauty is a burning fire
Unquenchable, Never does it tire
Beauty flies like the eagle
Soaring higher and higher

Beauty shows herself in the moon
Before the day comes, and she leaves all too soon
It is as light as a cloud
Always seen in the eyes of a child
Beauty is inside your soul
As vibrant as a young doe

Ettie Marlet Christian
New Site, MS

[Hometown] New Site, MS; [DOB] September 1, 1998; [Ed] high school sophomore; [Occ] student; [Hobbies] sports, writing, reading, debate; [GA] successfully managing Type 1 Diabetes

When I received a letter from Eber & Wein inviting me to submit my poem for this book, I knew this was an opportunity I couldn't refuse. The inspiration for my poem came while I was thinking about how pure and innocent beauty really is. Beauty is so unique and original, it almost seems unreal. To my family and fellow poets, thank you for your support. However, above all, I thank Jesus Christ for blessing me with this opportunity. May my words inspire all readers and poets alike.

Rainbow

Rainbow low in the sky;
Your gleaming beauty dazzles the eye.
Your beautiful prism colors
Of red, yellow, and blue
Strike a chord of harmony
That beams so true.

Rainbow, rainbow, in your radiant glow;
An arc of beauty, to us you show.
With an aura of color by God divine;
Your spectral light, by His design.

Rainbow, rainbow, where did you go?
You were here a while ago.
So now you fade and disappear;
By His light divine, and to us so dear.

Vernon Bogle
Manchester, TN

My name is Vernon Bogle. I now live in Manchester, TN. I was born in Lascasses, TN on April 28, 1943. I finished high school and took a course on broadcasting. I have been an avid collector of old 78 Victrola records, for over fifty years. My hobbies are solving difficult cross-word puzzles and playing the guitar. My greatest achievement was radio. My inspiration for this poem "Rainbow" just came to me, and so I just penned it down. Just looking at a rainbow gives one an aura of enchantment—like an arc to Heaven.

The Oak Tree

The oak tree grips the earth,
With a strong and silent hand.
The ugly weed spreads its seed,
Across the patient land.
Young birds scream with hunger,
The lurching beetle settles under,
The stolid rock seeking shelter,
The grunting pig for roots will dig,
In the summer swelter.
The patient earth a sweet life gives,
The hungry pig for eating lives.
From this earth comes a straining flower,
The tough and hoary oak
Lives in steady growth,
He has taken no solemn oath.
Springtime brings us flowers,
With the soaking by April showers.
After summer the trees turn bright,
Only one law all must know
Is to grip the earth and grow, grow, grow
Until growth turns into might.

George Thomas Palmer
Watts, OK

[Hometown] Watts, OK; [DOB] January 1, 1959; [Ed] bachelor's in psychology; [Occ] unemployed; [Hobbies] reading, the Internet, writing; [GA] winning in the Talequah Library Anthology Contest

I like to think that when I die I will leave a commentary on life behind me. That is why I want my poem published in this anthology. Sometimes I think of myself as a wordsmith, a man who shapes words into useful implements. I hope to leave my many well-fashioned articles behind me. It is the mission of the writer to give the direction for which humanity is to strive. The writer's words are put out and judged. Those that point the right direction are heralded. This is my submission. I hope you like it.

9/11

Flames burning bright
Smoke in the streets
Ash falling into a crowd of disbelief
Tragedy just struck
Everyone in shock
Grief in everyone's eyes
As they wonder if their loved ones are alive
A speck of hope remains
Until the second plane crashes
Then both buildings crumple to the ground
The nation comes together to get revenge

Nicole McCombs
Harrington, DE

[Hometown] Harrington, DE; [DOB] October 8; [Hobbies] music and poetry

Saturday Night Sauna (Steambath)

With no running water
Or electricity in our home
Neighbors would gather at Joki's
For our weekly sauna.
Men and boys went to the south door
Women and girls to the north.
Hot rocks were lathered with dippersful of water.
We girls sat on the bottom bench,
Chattering like chickadees,
Rubbing the dirtballs off our stomachs
While Mother shampooed the sand
Out of our blonde heads.
Then she poured a cool pail of water
Over our shoulders and we watched
As the soapy water ran past our toes
Through the wood slats
To the cement floor below.
We heard the wooden floor on the men's side
Creak and slam, with a whopping and stomping
Like a herd of moose.
As the braver men jumped into the belly
Of an icy lake.

Jane P. KenKnight
Cincinnati, OH

[Hometown] Rochert, MN; [DOB] January 20, 1937; [Ed] master's degree—Fullbright to Romania teacher; [Occ] teaching high school English, journalism, and creative writing thirty-two years; [Hobbies] sewing, penpals, baking pies, bread; [GA] raising three daughters and three foster teenagers

I have been a high school English, journalism and creative writing teacher for thirty-two years. I grew up in Northern Minnesota, where we didn't have electricity or running water until 1946. We had an outdoor pump, outhouse and kerosene lamps. I had lambs to feed, plus chickens, a cow and a pig. Our neighbor, Joki, had a large steambath, which was used by the whole community of Finlanders. It really got us clean. We kids usually sat on the bottom wooden bench. The higher one got to the top bench, the hotter it got. That was the domain of adults.

Afraid

We can be such fragile creatures
It takes so little to bring us down
We put up walls made of steel and fire
Those who get too close get burned
Those who try to climb get hurt

We think we know best
Hiding within our amour
Not everyone can be stone
And in that moment when we turn to glass
The smallest things can make us shatter
And the person that hides in the amour slowly turns to ice

There comes a time
When the fire burns too bright
The walls become too high
And the person who lays trapped inside slowly begins to melt
Till there is nothing left but a shell of the person they once were

We are such stupid beings
Doing this to ourselves
Too afraid of what's to come
So instead of facing it we hide
Lock the doors
Light the fires
And wait for something, anything, to happen

Chandler Siek
Paeonian Springs, VA

[Hometown] Paeonian Springs, VA; [DOB] December 31, 2000

I Cry

I cry with my eyes open
I cry with my eyes closed
Here I sit in this dark room
So no one knows

Not even a light
Not even a blink
The tears just keep flowing
As I sit and think

The thoughts in my head won't go away
The pain in my heart is here to stay
So I'll cry with my eyes open
And cry with my eyes closed
I'll cry till the end of time
And no one knows

Elizabeth G. Berigtold
Bel Air, MD

[Hometown] Bel Air, MD; [DOB] January 25, 1949; [Ed] high school, community college, veterinary assistant degree, medical terminology courses; [Occ] senior medical transcriptionist; [Hobbies] my cats; [GA] my first poem published about M's Kitty

M's Kitty has been gone two years now. This is for her. I will miss her forever.

The Mistake

She yelled at the old man to get out of her chair;
   he said anyone could sit in it.
      His refusal to move only infuriated her further.

At their next encounter she was sitting in the chair.
   She told him to get out of her sight;
      she didn't like him and did not want him near her.

He couldn't understand why she was upset.
   He had only been a resident for ten days;
      never had he been treated with such loathing before.

Dejectedly he sat alone on a bench around the corner.
   His thoughts went back to happier days in his life;
      perhaps he had made a mistake coming here.

He didn't know earlier residents at assisted living
   considered certain chairs or seating areas as theirs.
      Beward those who would dare to intrude!

No one is welcomed with open arms and smiles for long;
   you must play by unspoken rules, no ruffled feathers.
      Acceptance can be extremely hard to attain.

Vicki Starkey
Longmont, CO

[Hometown] Longmont, CO; [DOB] old enough; [Ed] University of Colorado, life; [Occ] administrative assistant; [Hobbies] reading, writing, music, nature; [GA] still working on it

A widow with four daughters, I read to each of them to instill a love of books at an early age. I enjoy the beauty of nature and watching people interact with each other and their animals. So much can be learned by observing the activities surrounding you. I love writing poetry that makes you think. I watched the encounter described in "The Mistake." Cruelty to others breaks my heart.

Every Living Thing

The worker at Casella's dump
pockets my money, and heaves
my bag of wilted lettuce, chicken
bones, coffee grounds onto the pile.

He's seen me here before—is comfortable
confessing that he's lost his job, confiding
that tomorrow he'll be gone just like the
screaming crow he once found stuck
between his parlor-screen and window.

With flapping wings, he acts out
the bird's escape once the unhinged
screen was yanked away. He tilts his
grizzled chin like the muzzle of a gun
and aims his laughter at the garbage-gulls
who screech for scraps, mimicking his gestures
with their whacking wings.

A long white feather falls between us.
He picks it up and tucks it on his ear
as if it were a quill he'll later dip in ink
to write important words of basic creature-needs—
food, shelter, someone to hear our cries.

Regina Murray Brault
Burlington, VT

Regina Brault is the recipient of over 250 national and international poetry awards and two Pushcart nominations. Her poem, "Timesweep Cantata" was awarded first place by the Salem College Center for Women Writers 2009 International Literary Award Competition. She was named 2009 Vermont Senior Poet Laureate by the Angels Without Wings Foundation as well as receiving the 2008 Creekwalker and Euphoria poetry awards. Her poetry has appeared more than 250 times in more than 130 different publications.

A Little Time

He only had a little time
Before she came.
He put her name
Into some verses with a rhyme
And massaged all the words until they fit.
So little time! He made the most of it.

They only had a little time
Before she left.
But they were deft
When it came to the things sublime.
Blushing, she read his poem. 'Twas candlelit.
So little time. They made the most of it!

Robert P. Tucker
Lakeland, FL

[Hometown] Lakeland, FL; [DOB] November 12, 1949; [Ed] PhD, University of Chicago; [Occ] retired professor of religion, philosophy, ethics and logic and ordained pastoral minister doing pulpit supply; [Hobbies] reading and writing poetry; [GA] retiring as minister emeritus after thirteen years serving the Unitarian Universalist Congregation of Lakeland, FL

Healing (Under the Weather)

You sound so sick let me try to make you feel better
Let's pray and draw you God and I all closer together
Did you notice I speak in God's rhyme
I want to care for you at this time

I'll get you medicine and that kind of stuff
And all of your pillows I will fluff
There is something I want you to know
That Jesus can heal, the word tells us so

I will touch you with my gentle hand...
And the sickness will leave is what I will demand
All you have to do is have enough faith
While my gentle hands softly touch your face

The spirit of God will be so strong
Away with the cough, and the sickness is gone

Pastor Michael Warren Hartl, DMin, DSc
Christian Media Ministries

Pastor Michael Hartl attended The Pennsylvania State University for undergraduate and graduate school. Michael has worked for the Walter Reed Army Institute of Research in the Department of Molecular Pathology (Department of Defense, United States Army). He has also worked at the Penn State Hershey College of Medicine as science associate in the department of pharmacology. Michael writes poetry for Christian Media Ministries (an Independent Charter Ministry). Michael has a doctorate in ministry from Trinity Evangelical Christian University (professional certification in media ministry). Michael was awarded a doctorate of science (Diplomat Christian Education and Counseling) through Holy Catholic Church International, St. James Seminary.

Construction Site: Baby Being Born

Hello, my name is Sarah Ann
I've heard God has a wonderful plan
I live in Mommy's tummy where it is nice and warm
But someday soon I will be born

So I can see the bright noon sun
And grow and learn and have some fun
There will be so many things to see and do
Mommy and Daddy can take me to the zoo

I can see lions, tigers, birds and bears
I'll be so happy, I'll cry happy tears
I can smell some flowers and catch butterflies
Roll in the grass and play games I surmise!

It will be fun to take my first step and walk
Imagine when I actually learn to talk
I wonder if my hair will be blond or red?
Maybe it will be black or brown instead

I wonder how many pounds I'll weigh?
Time is now ticking away
Maybe I'll be born at 8:00, 10:00 or noon
Whoops! I think it may happen very soon!

Victoria Damiano
Toms River, NJ

Victoria Damiano lives in Berkeley Township, which is located in the New Jersey shore area. She has previously worked in real estate and is presently enjoying her retirement. Vicci's interests are piano playing, songwriting and poetry. She has recently authored two books: Trees of Righteousness and I Am His Daughter, A Book of Plays. The poem "Construction Site: Baby Being Built" has special meaning to her, since she is blessed with twelve beautiful grandchildren.

Fear

Fear if you have it
Stand up to it.
For if you don't
It will destroy you and your life.
It will rip your heart out
And shred it to pieces
Right in front of you.
It will stop you from
Having what you want
Most out of life.
It will creep up on
You when you least expect it.
It will keep you in tears.
For *fear* is
The *destroyer* of *all* things.
It will let you
Think that it has gone.
But when you reach
For something
It will slap your hand
And rear its ugly head again.
So I say if you can
Face it and stand up to it.
But most of all
Push it aside.

Lora Wheeler
Willoughby Hills, OH

Making Motion of Poetry

How water flows
Poetry flows in my mind.
Thoughts in my mind glows
Keep words open for me to find.

Water flows shows its sign
A motion that it goes (along).
Even poetry has its design
Keeps the mind going (along).

I like every moment
As I go on making a change.
This does show some improvement
Why? So nice to arrange.

Thinking of poetry in motion
Staying close to me.
I think of my devotion
How it feels so gracefully.

Poetry in motion
All that I adore.
I have no other notion
Makes me like this even more.

(My Own Idea)

Arvid Homuth
St. Charles, IL

[Hometown] *Valley City, ND;* [DOB] *February 13, 1929;* [Ed] *bachelor of arts, two-year printing trade;* [Occ] *linotype operator, twenty-five years;* [Hobbies] *oil painting, piano player (Big Band 1953);* [GA] *Illinois State Art Show 1966*

I was born deaf with little hearing. My parents put one hearing aid on me in junior high making the other one go deaf. Coming to Illinois Rehabilitation helped me get both ears alike, putting two hearing aids on me to improve my hearing. My poetry had several entries to other poetry places. I came across Eber & Wein Publishing once, and that was it. I made up a poem of mine here. When I visited Jamestown, ND I saw Louis L'Amour Grade School. I graduated from Jamestown High School in 1947. I was a linotype operator for twenty-five years for several newspapers.

Perception

To see the beauty
where it's not evident,
when a rough exterior
covers gold.
A wondrous story
under a tattered cover
is love much deeper
than the shell beholds.
Observing these sights
takes depth of perception,
all have the power
though most ignore.
Facing the fear
which seems is before us,
opens the door
for the greatest rewards.

Lisa J. Emery
Hamilton, ON

Lisa Jane Emery Hamilton, Ontario. I am a survivor of multiple traumas and childhood sexual abuse. I am an advocate to end the stigma of mental health issues and an advocate and voice for animals and those who do not have a voice. I am a poet, free spirit, and wanderer. I live in Hamilton with my cheeky kitty and have two beautiful daughters. I strive to bring peace, justice, and equality where I can. Namaste.

Earth's Garden

Nature is filled with such ornate imagery
Earth is the canvas on which this finest work of art is made
Such intricate beauty has been passed down
Throughout the ages
With an effective combination of colors and sound

Every day I see an original piece of art
Just as the stars are different from another
So are the inhabitants of nature, adding their contribution
I wonder what kind of wandering spirits pass through here each day

The wind and sun add color to the garden's face
Moisture and heat have swollen the garden
Into a marriage of ornamental beauty
Each has taken up permanent residence

As I gaze upon the garden, I get a just sense of its worth
It's a powerful emotion of a great symphony
A harmonious combination of elements
Causing great harmony of feeling here

The source has delineated the plan of this garden with great care
All this splendor dressed upon the Earth
In fine array
It is magnificent

Tracy A. Banks
Brooklyn Park, MN

[Hometown] Woodland Park, MI; [DOB] April 19, 1965; [Hobbies] writing, reading, making crafts

Vacuities

An ache in the abyss of darkness
Spawns a pernicious cavity
Catalyzing a flood of saline
Arrested by a seawall of inner strength
Stemming the escape of enigmatic
Agony raping the spirit of solace.
Nurturance
Sustained in the ebony fissure
Effectuated by lasting credence
Induced my mature exemplification
In the beautification of faithful
Discipline to the heavenly decrees
Initiates therapeutic solace

Catherin Elizabet Belle
Ft. Walton Beach, FL

Ms. Belle, born in a Sante Fe boxcar on a side rail near the town of Sweetwater, TX, spent her youth on the family farm and ranch near the German community of Rowena, TX. Spending her adult life in the corporate world, she maintains her heart and soul is still mired in the land and the animals that inhabit it. She has attended numerous educational facilities but insists that her best education came from her father and the "School of Hard Knocks." Her professional career has been a kaleidoscope of experiences in varied career fields leaving her well versed on a variety of topics and a strong curiosity of others. She revels in the joy of learning and strives to learn something new every day. In 2005 she closed the doors on her desktop publishing business, retiring she embarked on a new career with a new challenge… writing. Ms. Belle firmly believes that "each day is an adventure and should be enjoyed to the fullest."

Memory of the Heart

To the 70th anniversary of the end of World War II

About the cosmos, I don't write—I was not
in sky-high edges even for a day.
But I saw blown-up heavens so glum and hot
above the bank of native river's bay,
the human pain, blood, death, dire roads of that war...
And though I was a boy, I understood
the power of people's accord—thus they bore
everything...the faith helped to tote their rood.

Today all this has become history's part:
the bloody dawn, ocean of troubles, tears—
this vastness of human suffering, too hard...
The second World War overfilled our Earth
by bitter sites of fire and people's backs bent
with grief on dear military graveyards
where heroes laid to rest—our loved mother land,
they could protect those troops of fearless guards.

And nothing is forgotten—the hate, as seas,
took over our world, seeping into hearts.
That does not bring the solace with desired peace—
they are so fiery, these hatred darts.
It got stronger—years rush crushing any bars,
but can't relieve this loathing to the end.
They firmly ache and don't forget, these soul's scars
of people who love their great native land.

Leonid Vaysman
Los Angeles, CA

Gratitude

Every day at any moment
We are amid reasons to be grateful.
Such humility has no special time or season.
So many blessings, great or small, are given to us.
Do we take the time to reflect on or take in
The little things in life?

Gratitude promotes happiness and good health.
It makes us divert negative to positive.
It humbles us to cope with the stresses of life
And the energy to cope day by day.
Being aware and appreciating simple things
Creates such a well being.

Look for the good moments in the days
And share appreciation for the smallest deeds.
No matter the effort, the grateful one
Receives untold rewards, for the attitude
Opens many doors for positive lives.

Knoxie A. Gore
Brownwood, TX

[Hometown] Brownwood, TX; [DOB] November 29, 1935; [Ed] BS degree; [Occ] teacher; [Hobbies] decorating; [GA] my family: husband of fifty-four years and three sons

Although retired after thirty-two years in a high school classroom, keeping busy is a priority for me. It makes my body and mind continue to function. Thus, this poem has a message to all of us to keep positive attitudes and enjoy life.

Wild and Free

I am...
Wild and free
Running, grazing
With eyes to see
Fences trying to
Hold me in, breaking
My spirit to tame
Within fighting with
All my might the wire
And post cold metal
Crushing, breaking... my teeth, gritting
Fierce, strength within
Giving all for
My spirit to be
Wild and free
Once again

Rose Michelle Poppelreiter
Saltillo, MS

[Hometown] Saltillo, MS; [DOB] June 27, 1967; [Ed] working on a BA in secondary education (English) at Blue Mountain College

I have been married to Andy Poppelreiter for twenty-seven years. We own and operate a small family farm, where we raised our four children. I love to write, read, sew, cook, can, garden, ride horses, and spend time with my family.

Transmutation

Lost
Built a bridge
Flesh to spirit
Underwent transmutation
A transformation
Constructed a soul connection
Of self-reflection
And redirection
With introspection
Felt my way through life
Blinded by circumstance
Alive, no will to survive
Had to find a way
Nobody to help
Blessed
Followed that bridge
Found my "self"

Dana Bradshaw
Cypress, TX

[Hometown] Pittsburgh, PA; [Ed] BS in MIS Penn State University; [Occ] writer, entrepreneur, IT professional and investor; [Hobbies] software programming and volunteer work

My Love

You take me as I am
Not as everyone else sees me.
You love my imperfections
You don't care what they see.
I got lucky when I found you
I ended up with the man of my dreams.
Nearly four years later
I still feel just as lucky.
You make me smile every day
You carry me when I fall down.
I'll trade my forever for yours
What do you say, now?
I've never met anyone that cared so much
You put me before yourself
But I can't let you do that all the time
I'll take care of you as well.

Breanna Rawson
Des Moines, IA

[Hometown] Des Moines, IA; [DOB] November 17, 1997; [Ed] high school

Heaven's Above Your Earthly View

I wish I could
be an angel,
topmost your noble tree.
For then I could
behold
your light below.
For then I could
stand watch
should your candle burn low.
For then I could
sing
to you until you sleep.
For then I could
grant
the wishes you keep.
And I surely would show you
love,
show you it is true,
Heaven's above your Earthly view.

Sara Laureen Bursch
Buffalo, MN

In the First Five Minutes

The sad secrets shared
Somehow, someway she knew I cared
She said it was her fault all the things that she did
How could it be? I say, you're only a kid
Loved ones who abused her show no remorse
Will selfishly go on their way, of course
How many years of therapy will be needed?
How much hurt and shame will be deeply seeded?
Next week she will be adopted, I was told
Will love for her life then gently unfold?
More secrets held inside, ashamed they will know
Will the new parents love her or make her go?
I tell her she's special and supposed to be here
All the years of pain and sorrow I hope will be cleared
Will my words and concern make a difference in her life?
Please, God, grant me the wisdom to lessen her strife
I don't know why things happen to children this way
I only know they are put before me and I pray
In the first five minutes

Luranne Parker-Betts
Marinette, WI

[Hometown] Marinette, WI; [DOB] July 9, 1956; [Ed] BS in hotel/restaurant management, Oklahoma State University; [Occ] substitute teacher, grades PreK–12; [Hobbies] writing, reading, cooking, scrapbooking, traveling; [GA] raising two wonderful boys

We do not meet people by chance; they are gifts presented to us at the right time and place.

Nicholas Louis

Ten little fingers
And ten little toes.
Into a man
You will grow.
What will be?
No one knows.
For these ten little fingers
And ten little toes.

Julia Hittle
Keizer, OR

[Hometown] Salem, OR; [DOB] March 14, 1936; [Ed] country school, high school; [Occ] retired; [Hobbies] gardening, sewing, writing; [GA] having my poetry accepted by Who's Who

I was born and raised on a farm in Iowa. My ancestors help settle the area. My parents were farmers. My poem is dedicated to our great-grandson. Oregon has been my home for over sixty years.

Indian Summer

On that fine day, I was walking around
in the mist, when I walked around a tree and there
you stood in the center of three rainbows. It
made you shine with different colors. Then
our eyes met and I knew the reason why I was
put on this earth. It was to meet the other
half of my soul. It was like I could feel our
souls coming together as one, like they had
been looking for one another and would be one
for the rest of eternity.

Sara Fay Ives
Carrollton, MO

Precious Baby Boy

Precious baby boy, you teach me how to live.
You also every day teach me how to give.
You may not talk much, but you know the language of love.
You are so loving, my precious angel from above.

God smiled really big when he made you
Because he knew the little things you would do.
Your precious cute smile is a ray of sunshine.
Jesus said himself, "You're a precious child of mine."

I believe God made you to teach me things.
Like being sad, yet still having the strength to sing.
Because I need to learn to be victorious and praise Him.
Even when there's emotional darkness inside, caused by sin.

Precious baby boy, I love your sweet kisses and hugs.
God has a purpose for you, for you know how to love.
Instead of thinking of myself, I want to think of you.
So that's why God gave us so much to share and do.

When you grow up, how proud it will make me
to see the brilliant young man you turn out to be!
I hope you will teach me a lot of things
Because I believe you're gifted, and what a joy that brings!

Patricia Edwards
Morristown, TN

This is a poem about my son, Elijah Michael Edwards. He's about three years old. He has a powerful personality, a sweet little heart, and a cute little face. When he's happy, I can't help being happy. He knows how to communicate directly, even though it is nonverbal because he has speech delays. But he is my precious gift from above, my only child. Praise God for my baby!

Etched

Be careful what you do and say
For you are leaving memories
Time stamped and etched on someone's life
Smiles or frowns or joy or strife?

What you leave is on the mind
Filed deep away and hard to find
But it is there and adding up
What do you pour in someone's cup?

What kind of mark is that you leave
For someone's brain to file...retrieve?
And when it's time and you are gone
What did you leave to carry on?

Good memories—bad—or in between
Were you kind or were you mean?
Sunny days and skies of blue
Or thunder clouds and earthquakes too

And looking back when you are old
What picture is there to behold?
We're all just trying to survive
So etch your best while you're alive

Tracey Travis Lee
Perryville, MD

We should all be mindful of what we do and say, and the effect that it has on others. Read James 3 in the Bible for information on taming the tongue. And remember, "A word fitly spoken is like apples of gold in settings of silver" (Proverbs 25:11).

The Feel of Sorrow

I stood where my mother stood
with her broken heart
Ninety-five years ago
in a country graveyard
On a cold January day
to see her firstborn child
Lowered into the ground
To be covered with red clay
To lie quietly for eternity

She could not have known
Five other children would
Come to her arms, me her last

Many times I heard her pray
"God I only ask to live to see
My children grown"

Sorrow lay heavily upon me
As I stood and saw
A small marker that read
"Infant son of T.G. and Lula Brazeal
Jan. 25, 1919
Only sleeping"

A small bouquet of artificial flowers
Placed by the stone seemed to make
My brother not so alone

Taney A. Brazeal
Fairhope, AL

I am eighty-two years old and did not try to write poetry until after my seventy-fifth birthday. I was born in Reform, AL to parents who farmed. I have a BS degree from the University of Alabama, where I majored in business administration. I started and ran several small businesses during my career. I am married, and we will soon celebrate our sixtieth wedding anniversary. We have two children, both with successful careers.

The Kingdom of the Pine

As a child, I peeked into the night while the moon was in full shine.
There I saw the little folk, from the Kingdom of the Pine.

Fine ladies wore their feathers bright, in shades of red and blue.
The little maids in waiting were the wrens and sparrows too.

The squirrels seemed like jesters as they played with such delight.
Small munchkins searched for nectar, darting quickly left and right.

The crickets were the minstrels while the songbird sang her song.
The bullfrogs and the katydids all seemed to sing along.

An old owl like a wizard, deep in thought and oh so wise.
The moonbeams did the lighting with the help of fireflies.

The night was full of magic as the old crow told his tale.
Up high the lone hawk soared like a ship in its full sail.

Then I saw the eyes approach from the shadows just beyond.
There appeared the Queen herself and the little Prince, her fawn.

I watched till I grew weary and lost all track of time.
In dreams the folk still visit me, from the Kingdom of the Pine.

Daryl D. Brown
Burlington, IA

[Hometown] Burlington, IA; [DOB] April 30, 1941; [Ed] master of science; [Occ] retired school teacher; [Hobbies] cars, motorcycles, casinos; [GA] first place in Iowa state track meets four times

I am a retired school teacher and coach living in Burlington, IA, with my wife of twenty-eight years. This poem was motivated by the idea of a small child watching a full moon rise behind a pine tree in the middle of the night. In this light the child discovers the citizens of this little kingdom—hence, "The Kingdom of the Pine."

The Trap

'Tis an entangling evil world
Full of greed and self-centeredness
Around every corner the demon sows his bait
Then awaits...to devour...
The weak, damned and inexperienced
'Tis a painful splinter when one finds
How blind one hath been.
'Tis a sodden field, one shall need to plod across
When one walks straight into the trap
Becoming evil's catch.
Evil shall undoubtedly cross each and every path
Will one be blind or will one see it?
On that bitter cold, dark lonely day
Should one find they've been swept up inside
A prison where so many descend into
Hereinafter when one has fully awoken
Contemplating freedom beyond the walls
Wondering how thy could hath been so blind
Evil 'tis destroying their life, devouring their flame
Yet one day when time is served
When the lock is unlocked and free one does walk
Will one be joyous to drift and wander free?
Star-crossed with desire for the trap
Sickly and woefully?
Or relinquish to death for one's remedy?

Loreta Stella
San Diego, CA

[Hometown] Camdenton, MO; [DOB] February 3, 1966; [Ed] cosmetology; [Occ] pet sitting; [Hobbies] writing poetry; [GA] acquiring cosmetology license

Abuse has trickled down my broken family tree contagiously. One day in the winter of 2014, a package of whatnots and thingamagiggers arrived via mail from my beloved sister. At the bottom of the box lay a newspaper clipping about a poetry contest by Eber & Wein Publishing. 'Twas a time in my life when I became aware abuse can be disguised in a snaky, crushing, hurtful, destroying form—verbal, mental, and emotional. I wrote my first poem, "The Demon," that winter, and out of my head rained many other poems cleansing and repairing my soul and sanity.

Silent Tears

Spices of the season
Penetrate the awaking day
I watch the snowflakes
Gently fall
As joy dances
Through my mind
Yet deep within
Are silent tears
Evening candles
Are now lit
As distant melodies
Fill my heart
To sing
Yet deep within
Are silent tears
In the stillness
Of the night
The aroma of sweet oil
Penetrates my heart
Bringing a song
For me to sing
Now deep within
Love has dried
My silent tears

Jo Worthington
Lakeland, FL

[Hometown] Baltimore, MD; [DOB] January 13; [Ed] master of divinity 2002; [Occ] minister; [Hobbies] reading and walking—each old and new place takes on a life in my writing; [GA] when I finish and publish my book

As soon as I learned to hold a pen, I began to write down the thoughts that I had daydreams about. For years my poetry followed the way I was taught, until one day suddenly my writing changed and a birthing began in me and through me as Holy Spirit began to teach me. Like a tapestry, different threads yet one design are what I write and what I teach. Also I am a prophetic intercessor and street evangelist, and these are also threads in the tapestry that God has designed for me to draw the lost into His kingdom.

Between Night and Day

It is that time between night and day
Where things appear from the haze
Like thoughts in a clouded mind
An awakened spirit that needs more time

The confusion of the beginning day
Where light pushes through darkness gray
Mirror's reflection appears in color
The digital clocks red in the open parlor

The white of day on the closed curtain
Awaiting the orange glow of the sun that is certain
Furniture appears out of nowhere
As the light grabs time's share

It is quiet time when monks reflect
The dogs stretch and crick their necks
Bark for their masters to awaken
The masters think the dogs must be mistaken

"Quiet!" An hour more is needed
The dogs know his voice must be heeded
Darkness succumbs to light's demands
Noise makes its bold commands

Garbage trucks and airplane noise
Neighbor's clamor breaks your poise
Slowly you give in
You let the day begin

Timothy M. Nugent
Las Vegas, NV

I am a traveler and retired gentleman. I ride a Honda Goldwing around the country, meeting new friends and opportunities to enjoy fresh and new experiences. I am sixty-five years young, living in Las Vegas and enjoying breathing life in.

Friends

Once in a lifetime a gentle breeze blows through
And caresses one's soul
And in that moment a life is changed
It's almost as if that life had organized time and events
Just for that moment
To come together with that one it has known for eons
To peer into their eyes and see a soul like its own
Walls that have been built to protect
Are suddenly torn down
And though the life is vulnerable, it feels safer than ever
Words need not be spoken
For each life knows the other inexplicably
And even though these two lives
Will eventually travel different paths
Both know that as time weaves its way through eternity
They will return to each other again and again
Renewing the bonds of true friendship
These two spirits forever intertwined

Kim Davis
Jersey Shore, PA

The Question?

They sit in a huddle comparing their notes
Each seeming to be horrifically composed
Each looking to a fellow shoulder to show a smile
A friendly face in the trees of bleakness
The question?
The people who have come to test the legal system
The sentries are always on duty keeping the watch
Men and women all in the same colored suit
One taller one skinnier one wearing glasses
Some smile, others with just a thinking expression
None of them show signs of an out-of-season tan
Every move is calculated
Their pacing so rhythmical
Leather shoes make no sound on a marble floor
Legal files showing riveted edges
Yellow legal pads slipping top to bottom
None of them seem to show signs of a victory
The question?
The lawyers
Who then in this daily structured gathering is the victim?
The question?
The judge—of course

Sharon Rinaldi
Toms River, NJ

[Hometown] Springfield, IL; [DOB] May 1, 1950; [Ed] high school, some college; [Occ] avian specialist; [Hobbies] writing, my horses, birds; [GA] my children, Shawn and Cortney

I was a legal secretary and worked for an ambitious lawyer who set his sights on Congress. He was elected and, due to me being a loyal and really good campaign slogan writer, I was deemed the administrative assistant for the district. Gerald Ford was president then with Nelson Rockafeller. Opened doors and opportunity were so easy for me to obtain. But along with that came the back-biting, cruel and very active attacks on me from everyone that wanted to be on that political payroll. I started writing personally just as a way to survive. I do love politics.

Frozen

What birds can survive...
Where do chipmunks hide...
Hairless squirrels limp about
Branches break though once stout...

Geese in formation, northward bound,
Decide they must, and turn around...
"We'll have none of this!" they cry,
And head once more for the South...

Following me into the bank...a mole
Back out again into the snow, and his hole...
A cottontail burrows beneath McKight Hall...
Niagara's rapids refuse to fall...

Deer huddle by houses and sheds...
Sun shines on a once-watery scene...
A tiny sparrow shatters over my head...
A sturgeon, stirring in mud...plunges upstream...

Tobi J. Kumar
Fairport, NY

[Hometown] Baldwinsville, NY; [DOB] September 30, 1939; [Ed] BA in liberal arts; [Occ] photographer; [Hobbies] art, travel, poetry, adventure; [GA] inclusion in Marquis Who's Who in the East 24th Edition

I am basically a photographer. I have worked for companies like American Photograph Corporation in New York, and years ago for Karl Mann Associates on West 13th Street in New York, as an artist. I love travel and adventure. Most of my poems are related to these things, as per my book, Unfold the Sky, which is available online. Writing poetry began for me in the solitary winters of western New York. The poem "Frozen" was inspired by the horrific, yet magnificent, winter of 2014, when Lake Ontario froze end to end, and Niagara Falls became a statuary wonder.

Mr. Poet Man (an Ode to a Poet)

Your words are very clear
And I do understand
Although they are different
My fellow man

But, then again
We all aren't the same
Nothing's wrong
And who's to blame

Our lives they do vary
As do our words
Our hearts are free
Souls of birds

Our spirits high
Our words they claimed
The crazy thoughts
That left us maimed

The hurts in passing
The life is here
My fellow man
Your words are clear

Tony Burgos
Stockton, CA

My name is Tony Burgos. I live in Stockton CA. I am a Mestizo by blood (mixed blood, Filipino and Mexican), born April 8, 1960, a truck driver by trade for now. I enjoy martial arts, fishing, and people watching. My greatest achievements in life are being able to believe in God, my family, and being able to be a liver doner.

Frown

When you frown you frown alone,
Forehead wrinkled, eyebrows telling
Of displeasure, your lips in downward
Curve. But wait, all that changes.

Come eventide you are slow dancing
With your charming and lovely lady
To the wonderful music of yore after
A long, hard day and the frown is turned
Upside down.

James C. Clemons
Fredericksburg, VA

[Hometown] Newton, IA; [DOB] September 8, 1926; [Ed] 1974 grad of University of Maryland; [Occ] USG and logistic management; [Hobbies] bridge, going for walks; [GA] getting things done

I grew up on an Iowa farm in the 1930s, a one-room country school and high school in Newton, IA. I was drafted in 1944 to infantry in Europe and discharged to Vienna, Austria in 1946 to work in intel. I married my Vienna girl in July 1948 and returned to the US. A career in foreign affairs took my family to Europe, the Middle East, and Africa. I graduated from University of Maryland in 1974. I worked in communications, logistics, project management, and as an investigator. I retired in 1979 having another career as a logistic support consultant and tech writer. I love the outdoors, the Alps, and Iowa too. All of the above inspired stories and poems.

A Second Chance

It's a shut case a cleansing of the soul
An Ash Wednesday where Lent has a
Fastening a second chance
Like snow blessing the land
Washing away the sin like a snowman melting
As if to say now do it right
Let the regrets get lessons to live by
Until life grows new wings
Modernizing the truth of another life
Where wings are grown to fly
Without leaving the ground
Heaven is here on Earth
Remember when there was no leg to stand on
And dizzy spells had us thinking of the way
The trees would come back to life or
The grass turning brown would come back green
Half a dream away from
The one hundred billion stars bringing on
Super nova explosions with the rain
Bringing us into a dream world
As the sun and the moon were changing tides
The second chance of cleansing the soul

Vincent Palumbo
Calverton, NY

Will You Make a Difference?

Do you wake up each morning with a smile on your face
Feeling humbled by what He gave to embrace
Or do you wake up knowing it will be a bad day
Just because yesterday didn't go your way
Do you plan to make a difference and give it all you got
Or are you going to give up and complain a lot
Do you hope to put a smile on someone's face
Or do you not care without a kind word to say
Do you realize your attitude and the choices you make
Play a huge role in this world we create
When you come in contact with another soul
You could leave a scar or make them whole
You could make them laugh or make them cry
Give them a reason to live or a reason to die
Zero is the weight of a human tongue
But once provoked it's the hardest to hold on
It will rear up in anger with too much to say
Spitting deadly poison upon its prey
Be cautious of how you make someone feel
They could carry it with them and never heal
We are all connected somehow someway
What you do yourself could affect someone's day
So remember tomorrow when you get out of bed
It's not just your world we were given to live in
But a world we create by what's inside our head
And a world we control by what we are feeling within

Brenna (Danette) Bonner
Mesa, AZ

[Hometown] Mesa AZ; [Occ] grocery retail management, Sprout's Farmers Market; [Hobbies] writing poems/ songs, building/creating unique things out of "junk," playing the spoons

I am the middle child of two brothers and two sisters. I have never been married or had children. I have struggled in my life trying to find answers as to why I am here. What is my purpose? Out of high school I modeled for a short time but found myself spiraling downhill from the choices I was making due to peer pressure. One day I opened my eyes and realized I was better than the life I was living, and put my heart and soul into being somebody other than a pretty face. I advanced in my new career quickly and considered my job my soul mate. I was single, independent, driving BMWs, financially stable for many years. Then one day, my world flipped upside down. I lost my job and was out of work for more than seven months. I not only lost the material things that made up my so-called success, but I lost my soul, confidence, faith, and trust in people. What I have realized is that it doesn't matter what we have accumulated if it's not what we can store in our hearts when our journey has ended.

As I Kneel to Pray

My walk through life has been broken hearted
Everywhere I turned the burdens started
Constantly feeling like I've been discarded
Why can't I break free
This life, it cannot be
Someone please save me
As I kneel to pray
Father please take this pain away
Change my heart and my ways
Help me live for You today
It's a bumpy road that I am on
Life it seems is so far gone
I sit and wonder where did I go wrong
Everything keeps on happening
My whole world caves and is trapping me
Please set my soul at ease
As I kneel to pray
Father please find me so I don't roam
I can't do this on my own
Without you I feel alone
My eyes are open and it's begun
The chains and locks have been undone
The never-ending race has been won
I look around and see Your glory
Now I tell a different story, of how Your son paved the way for me
As I kneel to pray
Father I want to thank You every day
I want to praise You in every way
Father You are my potter and I am Your clay

Jessica Davis
New Kensington, PA

I've been writing poetry for twenty years. I have multiple publications and awards. Writing helps me express myself where my voice can't.

Our Love

Tell me that you love me
Show me that you care
Take my hand and lead me to
A place where we can share our love
Forget about times gone by
Remember not the things of old
Lead me to that special place
Of ecstasy untold
Carry me down the road of passion
Across rivers of joy divine
Wrap me in your blanket of love
Prove to me that you're mine
Tell me that you love me
Show me that you care
Take my hand and lead me to
A place where we can share
Our love

Lisa Howard
Summerdale, AL

[Hometown] Elsanor, AL; [DOB] September 8, 1965; [Ed] high school; [Occ] department of transportation; [Hobbies] fishing; [GA] my family

The Darkness Is My Friend

As I gaze through my window
Once brightened by the light of day
The murky shadows descend like foes
As they hasten the last sun rays away.

Soon, the somber night will come
As light slips away and the
Undefined once again will descend
But I am not afraid for the
Darkness is my friend.

The yielding beams of the perfect moon
Playfully cast an illusion of art on my bed
While millions of tiny stars twinkled
Around my head.
I am safe in the comfort of God's loving
Grace and clothed in all His glory
Awaiting sleep soon.

The body and the mind must daily
Proclaim release.
For the labors of mankind will never cease.
The drapery of darkness will fall,
Without fail or end,
But I am not afraid,
For the darkness is my friend.

Delores J. Whitley
Murfreesboro, NC

[Hometown] Murfreesboro, NC; [DOB] April 27, 1941; [Ed] high school graduate, two years nursing school; [Occ] housewife; [Hobbies] painting, flower arrangements, writing; [GA] my two children, Deanna and Jim

I developed a deep love and respect for the great poets like Browning and Edgar Allan Poe when exposed to them in senior English class. I have loved poetry ever since. I have written my life's experiences in a journal daily. Writing is just one of the keys that opens the mind and heart. I enjoy admiring the beauty and wonder of God's creation, our beautiful world. It never ceases to amaze me.

The Vietnam Vet

Alone
and in a wheelchair,
the Vietnam veteran
with a grayish and autumn beard
lives on…

With a multitude
of bad flashback memories
daily tormenting
his Purple Heart and spirit,
he endures remaining days…

Alone, he drinks beer
listening to a sad-assed
cantina oldie…

Arturo C. Hernandez
San Antonio, TX

[Hometown] San Antonio, TX; [DOB] 1947; [Ed] associate of arts; [Hobbies] reading, writing, photography

My greatest achievement is that I am the author of two books. How to Recognize and Challenge and Defeat Workplace Discrimination *was my first book. My second published book is titled* Photography and Poetry of a Chicano. *Both are available in hardcover, softcover, and for the Kindle on Amazon.*

Just One Person Out of Line

Let no more be done or said,
for the unsaid has been done.
And let us not be afraid,
we are once again as one.
It is not your fault or mine,
nor the system or the time.
Once again the sun will shine,
just one person out of line.
Just one person who awoke,
seeking his moment of fame.
And in doing so he broke
a million hearts at a time.
Once again we paid the price
for being caught unaware.
Let us now believe that justice
will make him pay for his dare.
But our noble justice system
has to protect his due rights.
His grin tells me that he knows them;
he won't go through sleepless nights.
Our hearts grieve for the deceased,
their families and their friends.
For what they have left unsaid
will be spoken through our tears.

Felipe Chacon Jr.
El Paso, TX

[Hometown] El Paso, TX; [DOB] September 23, 1951; [Ed] University of Texas–El Paso; [Occ] retired from El Paso transportation department; [Hobbies] singing, songwriting, guitar music; [GA] Vietnam era veteran of US Navy

I have spent most of my life like most average people: trying to achieve the American dream, keeping up with the Joneses. This didn't leave me a lot of free time to write. I developed a talent, a passion for writing at a very young age, because of my deprived childhood. I was born into a very poor family, I don't think I was ever a child; my father forced me to mature before my time. My mother is my hero; she pulled me through. Because of her, I am somebody. I am now a musician, singer, songwriter and poet. This poem I wrote in memory of all the victims and families who have suffered because of the violence in our sick society. God bless our USA.

Easter: A Puppy's Point of View

Easter is coming... such a glorious day...
A day for me to bunny-hop with my friends as we play.

The problem with that dance is the paws left and right...
While one paw is dancing, the other needs a bite.

When my pup friends arrive as I'm out on my walk...
We all get so excited, you'd think we could talk.

It's one bark here and one bark there...
And so it continues until there are no more to spare.

When Easter is over, I'm very tired, I must say...
But my friends and I think it was a really great day!

Now, before putting my head on my bed...
I must lovingly thank you all for your friendship instead.

Love, Button

Boni Berg
Sebring, FL

[Hometown] Glenwood City, WI; [DOB] October 8, 1939; [Ed] college degree in education; [Occ] retired teacher; [Hobbies] golf, creative stitchery, poetry, reading, spending time with my puppy, Button; [GA] my life with a loving husband for fifty years

I grew up in a small farming town of seven hundred people. One of seven children, I was raised in a low-income family. My parents were talented, hardworking, gentle souls who did their best with what they had. I was a very successful student, graduated as class salutatorian, and worked extra jobs to save for college. I managed to put myself through college earning my degree in education. My husband and I met at Stout State University and are about to celebrate our fiftieth wedding anniversary. We both taught for thirty-six years and are now enjoying retirement in a golf community in Florida. Button was a very special gift from my husband for my seventieth birthday.

The Flight of Peter and Greta Honker

Snow was in the wind as we gathered on the rippling lake,
Our patience was straining for our leader's signal to make.
Then, an excited call, wings beat water on the takeoff roll,
We were on our way to the Keys, our destination goal.
Climbing out, we proudly pierced the pillows in the sky,
Our leader found the prevailing wind for direction to rely.
The noise forced our positions at opposite sides of the V,
If in trouble, one could easily observe the other's plea.
Our wings felt like anvils after several hours in flight,
The leader sensed the dilemma and set the glide to alight.
We saw the stopover selected as we followed the descent,
A lake next to a corn field, not a single honk of relent.
We satisfied our appetites to every goose's delight,
Until a very angry farmer made us aware of his plight.
We ran and arose, wings beating on elevators of air,
Lucky to be alive, we were a thankful and happy pair.
Quick to the formation, we continued on our way,
Hopeful to feel the Keys' warmth by close of the day.
In vivid splendor, Long Key Bridge came into our view,
Then lustrous Seven Mile Bridge with its silver hue.
The leader set his wings for a reed laden lake ahead,
This was to be our winter home, the challenge was met.

Garry O. Hanson
Florence, KY

I am a semi-retired consulting engineer who enjoys writing poetry as a pastime. Every poem represents a challenge to me as to how well I can communicate to the reader, perhaps with a seasoning of humor, a particular feeling, impression, or act of nature. "The Flight of Peter and Greta Honker" is representative of the latter. I don't know of anyone who doesn't get emotional about watching and listening to a flock of wild geese migrating south for the winter. Surprisingly, the mechanism of their navigational system has never been satisfactorily explained.

What Can We Say?

Today I saw them leave
Young men, too young to die
Who have yet to see the world
Who love life as much as I.
As I stood with tear-filled eyes and watched them
sail away
I thought how heavy their hearts must be
Upon this fateful day.
They waived goodbye to those on shore
They called and said farewell.
What can you say to men of war
Who sail on to a living hell?
Can you throw them a glance, a cheerful smile
as though they go to play?
Where is a word to comfort them, these men
who go away?
How can we know what's in their hearts?
How can we feel their sorrow?
For where they go they do not know
They sail into tomorrow.

Natalie Meyer
Brooklyn, NY

I am eighty years old, and this was written as I watched a convoy sail out of the New York Port of Embarkation, where I was working, early one Sunday morning, during World War II. Unfortunately, these words still hold true today, all these years later. What have we learned? I graduated from Erasmus Hall High School in 1944, Drake Business School in 1946, and attended Brooklyn College at night for two years studying literature and poetry.

Love

I felt love for him in my heart only because he showed he cared
My heart was broken many times by the ones I trusted most
He talked me through the hurt and pain and showed me what I am worth
Through all my frustrations hatred of being deceived I learned to shut out the world
He taught me how to set aside my anger by expressing my true feelings
I had learned to open up and trust through what was once broken
I was able to speak openly for the first time by sharing my emotions
I learned I am best being who I am and not an imitation
I have learned to speak my mind and not from altercations
I feel better with who I am and not from others' expectations
If only I had spoken what I feel now it would be a start to a new beginning
Why do I feel so guilty about being in love, while our actions act freely?

Angela Khristin Brown
Las Vegas, NV

[Hometown] Las Vegas, NV; [DOB] January 5, 1969; [Ed] doctor of humanities; [Occ] gaming lab assistant; [Hobbies] professional author; [GA] writing poetry

I am a middle-aged female who has a need to have her voice heard. I want to touch others' lives with the words I speak. I ask to close your eyes and open up to what is being said. You may not understand, but you will relate to what is said in my lines of poetry. Women feel pain, love, and loss...these are the words I write in my lines of poetry.

No Letter to Santa This Year

Two years have passed since that tragic December day.
The actions of a madman, precious lives were taken away.

There will not be any letters to Santa this year
but in God's heavenly choir twenty angelic voices sing carols so loud and clear.

A town still mourns, a parent sheds a tear.
A friend gives support for those they hold dear.

A classmate remembers an event on some special day.
They spend with a first-grader before he was tragically taken away.

For the heroic deeds of the educators on that horrific day
gave the ultimate give so that others may stay.

Now in Heaven their guidance goes on
to mentor each angel when they sing a new song.

In the blink of an eye those angels were gone.
The teaching, learning at Sandy Hook will carry on.

First-graders will pass through then go on to learn more.
The departed will never be forgotten and that's one thing for sure.

Effie Noseworthy-Kasell
Perry, FL

[Hometown] *Green Island Brook, Newfoundland, Canada;* [DOB] *March 29, 1952;* [Ed] *RN diploma;*
[Occ] *retired registered nurse;* [Hobbies] *knitting, card playing and board games, especially Scrabble*

I feel my greatest achievement is the satisfaction I obtained from my nursing career of forty-plus years and the appreciation that touched my heart. I am so thankful for all the lasting friendships I've made through work and along the way. I'm also glad to have the opportunity to touch the hearts of readers from the words I write. In regards to the poem of the Sandy Hook tragedy, I, like so many others, ask why?

There's Always Hope

Life can sometimes be very cruel,
But you are nobody's fool.
    There's always hope!

Often times your life can go wrong,
So carry on, for you are strong.

Put a smile on your face,
And stay in that race
    There's always hope!

Go the extra few miles,
Try to do it in style.
    There's always hope!

God will bless you in all that you do,
He's sure to carry you through.
    There's always hope!

Winifred J. Love
Abington, MA

[Hometown] Abington, MA; [DOB] February 7, 1941; [Ed] high school; [Hobbies] drawing, writing and reading; [GA] drawing a religious picture freehand that hangs in a convent

I've had many a so-so job all my life but managed to get by. I've always loved writing poetry, and I'm working on a fictional murder mystery, untitled as of yet. I draw and paint pictures. I have to be in the mood. I love animals—rescued a mama cat and her five sweet kittens. They are all doing well. My poems just seem to come on a whim.

West Virginia State of Mind

An old man sits in his chair, eyes a glassy stare,
Thinking of a place that's no longer there.
The city of his birth, two rivers running through,
With barges, tugboats and paddlewheels too.

Gone is his school, church, homestead and more,
Erased by construction of Interstate 64.
Movie houses closed, streets are one way,
Families all gone, no place to stay.

Seven decades flash before his eyes, now dim;
Yet when closed, the past comes alive again.
Rhododendron is its flower, a cardinal its bird,
And John Denver's music can always be heard.

So where is this place no one can find;
Or is it just…a state of mind?

Jack Iman
Zionsville, PA

[Hometown] Charleston; [DOB] June 10, 1933; [Occ] army and banking; [Hobbies] writing and oil painting

I left to join the army in 1951. After being discharged in 1954, I married a local girl in Phoenixville, PA, obtained a job in banking, and remained in that occupation until retirement. I was able to acquire an education paid for by my employer and obtained position of vice president. Writing is a passion of mine, which includes three books on my background and family history written for our children. My poetry started on the death of our youngest daughter, and only comes from raw emotion.

I Followed My "I Do's" Happily

The girl who was my playmate at age five
Became my wife when she was age seventeen
She began as a little blond cutie
That captured my heart permanently.
If you tell your sweetheart you love her frequently
And continue to tell her daily in marriage
You won't have time for a roving eye.
A sudden surprise, now and then
Adds delight to the day as well as the night.
Surviving WWII we expanded our future
And raised a family, she was more beautiful pregnant
And continued to be through sixty-nine years of marriage.
One day in the Army I received a photo of her and my buddies
Thought it was a movie starlet, but I said, no she's mine.
She went to Heaven in 2012, I feel her presence many times
As we often said—"I'll love you always."

Morris Eldon Ward
Union City, CA

[Hometown] Lynwood, CA; [DOB] October 10, 1923; [Ed] high school; [Occ] welding, manufacturing of special truck bodies; [Hobbies] archery, poetry; [GA] marriage, family

I graduated from Inglewood High School June 1941. I went to work building garage doors in my brother's business and joined the army September 1942, visited my future wife and family in 1942 and married her July 31, 1943 before I was sent to the Solomon Islands. I was in high-frequency radio communication in 13th and 5th Army Air Forces, through the Solomon, Philippines, and into Tokyo two days after the Armistice. I returned home December 1945. I worked in truck body manufacturing for the next twenty years with my brother. We had two plants—one in Los Angeles, one in San Diego. I managed both. In my off hours I was Vice President of Foothill's Loyal Order of Moose

Mama's Shoes

I walked a mile in Mama's shoes
Ouch! Ouch! My aching heart and feet
Oh never, never shall I ever choose
The long day's journey to repeat.

Ollie V. Zoller
Amarillo, TX

[Hometown] Amarillo, TX; [DOB] February 16, 1931; [Ed] high school in Pryor, OK and two-year correspondence course; [Occ] retired; [Hobbies] reading, writing, music, TV; [GA] growing in Body of Christ

I was feeling extremely blue one day and remembered the long rocky road Mama traveled. I got to feeling ashamed of myself, so I picked up my favorite pen and wrote this mini-poem.

Eber & Wein Publishing

Autumn

You can hear autumn in the air
the rustling of the leaves
the wind that blows through your hair,
you can't really see it
yet, it is everywhere.

Summer has passed you by
the leaves are beginning to fall
some leaves are golden brown in color
some leaves barely
have any color at all.

You can hear autumn in the air
as the birds go south to roost
leaving behind the approaching
cold weather, as if there were
a truce.

Rain is on the horizon
dark clouds are rushing above
signaling a storm is near:
wind, rain, rustling leaves,
indicates autumn is here.

Bobbie Greer
Sacramento, CA

[Hometown] San Augustine, TX; [DOB] October, 1938; [Ed] high school, one year of college; [Occ] retired legal typist; [Hobbies] writing, reading, traveling, bowling and poetry; [GA] caring for disabled son

I am a seventy-six-year-old mother and grandmother. I worked for the state of California as a legal typist for thirty-three years and retired in 1999. At the same time, I cared for a disabled son, suffering from muscular dystrophy. He passed away in 2009 at the age of forty-nine years and three months. It was a privilege to have cared for him those years. My poem "Autumn" was inspired by the beautiful colors of the leaves on trees God presents this time of the year. The reds, yellows, oranges, browns, purples and greens all mix together making our surroundings a beautiful scene along with light breezes of the wind. It is awesome, breathtaking and enjoyable. This is my favorite time of the year.

The Crazy Eights (8s)

There were two zeros
Jumping up and down
Then one odd thing happened
One fell but not on the ground
Landing on top of the other
Like wrestling with one another

Their value was no longer zero
Their combined strength was eight
Intrigued as to what had happened
The other two zeros couldn't wait

Deciding to stand close together
Glued like birds of a feather
Forming a mighty eighty-eight
Extremely proud make no mistake

Inflated egos they were flying high
Enjoined together they looked like a butterfly
Flying away the crazy eights could be seen
Like millions of monarchs harmonizing
Happy Birthday, Sweet Sixteen

Jose Hernandez
Donna, TX

[Hometown] Donna, TX; [DOB] March 3, 1943; [Ed] business college; [Occ] accountant; [Hobbies] golfing, reading; [GA] four aces of home course par 3's

In the beginning, God created the heavens and the earth. We can all remember the early childhood games we played. In my case, playing marbles, tops, jacks, hide and seek. The simple game the zeros were playing changed their lives. When I asked the Lord to be my Lord and Savior, He did away with my low self-esteem by making me a new creature. Like the zeros ascending to the skies, I too await the day of the rapture to join our loved ones that have preceded us.

The Answered Prayer

Patience the Lord said to me
All will come that's held in your destiny
You must accept the things that I have planned
For I hold your life in the palm of My hand
Be aware you're not alone
The devil he has plans of his own
He will tempt you today
He will tempt you tomorrow
He will try to drown you in a life of sorrow

You must have faith in My love for you
Like so many others already do
Do not try to understand each passing day
Look at the whole picture along the way
Patience the Lord said to me
All will come that's held in your destiny

Rick Rhythm Williams
Brooklyn Center, MN

[Hometown] Brooklyn Center, MN; [Ed] high school; [Occ] PCA food service manager, IE LC Pizza; [Hobbies] poetry, classic cars, playing the blues; [GA] playing music on stage with international musicians in front of five thousand people

I am a singer, song-writer, musician, and poet. I have published and recorded my work and received several awards. I have been published in twenty-five international poetry books and received six Editor's Choice Awards, one Accomplishment of Merit Award, International Poet of Merit Award, 2000 Poetry's Elite Award, Best Poems of 2000, The 2012 International Who's Who in Poetry Award, and The 2012 Best Poets and Poems Award. I have been a member in good standing throughout the years with several poetry organizations. I have been on the radio and have played music on stage with several well known blues musicians. One of the biggest crowds I have played in front of was over five thousand people. My home is in Minneapolis, MN. Most of all, my family is my first passion and number one love.

Self-Preservation

I'm not surrounded by people who have much good to say
My environment...I pretty much, sway away
At the age of 62 there are a few who could entice me to play...
in "their" worlds
These younger people enter and exit my life, filled with strife,
"my job, my life, I need a wife!" I ask...why?
Do they search me out as a mentor? My own existence I cannot center
Envious? Jealous? No—I oft times pity them...
been there, done that and have progressed along
I'm continuously soul searching – I go through all the steps,
filtering through my music collection seeking that perfect song
So often I feel I don't belong...
I have a reservation for my "self-preservation,"
I might have to pass you by
It's me, myself and I who I depend on and rely
Most people fear being alone, incessant on their cell phone
I will be my best friend until the bitter end
Stop to see the muse, outside...
enter inward and find a personal fuse
Makes no sense, at my expense
How many times I've lost myself in someone else's life!

Nancy L. Cox
Denver, CO

[Hometown] Cleveland, OH; [DOB] February 11, 1952; [Ed] high school graduate, one year college, three years metaphysical studies; [Occ] retired, secretary of HOA board, on-call building manager, writer; [Hobbies] crafts, poetry, life; [GA] being at peace within

What can I say about my life...it's been full! I've only been able to travel the US and parts of Canada...enough personal relationships, marriages and changes of residence to almost last a lifetime, to some. I have been a professional astrologer/Tarot reader for twenty-two years, outgrew that journey, then seeded a son that seeded a granddaughter. Now I write. Unpublished short stories, a novel, and poetry are my avenue. If God meant for me to be with money, someone would be reading my first book.

Teenager's Dreams

Assembled radio sets in my middle school,
She extended my ears over thousands miles.
Lying down in a knowledge cradle,
I was fed with nutritious of sciences.

Built airplane models in my high school,
She made my body grow a pair of wings.
Never stopping flying in the sky,
I was piloted to see various mountains and rivers.

Educated on surveillance radars in my university,
She elevated my eyes onto skyscrapers.
Directing their antenna to rotate,
I was fascinated by information from ocean to space.

Xubao Zhang
Kitchener, ON

The Brave Warrior

Armored in the glowing aura of justice and truth
The brave warrior faces his final mission
To soar beyond the limits of darkness
On majestic wings of a snow white dove
Acceptation framed with doubt
The heart cannot deny
Leaving this place, this moment in time
Leaving behind those who shared each breath of life
Bonded forever, linked by devotion
Deeply saddened they stand by his side
Assuring the brave warrior as time draws near
Mission accomplished
Reward well earned
The spirit departs
His last words
I am ready, I am going home.

Joyce H. Long
Crozet, VA

[Hometown] southwest VA; [DOB] November 9, 1932; [Ed] sociology degree; [Occ] police officer in Washington, DC; [GA] the lessons learned from the ultimate teacher, life

Upon graduation from college, I accepted a clerical position in a government office. In time I decided to try something different and applied to become a police officer with the Metropolitan Police in Washington, DC. There I met the love of my life, a detective, who possessed all the qualities I admired: a dedication to his profession, an air of assurance and self-confidence, and an engaging manner toward everyone. During our forty-six years of marriage, he stood by me through life's challenges, including serious illness. This poem is dedicated to him. Writing poetry has challenged me to attain a deeper understanding of myself, of life's purpose and the endless search for truth.

Come Here

Come here to me oh lover scorned
So I can mend your heart
Stop those tears for whom you shed
For now you are apart
Come here to me I'll hold your hand
Some comfort is all you need
Lay your head upon my chest
Your hurt will soon be eased
Come here to me you wounded soul
For soon you shall forget
Let the pain and sorrow go
You surely won't regret
Come here to me oh precious one
Our time has come at last
We'll heal what has been broken
And leave it in the past
Come here to me my dearest love
I've waited far too long
To hold you tight within my arms
And sing to you this song

Virgin Matos
Suffolk, VA

I currently reside in Newport News, VA. I grew up in the great city of Chicago, but I was born in Ashtabula, OH in April 1960. I enjoy writing poetry as a way of expressing myself. I'm working on a book about my life experiences hoping to help others who are going or have gone through similar situations. I would say my greatest achievement is my daughters. They have stood by my side and given me the strength to carry on when I had no hope. I thank the Lord every day for all His blessings. This poem is dedicated to my sister Tina Marie Garcia who passed so suddenly this year.

Grandmother's Portrait

A black and white picture hung on our wall
puzzling me—it didn't look like Grandma at all.
But it must have been, who else could it be,
sitting so still in her chair, but sad without me.
It was Whistler's Mother, years later I learned,
a famous portrait.   Perhaps she yearned
for her son just to climb up to sit on her lap
as she sat prim and proper in her white lace cap.

    My grandmother rocked in her favorite chair
by the window often inviting me there
to climb onto her lap where we two would be
chatting and rocking while I perched on her knee.
As I listened to her tell stories she knew,
remembering when she was a little girl, too,
picking lingonberries or watching the sheep,
her voice soft and low often put me to sleep.

    My favorite times were when Grandma called me
to come share an apple as I sat upon her knee,
cut in two, she scooped its sweetness with a spoon
to feed me that sweet apple in the late afternoon.
I never knew her memory no longer was clear
as she rocked back and forth holding me near.
She wore no lace cap covering wisps of gray hair
but her old faded apron held me close in her care.

    Her rocking chair reminds me of her loving embrace.
Did Whistler's Mother ever have a smiling face?

Susanna Mason Defever
Anchorville, MI

[Hometown] Anchorville, MI; [DOB] May 11, 1934; [Ed] MA in English; [Occ] retired teacher; [Hobbies] collecting art, especially by Michigan artists; [GA] making a difference as a teacher and on community boards, like mental health

My mother was a remarkable person and a great teacher. She inspired me to love reading, writing and the arts, especially theater. I became a teacher who shared that love with students, encouraging many to submit work for publication. For years, my motto seemed to be "give me an occasion and I'll write a verse," thus, becoming known as "The Occasional Poet." Weddings, births, retirements, memorials, seasons—many poems celebrate people, places and events, especially family and friends. In this poem, I recall a picture I once believe to be of my grandmother.

Gullible Girl

Gullible girl how incapable you are of knowing his lies. Believing every word whispered into your innocent ears, because it makes you feel good. You take what you can get and forgive him for the tears he drains on your face.

Gullible girl you now know all his lies but yet still take them. Seeing every girl he sees on the side but you still stay because he said he loves you. You stay because you think you love him too. Little do you know you're not in love because if you were you wouldn't have so many tears. Every day wouldn't be gray.

Gullible girl pull it together you deserve better and you're worth way more than how he treats you. You deserve someone who will show you off and sneak you a little forehead kiss. You deserve happiness!

Mykalyn Mosley
Houston, TX

I wrote this for many women that experience pain and can't see they can make it through.

Fire

The flame, the fire that burns within
So safe yet dangerous, flares brightly
An all-consuming inferno of searing heat
A fierceness that glows like the rising sun
We seek to control, capture, reign in, and rule
However, in time we find it burns
Too hot too fast too far too bright to tame

Anjuli Morgan
Spokane, WA

I was born in Austin, TX where I studied creative writing at Austin Community College. I have enjoyed reading and writing poetry since childhood. I recently embarked on my life's greatest adventure by moving cross country to Spokane, WA in search of inspiration.

An Inevitable Denouement

On a dim, blistering winter night
An elderly man stands readily, before the whitened snow
Hands and feet, uncontrollably quivering from the cold
His vision limited from the approaching blizzard

A blurred image of an unknown distant figure
Lies just meters ahead, down a rugged and broken path

The man pushes onward, against the uneasy weather
Unsure, yet convinced...he must reach this distant object
Grabbing nearby tree limbs to maintain his balance
Harsh winds and razor snow, bring him blistering pain

Unsteadily he strives, pushing himself to breaking limits
In the distance ahead, it continues to remain ever so still

Now, no more than a meter ahead, the figure reveals itself
A shrouded and dark appearance, with its back turned to his face
Neatly dressed with mirror-shined shoes, a fine coat and top hat

Slowly stepping toward, what appears to be a man
With a slight sudden touch, the man dismantles his coverings

The bare body of an elderly man hastily turns around
Now staring into the eyes of his very own self
With a quick rush of heat to his heart, he lies still and alone

Bryce Abbott
Yorba Linda, CA

[Hometown] Yorba Linda, CA; [DOB] June 7, 1990; [Ed] high school diploma; [Occ] warehouse worker; [Hobbies] hunting, fishing, snowboarding; [GA] being featured in Eber & Wein Best Poets of 2014

Poetry has always been something that came naturally to me. Since I was a preteen in middle school, I've always found myself taking an extra interest in rhyming words together to create sentences and then arranging those sentences to form a short story. Most of my writings were fictional at the time. But as I grew older, I began writing about things I have experienced or have seen others go through. Today, poetry remains a sanctuary in my mind, where I can release my inner thoughts and free my mind.

What Do You Choose?

The dealer's on his side,
You on yours.
Down to your last dollar,
What do you choose?

When I say last,
I mean very last.
The other dollars gambled away
In a darkened past.

This last dollar,
It's enough to get you by.
Then again,
There are a lot of memories stuck to it
That still make you cry.

Do you throw it on the table?
Just let it go?
But it's your very last dollar.
Somehow you just know.

The dealer's on his side,
You on yours.
Down to your last dollar,
What do you choose?

Danny Gunter
Independence, MO

If you're wondering, I decided to keep my dollar.

Organization

Bill was a very organized old man,
Attending to all the things one can.
Positioned teeth, glasses and hearing aid, too,
Along with medication on the night stand new.

His nightly routine was very easy to master,
With things nearby made his routine go faster.
He could almost meet his needs in the dark,
Since all his stuff had a good place to park.

Bill tried to listen to his radio at night,
As it was by his bedside placed just right.
He found it very difficult to hear well,
Checked hearing aid battery and off to sleep fell.

He was an early riser, so did his routine fine,
Went into the kitchen so he could dine.
Turned on the TV, but couldn't hear the news,
Thought he'd call the doctor and get his views.

"Doc," Bill said, "I can't hear it thunder!"
Doc took a look and said, "No wonder!
You stuck your suppository in your ear;
Now, the hearing aid is probably in the rear."

Patricia A. Amburgey
Wichita, KS

[Hometown] Stilwell, OK; [DOB] November 18, 1929; [Ed] BA, MA, NSU, OK; [Occ] retired educator; [Hobbies] painting, crafts, poetry; [GA] daughter, Debra, and coping with a broken neck

Poetry is inspired by real happenings surrounding you and a figment of your imagination. Humorous events stimulate me to write, too. I published a book entitled, Poems: Mundane to Ridiculous. *I craft poems mostly for self-expression, therapy, and to project a positive viewpoint. I don't seek recognition, but am humbled when a poem touches a vein of thought or is published. I strive to improve my craft for self-satisfaction. I try to paint a picture with words, the sensuous element in poetry. Hopefully, my poems will be a legacy to my family, grandchildren, friends and others.*

Ode to Ms. Lewis

You taught me so much, Ms. Lewis:
To deduce and to explore.
You taught me math and history,
Reading, writing, and so much more.

You taught me daily journaling,
Introduced me to poetry;
You engineered my first encounter
With beginning chemistry.

Thanks for our concert field trips,
For excursions to Shedd Aquarium,
For tours to the great Sears Tower,
And the Adler Planetarium.

Thanks to you I'm now a teacher,
And when classes next resume,
I'll be teaching here at Lincoln;
They've assigned me your former room.

Your instruction was enriching.
The depth of my thanks, hard to tell.
To my kids I'll pass all you've taught me,
And you've taught me exceedingly well.

Ms. Lewis, please come back and visit
Whenever you're so inclined.
My classroom will be your classroom.
You are welcome at any time.

Yvonne B. Arroyo
Vacaville, CA

As a retired bilingual teacher, I still enjoy reading and increasing my knowledge of Spanish—my second language. I am proud of my published book: How the Octopus Got Eight Arms (in verse), *and am presently working on publishing an ESL rhymer. This poem is meant to honor every great teacher I've ever had.*

The Wind

Drifting sighs and lonely murmurs
caught in the fickle spaces
between high noon
and the midnight sun:
raise your sails—spin dizzy,

spiraling pinwheels
calibrated to the keening
of dervish trees—dip the loose
shutters on my window; they dance
deep eyed and hollow.

Coiled for a sleepy moment
in a chambered shell, your breath
sounding like the whispering
sea; only to bluster awake

with a pirate's laugh
before rustling away
into the vast, secret pockets
of the sky.

Kimie Gill
Sierra Vista, AZ

[Hometown] Sierra Vista; [DOB] May 7, 1957; [Ed] high school; [Occ] writer; [Hobbies] hiking, exploring nature, free diving; [GA] summiting the Koolau Mountain Range

I'm a naturalist specializing in the identification and classification of endangered plants, birds, and animals found only in Hawaii. I started out hiking and summiting the amazing and sublimely beautiful Koolau Mountains of Hawaii. I gradually became aware of the very rare and endangered native species found only on Hawaii's mountains. It became a personal mission for me to try to save these species from extinction. I became an expert in locating and identifying these precious species so close to the brink. It is my fervent hope that people become aware of the perilous plight of Hawaii's endangered species.

Without a Penny

Some go without
I've seen many
That take not give
Without a penny
Some are lost
Some are found
Some have their world
Turned upside down
To give a lot
And not so many
Is not to give
Without a penny
Though some are fragile
Old and feeble
Some are hooked
Those use a needle
To help just one
And not the many
Is not to give
Without a penny
To help one less
And not the many
To leave behind
Just one penny

Louise Leamen
Etobicoke, Ontario

[Hometown] Don Mills, Toronto, Ontario; [DOB] April 16, 1959; [Ed] twelfth grade; [Occ] retired writer and grandmother; [Hobbies] walking, reading, knitting; [GA] my three children and first poetry book

In school, I excelled at English and art.

Integrity

The Lord God, Holy Lord of Hosts
From on High,
Held me in His arms today.
He said, "Integrity of thy very soul
Will lead you to a path of love;
As you send integrity outward,
Integrity will return to you
In the form of nobleness."
I took these words unto my heart
And felt a magnificence born
Which had been born with me at birth.
The Master's words of Jerusalem
Cleaved unto my soul,
The words of real wisdom
Spoken clear
From enlightenment that was real.
Goldenness of such depth
That in its integrity speaks volumes
Of love and spiritual richness
That is known to those
Who know
The Father
Resides in their very heart.

Morgan Bobbie St. Claire
Osoyoos, BC

Her Fight

Little girl was six years old when they told her the news,
Turns out she had cancer too.
The nurse took her in her arms and held her tight,
She said, "Hold back those tears. Don't show it your fear."
That little girl looked up, faint smile and all,
Said, "I'll win this ugly fight."

Little girl is now sixteen years old,
She walked up to the nurse from ten years ago.
She said, "Excuse me, ma'am, do you have a moment?"
Well that same nurse turned around,
Tears rolled down her wrinkled face as she fell to the ground.

Her hands clasped together, while she held them up in the air,
She spoke loudly, "Thank you, God, for answering my prayers."

Little girl helped her up and held her tight,
She spoke softly, tears in her eyes,
She said, "Now it's your turn to win this fight."

Katie Klinkkammer
Cedar Rapids, IA

[Hometown] Cedar Rapids, IA; [DOB] March 24, 1994; [Ed] AA in applied science; [Occ] college student; [Hobbies] reading, writing, photography; [GA] hiking Mount Rainier

Although I've been studying to become a medical assistant, I have always found time to further my writing passion. My poem was inspired by many family members who have fallen ill at some point in their lives. Their fight and determination has inspired me to explore new styles of my personal work.

Where Angels Tread

She has a rainbow over her head
And she walks close to where angels tread.
But don't get me wrong and be misled.
I didn't say she had a halo
Or was as pure as the driven snow.
I didn't say she was an angel you know.
Just that there's a rainbow over her head
And walks close to where angels tread.
That's all I said.
She makes my life shine
And sends shivers up my spine.
But I didn't say she had a halo.
Oh no no no.
I didn't say she was an angel you know.
Only that she makes my life shine,
Sends shivers up my spine,
And best of all—she's mine.
She has a halo over her head—
No, wait! She has a rainbow instead.
Yes, that's what I said.
And when I'm sad and feeling blue
And don't know what on Earth to do
She whispers in my ear, "I love you."
Then, I feel like there's a rainbow over my head—
like I'm being heaven led.
And then, I walk close to where angels tread.

Noah Padron
McKinney, TX

Keep On Writing

Keep on writing my friend
even if you feel that it is to no end
Continue to move forward
even if at times your destination seems too far to travel towards
Persevere at all costs
even if there are tears at what is lost
Keep on writing my friend
even if there are times when you no longer wish
to continue fighting your addiction
No matter what it takes
no matter what you have to forsake
Keep on writing my friend for goodness' sake
Keep on writing

Barbara Hagen
Palm Desert, CA

[Hometown] Palm Desert, CA; [DOB] June 6, 1964; [Ed] AA degree from Pasadena City College; [Occ] writer; [Hobbies] writing, bowling; [GA] published a book called All For MJ: A Collection of My Favorite Poems

I am battling a compulsive gambling problem, and I want to help and encourage others through my poetry who are also suffering from the same problem. I am also an aspiring writer and comedian, and I want to encourage others to follow their dreams even through those times when they may feel sad or disgusted.

Lost

I've lost
I've lost the will to live
The pleasure to give
The feeling of love
The sounds of laughter
Tell me something… what are you really after?
I gave you secrets from my heart
Memories that will never part
Laughter…
I don't think you care
You are a sad tear
Full of jealousy and power
You will never fall
For your tears are made of ice
You think yourself and nobody else
A sad tear is what you are
Leave me alone my friend
I never knew you were such a devious animal
(Always) scratching and gouging at my pride
You've taken away the secret person inside
See you've taken pieces of me and showed them to the world
You can't piece them together as they once were
Either can others who listen to your cruel words
Leave me alone, don't stare
I don't want to hear your voice, there's nothing left to tear
Just continue your life as if I was never here

Sherry M. Grimm
Kokomo, IN

[Hometown] LaPorte, IN; [DOB] May 30, 1978; [Ed] high school and training; [Hobbies] poetry, writing, artwork, music; [GA] surviving the death of a lifetime partner

I had six and a half years of training in property management, two years in woodwind musical instrument repair, and an apprenticeship as a clarinet technician. I had five years of private lessons on saxophone classical music training.

My Special Brother

Al was my favorite brother.
I'm sure the whole world could see.
I followed him everywhere he went
Because he was so nice to me.

He taught me a lot of things.
When I was real small,
He nailed little boards to a tree,
So I could climb it and not fall.

We played like we were having church.
Al held the Bible and was the preacher.
He might not have been all of that,
But he sure was a good teacher.

I hope we meet up in Heaven
Sitting close to Jesus' feet.
We will hug each other real tight.
Wow, won't that be real sweet?

I pray our family will be there.
They would make a big crowd.
Al could play his guitar
And turn the volume up real loud.

Only God knows our future.
We all know this is true.
We need to love and help each other,
Just like we've been taught to do.

Olive L. Childress
Pensacola, FL

[Hometown] Pensacola, FL; [DOB] October 27, 1925; [Ed] tenth grade in high school; [Occ] retired housewife; [Hobbies] sending letters to people in prison and poetry; [GA] playing guitar—Country Gospel

I went to work at the Naval Air Station in Pensacola, FL when I was seventeen years old. I was "Rosie the Riveter" for two years. Since I was small in size, I had to go inside the airplane wing to buck rivets. My father was sick with cancer and couldn't work. My poem was inspired by my brother Albert, who took up so much time with me when we were growing up. I wanted to be outside and do the things he enjoyed doing. He taught me how to spin a top, shoot marbles, and fly a kite.

The Master Gardener

The master gardener toils with the soil
Gardening gloves, a sun visor and pruning shears, her constant companions
Her hands pull the weeds from the already dead square-foot garden
Remnants of a tomato plant and basil deep below
What remains, a fresh canvas of possibilities
The tiniest seed is planted and covered up in great faith
A sprinkle of water and a healing touch to begin
A new crop
A season of waiting yields a small, green leaf that brings great joy

The gardener's eyes ever keen as she turns and inspects the harvest
Careful to remove anything that will choke and devour
Her fingers smell of sweet basil and green beans
The gift of growing that will feed many
The gift of peace that comes
As soon as her hands touch the dirt

Each garden tells a story, of love and friendship
Moments of great joy
And seeds sown with tears
Each patch planted leaves behind
Evidence of her time there
A constant reminder
Of the lives she affects
Ever pointing upward
To the Master Gardener Himself

Giana Gallardo Hesterberg
Brownsville, TX

[Hometown] Brownsville, TX; [DOB] December 29, 1981; [Ed] BA Central College; [Occ] stay-at-home mom and part-time private piano instructor; [GA] finishing the 2008 Chicago Marathon and the 2010 San Antonio Rock 'n' Roll Marathon, my children

This poem is dedicated to a dear friend, Angela McGowan Barnard, the "Master Gardener."

My Eyes

Eyes are wondrous things
Never know what sight brings
So to my surprise one day
I was walking down the hallway
My daughter in wheelchair
We had all been in despair
On the way to therapy
A man came out of nowhere you see
I asked him are you able to pass me
You are perfect where you are
As I turned back around in front of me
Nurses station bright as a star
Calm and peaceful light was glaring
Angel wings they were wearing
For the man who looked like Jesus
Walked over to my daughter as he pleases
Bless you my child words he spoke
Then he disappeared my face tears did soak
For my daughter fought her way back
A faith she has never lacked
Guillain Barre is a paralyzing thing
Eyes of the doctors a miracle she can do anything
This is a true story
So glad my eyes did see

Deborah Kathman
Cincinnati, OH

[Hometown] Cincinnati, OH; [Ed] high school graduate, graduate of Council on Aging Learning Advantages; [Occ] personal care assistant; [Hobbies] writing poems and songs, playing my bass, walking; [GA] performing gigs with my band

I've been a mother of two for thirty-four years of my life. I have a great son and daughter and am a grandmother of five smart grandchildren. My love for writing poems has been with me since junior high. I've been taking care of the elderly for five years. This poem is inspired by a vision my daughter and I did see. A determination, courage she beholds, along with a serenity prayer. My son is a loving, hardworking father of two. As you can see, I'm so proud of my family.

Home Is

Two left turns and one right towards a koi pond with fountains.
One left turn and two rights to get to the I-880.
A chain-link fence stands at the end of the block.
Concrete slope, dirty trickle of water, and a lost shopping cart.
Last month, we slipped through the fence
raced the cart and left it bent in the gutter.

The house is two stories, pale brown, 1,862 square feet.
Linguica sizzles through our grandmother's window,
but charcoaling barbecue wafts from two doors down.
The boat in the driveway has not tasted water in eons.
We crawl over its abandoned hulk—next week
we will jump from the second floor onto piled mattresses.

The neighboring kids play basketball in their driveway.
We play in the street, seven children and a soccer ball.
Four-door sedans honk their way through our asphalt field.
There is no white picket fence in our yard.

Kaytlynn Wilson
Chico, CA

[Hometown] Chico, CA; [DOB] 1989; [Ed] BA in English studies and linguistics

Most days I can be found walking my dog anywhere outside, whether it's on the beach or up in the mountains.

Friendship Beyond Love Eternally

To have a special friend
And if you want true
friends, you have to
pull up the weeds
plant the seeds
fertilize it
sometimes, uproot the
trees
fertilize it, water it,
but not too much
mulch it, protect it, be
delicate with it
protect it from pests
even from other birds,
from the nests.
You must do this
every day
without delay
forever and
ever, eternally.

Priscilla Thomas
Tampa, FL

Mrs. Lewis' Red Radio

From a polished wood pedestal it benignly ruled
over each first grade student at South Side School.
Regal in red plastic, mute all but one hour each day,
afternoon recess over children, now we will let the radio play.

Lights off and through out the soft semi-gloom,
strange beautiful music circulated about the room.
Open windows let in honeysuckle-scented spring air,
eyes closed, heads resting on crossed arms, a sigh here and there.

Oh, that tinkling, windsong sound of music layered us,
covered us with peaceful tranquil blankets warm and soft,
and Mrs. Lewis, petite behind her desk radiated a caring trust
so that one at a time we could slip to her side and quietly talk.

Inky had six puppies and little sister took her first step.
Momma baked Daddy a birthday cake and she let me help.
And Mrs. Lewis would nod and smile, simply because she cared,
as the little personal dramas of six-year-olds were shared.

Then came Emily and with hands clenched tightly in her lap,
bruised and frightened face whispered close to Mrs. Lewis' ear.
Suddenly—children, behave for me now and take a brief nap,
or just listen to the radio until I can come back here.

Her hand on Emily's shoulder they quickly left the room,
and the red radio played on, soothing music to quiet any fear.
My sleepy gaze drifted across the aisle to Emily's chair,
and there on the seat was a drying bloody smear.

Malcolm Lane
Camden, AR

Because of Mrs. Lewis, the first grade classroom at South Side School was not a classroom at all. It was a warm sanctuary, and she was the sainted overseer of little wounded souls such as myself...and Emily. And the music coming from her red radio, which so enthralled me, I later learned was classical, which I listen to almost exclusively to this day.

Life's Unknowns Are Knowledgeable Advancements, for Perusing in Curiosity

There will come a time when we will have felt, seen, and heard almost everything. But I fear the day when we have discovered everything. By then, we will know how to feel, what to see, and what is to be heard. We will go insane searching for anew, yet we have already known that there is no more to find. We will become lost in our own thoughts and understandings, but we will still try to find a way to make the conundrum a consensus. Perhaps...just maybe, this is why we have a limit.

There will be two or maybe three times in your life when you would have felt a certain way, and you will know it because you realized that you are a totally different person. The person you were in the past would not have known that you would become the person you are today.

Closure allows for self-fulfilling prophesies.

There is a timeline that is attested, it is woven into a thread that is unfurled at the end; and each individual fiber at the end is an outcome. Indefinitely spread, but still originating from the same dawning.

Farjam Ashrafzadeh
El Paso, TX

What Ifs...

What ifs and what fors
Are a thing of the past
Need to keep moving
To bring to light
Not perfect
But kind hearted
Naïve but true
Lessons learned
Can't pretend
But can't dwell upon the past
No more what ifs
What if I did this, what if I did that
What if I had this, what if I had that
Truth is life isn't on the what ifs
But on the here and now
Look around—nothing is perfect
But life is what we make of it
So live it—don't deny it
Enjoy it—smile it
Hold tight to the ones you love
They're not the what ifs
But the what *is*!
Love them even when they can't
Believe that in the future they will
Because "what if?"... they always have...

Corinne Soutra
Chicopee, MA

[Hometown] Hatfield, MA; [DOB] December 1, 1959; [Occ] payroll administrator and assistant swimming coach; [Hobbies] swimming and sewing; [GA] my children and competing again in swimming

My writing usually comes to me in the middle of the night. About five years ago, with the encouragement of my dear friend, Jack, I started writing my thoughts down. "What Ifs" is written for my children. Besides my children, my greatest achievement has to be getting back into swimming competitions at the age of fifty and qualifying to go to the 2013 Senior Nationals, and qualifying again to go to the Senior Nationals in 2015.

Unnoticed

An autumn leaf falling in the
summer breeze

Orange and brown with a hint of red
secretly cascading, falling from the tree

The autumn leaf entangled in the summer heat
drowning in front of everyone

The birds singing in the tree
sweet melodies of summer breeze
did not notice

She fell to the ground
orange, brown with a splash of red on the leaf

The beautiful hue going unnoticed
On a warm summer's day

The heat cracking the skin of the leaf
Attempting to dry the little bit of life left in her

She thirsts for recognition
and she hungers for love

The autumn leaf fell to the ground
on a hot summer's day

Bernadette Butler
Berea, OH

*I live in Berea, OH, and I grew up in the Chicago area. My first journal was given to me by my
mother, and I have been writing ever since. Writing gives me the freedom to express my innermost
thoughts. My writings are about my faith and my life experiences. My goal is to publish my poems
and my book about my son who has autism.*

Happiness: A Mirage?

Oh my tears, don't roll down!
Oh my sobs, don't come out!
No place for you in this world,
Within yourself, solace you find
Everyone has a tale of woe,
Maybe with a different note.
Dancing roses on the thorns,
Puffing in hot oven breads,
Tell us that happiness comes,
After going through such tests.
On such martyrdom does life thrive,
Giving this message at every step.
Covering tears with fake smile
Seems the way to happiness!
I wonder what happiness is…
Isn't it a mirage which all pursue?

Madhuwanti Mirashi
Santa Clara, CA

[Hometown] Maharashtra, India; [Ed] PhD in Indian classical music, master of arts in psychology, certificate in applied psychology; [Occ] instructor, lecturer, program executive, performer, teacher, private tutor; [GA] worked in Fiji Islands and traveled to adjoining nations, represented Indian music at International Drum Festival in 1990, obtained US citizenship

Ice Fishing

Grab your sled of fishing gear.
Pull it to the secret spot not so near.
Lumberjack's symphony
Echoing across the ice.
Thoughts of bringing home a trophy,
Wouldn't that be nice?
Rip 'em lips slippery silver bullet,
Slow jig, fast jig, sitting on a bucket.
Now stop... Give 'em a little dance
You're nearly in a trance
Rod tip down, quick jerk!
Heart racing, wondering, "Did it work?"

Michelle Jarvis
Port Edwards, WI

[Hometown] Adams, WI; [DOB] January 1973; [Occ] certified nurse's assistant; [Hobbies] kayaking and fishing; [GA] raising two honor student boys that have ADHD

Shakespeare

Shakespeare wrote poetry, immortal lines,
He, as the Muse, winging away from the fanciful,
Creating ripples as if the soul is stirred,
Vibrations in a wide expanse spreading along
The horizons of the distant sea from where springs
Foams fomenting the wounded heart healing on its own,
While ruminating lines writ from the great pen,
Shakespeare held to brush lines of blood and horror,
Painting tales, tragedy and romance with deft skill,
The like isn't born yet to lead life, again to relate man's lot.
His art so compelling, the technique chiseled to perfection.
Generations read him, visit his birthplace, Stratford-upon-Avon,
To see the stable boy making history—prophesying truth—
Soon blood and horror will agonize man with remote control.

Konduparthi Lakshmi Narasimha Swami
Melbourne, FL

[Hometown] India; [DOB] December 1929; [Ed] PhD Madras and Utkal Universities; [Occ] professor of English

I visited a few countries and it was my visit to Stratford-upon-Avon that inspired me to write those lines on Shakespeare. I am an author of a few books, and some of my poems are included in a few anthologies published in the US. I have two sons and a daughter, and have four grandchildren. I live in the US.

Don't Let Go

I see the way you look at her,
Your eyes filled with compassion & love
I see the way you move around her,
You want to protect her as much as you can.

I hear the way you talk to her,
Your voice, full of care & understanding.
I hear how much she means to you,
You know you never want to lose her.

I see the way you look at him,
Your eyes never leave his face.
I see the way you stand around him,
You never want to leave his side.

I hear the way you talk to him,
Your voice always loving & full of understanding.
I hear how much he means to you,
Your love is never wasted on him.

You mean so much to each other,
I see how much you react to the other.
Never let the little things get to you,
I see you two were meant to be.

Brittany (Keating) Speelman
Gettysburg, PA

[Hometown] PA; [DOB] February 15; [Ed] high school, some early childhood classes; [Hobbies] baking desserts and decorating them; [GA] published my own book

Although I never furthered my education, I feel I still have learned so much. I love making people smile and I try to do that through my writing. I have always been interested in writing stories and poems. In my spare time, I decorate cakes, cupcakes, and giant cookies. I am also proudly married and the mom of a cute black cat with orange eyes, named Puck. My published book is titled Our Turn.

When We Choose to Hate

People of faith can become people so cruel.
Instead of loving others hating is their rule.

Instead of giving a message of love to others,
We try not to save but hurt sisters and brothers.

People don't tolerate other faiths or those who are poor
As we gained our freedom we started closing the door.

The people in control want to control those who must depend.
Making working people who have to be ones who must bend.

We reward those who don't work and not those who do,
So hatred between classes of people started to ensue.

Out of fear and loss of jobs we fear those who come in,
But we wouldn't even be here if it weren't for our kin.

Hitler just used hatred for others to promote his case.
Many people wanted to hate those of a different race.

They looked away when they began to kill them all.
Soon this world will crumble and will start to fall.

The world's stage is getting ready as we near our end.
The world will suffer a lot if we don't start to bend.

Can we teach our faith through love and not by hate
As people of all faiths will start to share the same fate?

It will not be long as this nation changes from all faiths to none.
And we might have to choose what we believe at the point of a gun.

Catherine Farrell
E. McKeesport, PA

[Hometown] East McKeesport, PA; [DOB] May 18, 1951; [Ed] AS degrees in childhood education and computer systems; [Occ] taking care of a friend; [Hobbies] puzzles; [GA] daughter Angie

Tribute to Our Dad

He was a man well loved by all
A man of faith we came to call
Our steadfast block of stone he was
Always there for you, for any cause
A man of principle, family devoted
Grateful for friends, so long in knowing
He loved to teach lessons in dollars and taxes
Safety and math and bedtime relaxin'
So mannered and rational and usually mild
He laughed and he loved and sometimes got wild,
But always, our father, so grounded in earth
He led a true life from death back to birth
It's hard not to love such a man as was he
Invested in learning and teaching and family.

Robert J. Dutton
Omaha, NE

[Hometown] Omaha, NE; [Ed] two bachelor's degrees, master's in English; [GA] saying "I do" and watching the birth of my child

We love you, Dad! You will be greatly missed! I am forty-eight years old and work for a company that serves the needs of children with mental, emotional, and behavioral disorders. I have been in this type of field for nearly seventeen years. My writing has always come in spurts, using people or nature as common subjects because I am often affected by the beauty of either. Having a young daughter keeps the wife and me very busy as we dote on her, knowing all the while how we do not want to create a spoiled child in the process.

I Always Wanted to Be a Painter Man

I always wanted to be a painter man,
To color the leaves and paint the land;
To paint the chill of a frosty morn
Or a beautiful sunset or a field of corn.

To paint the sound of the hush of night
Or a morning sunrise or evening twilight;
To cover my canvas with crimson and tan,
I always wanted to be a painter man.

I paint old barns with rusty gates,
Stands of pines so tall and straight;
I paint the grays of winters bleak
Trickling streams and snow-covered creeks.

I paint the smell of freshly cut hay
Or the beginning of a brand-new day;
I paint these things because I can
You see, I was born to be a painter man.

Ronald J. Lay
St. Cloud, FL

[Hometown] Franklin, IN; [DOB] November 27, 1947; [Ed] doctorate in Christian philosophy; [Occ] archbishop, artist, teacher, poet; [Hobbies] playing piano, fishing; [GA] becoming a priest, winning international medal, listing in Who's Who in America

Ronald J. Lay, CPhD, has a very artistic background. He is an international medalist in painting, an ordained priest, a member of Academy of American Poets, a published artist in several national art magazines, and most recently listed in Who's Who in American Poetry 2014. *Whether writing, painting or any other endeavor he takes on, he is not only descriptive but also very passionate. This style of writing allows his readers to not only imagine themselves within his poems but allows them to recall or relate times within their own lives.*

Alzheimer's & Love: The Story of Raphael and Rose

His eyes were soft blue,
filled the hearts of all he knew.
Before the fog clouded his mind,
his wit was quick and his smile kind.

His aged eyes stared into space,
unable to focus on time and place.
As his mind became a maze,
his soft blue eyes drifted into the haze.

Soft blue eyes, once young and clear,
fell in love, a woman so dear.
Still a boy, he took his child bride,
creating a family that gave them pride.

She was the love of his life,
soft blue eyes always smiled for his wife.
Her voice, her touch could clear the haze,
for time she could guide him from the maze.

Soft blue eyes searching for home,
he couldn't leave his family alone.
The love of his life held him to her breast,
and whispered, "Dear one go to rest."

Their bond would not be broken,
soft blue eyes made a promise unspoken.
He agreed to go rest and wait,
together they would enter Heaven's gate.

Then eternity would be theirs,
finally they will be freed from all earthly cares.

Tammy Glen Perkins
Prescott Valley, AZ

[Hometown] Prescott Valley, AZ; [DOB] September 19, 1961; [Ed] industrial safety degree, associate of applied science; [Occ] retired industrial safety professional; [Hobbies] poetry and children's stories; [GA] my family, being Grandma

As a retired safety professional (copper mining), I now find the time to pursue my true passion—writing. My family gives me the inspiration I need to capture all the love I feel for them in the written word. My poetry is my gift to my loved ones.

God Give Me Strength

Father, give me strength today
To meet life's trials and troubles.
Some days I feel I can't go on,
When the whole world seems in rubble.

When you are here beside me
All life's pressures are subdued.
I shall take a little quiet time,
And spend that time with You..

Knowing You're beside me
Always makes me feel so strong.
Trusting You with all my heart
Keeps things from going wrong.

I know that You will hold me,
And keep me from all harm.
Please take away all cares I have
And embrace me in your arms.

So, Father, give me peace today.
I know how much You care.
I feel your strength within my soul
Just knowing You are there.

Clara M. Ashmore
Homosassa, FL

Clara M. Ashmore

[Hometown] Homosassa, FL; [DOB] October 9, 1937; [Ed] college graduate for teaching; [Occ] co-owner of a family business of natural pet products; [Hobbies] fishing the Homosassa River and the Gulf; [GA] raising four wonderful children with a great husband

Growing up the youngest of eight children, four of which died before I was born, my two brothers joined World War II when I was only five. My sister worked with the USO entertaining troops coming through Kansas. I sort of ended up an only child, but knowing the feelings in the life of my parents, we prayed every day that the war would end and my brother would be safe. Placing my trust in God has been a natural part of my life. God never let me down, so I take this time to thank Him with my poems.

American Dream

Amidst the sprawling homes, far from the tracks,
that perch along the hills and hidden behind
the blushing maple trees that turn their backs,
lies the other America. Unkind

and cold, without lyrics or harmony;
that doesn't sleep on fancy sheepskin sheets
while being waxed about poetically.
This America is where the rain meets

my eye, as the train slows through Baltimore
to get a closer look. Here, there are rows
of homes resting on legs of brick still sore
from all those years of running. The wind blows

a shirt, exhausted and fading that hangs
on a line drooping pole to windowsill.
Neighbors divide from neighbors—rival gangs
kept apart by link-fences that now till

parcels of land that, from the naked eye
don't look like forty acres. From the train
I spy one house, Old Glory, flying high;
as Sisyphus still climbs his stairs in vain.

A lone salute to dreams that still remain.

Michael Langford Whitlow
Long Beach, CA

Serendipitous Savagery

The smell of us is still on me and even though it breaks every
conventional rule of etiquette—I may skip taking a shower
altogether just to have the musk of us linger like perfume
to my senses throughout the day. Even now a picture of you
fades in my mind your skin your touch your strength
your unspoken desire—the way in which you hesitate to take
my hand as I am kissing you and kissing you and kissing you
all over but never on the lips—for mine savor in waiting for
yours like no other before. Our time is always the best affair
as we draw caution to the space around us as a fan oscillates
the air in a whirlwind breeze just beyond this spot on the floor
where you and I sweat savage to a serendipitous sunrise.

Ricardo Lazaro Serrano
Sun Valley, CA

[Hometown] Los Angeles, CA; [DOB] September 16, 1973; [Ed] medical massage therapy; [Occ] live-in caregiver; [Hobbies] symbology; [GA] 2012 publication of my first poetry book, Scarlet Verse *(River Road Press)*

Tears Did Fall

My eyes were cracked canyons
Incapable of containing
The smallest drop of water
But when they spilled the news
A tsunami crashed over every corner
Of my life
Of all our lives
And finally
Days later
Tears did fall
A downpour

Mackenzie Krol
Vienna, VA

I am a high school student in Vienna, VA. My teacher freshman year pushed me to enter all kinds of poetry and writing contests, and I've been doing so ever since. I love how the written word creates stability in a world of chaos. When I'm not writing, I'm competing on my horse or drowning in a pile of homework.

I Had a Dream

In my mind and heart I had a dream.
When I try to grasp it, far away it seems.
I could almost feel the sensations...
Then they would escape me,
as though they were temptations.
I could almost see me in a paradise...
Then the tears blur the vision in my eyes.
I cry out, "Please! Let me have my dream.
Please! Let us work toward it as a team."
I see myself standing in a doorway, reaching out.
There is beauty everywhere and no reason to doubt.
I could almost hear the beautiful song
I wanted to sing...
Then I am jolted back to reality and its ugly sting.
Oh! I so want to walk in peace and quiet.
I want to gaze at the starry night.
I want to hear the songs of the birds,
in all their splendor.
I want to sit and watch the antics of the creatures,
at my back door.
I want to see no more jury cases.
I want to see people with happy faces.
Yes, I had a dream in my mind and heart.
Will I ever see my paradise and play my part?

Lillian Hart
Spokane, WA

[Hometown] Ulysses, KS; [DOB] February 1930; [Ed] high school; [Occ] retired; [Hobbies] writing short stories and poetry, cooking; [GA] being married sixty-five years before my husband's death

I was born into a very large family of fourteen children, which gave me much to write about. This poem was inspired by wishing that this world was not in such a big unfixable mess, so that we could all have a tranquil life.

A Unique Proposal

My Dear Darling,

Most of our lives I had been away since our early childhood days there in Kentucky at school, we walked, talked, laughed and played, now it seems as though it was only yesterday, since I up and moved away. With our spouses both now gone, I returned once more to my old Kentucky childhood home. In telephone conversations thou saith to me many times, thou don't know how much I really love thee, finally I saith to thee, honey how much doeth thou love me? Thou saith an eternity forever and ever.

And ever, and ever, and ever, and ever, and ever, then thou saith to me, honey, how much do thou love me?

I saith, oh I suppose a lot, thou then saith yeah! See I love thee much more than thou love me! Kiddingly, I saith I know that if I had a nickel, I'd spend it on candy and give it to you, honey, that's how much I love thee, thence, thereafter all was laughter.

Verily I now saith unto thee I'll love thee for the time we might have had, but could not have, and wasn't ever meant to have, thenceforth, I'll love thee for all the time our heavenly Father allows us upon this earth, until He giveth us a new heavenly birth, let us now and forever pray that He grants us many serenity days an abundance great in number, before He lays us down to slumber.

I saith unto thee wherever sundown finds us that will be our home, my home will be thou home, thou home my home, my children thou children, thou children my children, my church thou church, thou church my church, verily I saith unto thee I believe God planned this be our destiny.

I now ask of thee will thou marry me?
If thou take this ring I truly stake my claim.

James Oliver
Akron, OH

[Hometown] Inez, KY; [DOB] January 2, 1929; [Ed] grade school and some home school by mail; [Occ] retired rubber worker; [Hobbies] playing my guitar and mandolin

Vicie and I went to school together in Kentucky. My family moved to Ohio, and I got married and raised a family. She married and raised a family. Her husband had been dead nine years when my wife passed on. I went back home to the camp meeting and went to her home. We talked a couple hours and then dated for a while. I was at my winter home in Florida when I bought an engagement right, wrote the poem, had it notarized, bought a little boy and girl doll, and put the ring in the boy's hand. I called Burgess, the girl I called Vicie and mailed it.

Tim and the Little Circle

I took a metal paper punch
And with that punch I punched a bunch
Of little circles for my art.
I say, it made me feel real smart
To punch and make the circles fly,
I laughed. It almost made me cry.
Across the table the circles flew,
And not just one and not just two.
Those circles popped now here, now there.
They popped and popped just everywhere!
But when I tried to glue it down,
That circle turned into a clown.
The circle tried to play with me.
Where did it go? I could not see.
It stayed right there upon my thumb.
"It won't come off," I said. "How come?"
I picked it from my thumb and then
It wouldn't leave my hand again!
I giggled, struggled, laughed out loud.
That little circle must be proud
Of how it hung onto my hand.
I picked if off and made it land
Upon my art work. Now I'm done!
I clapped my hands for I had won.

Carol Kaufman
Portland, OR

[Hometown] Waveland, IN; [DOB] November 22, 1942; [Ed] BS in K–8 education, MS in deaf/blind education; [Occ] itinerant teacher for blind and deaf/blind; [Hobbies] arts and crafts for students; [GA] seeing former students become amazing professionals

I have worked with so many incredible blind students. So many of the these students were musically talented. Some wrote amazing poetry. This poem was inspired by a blind student I was supporting in his art class. Our students were in their home schools with their visual classmates. An itinerant teacher drives from school to school supporting those students with what they need to succeed with their peers. Tim plays the drums and piano. I truly enjoyed working with these students.

Together

Together I feel
that I am you
and you are me.
We seem to blend
in perfect harmony.

All of the things
that I like to do
often you say,
I like to do
those things too.

We talk for hours
never watching TV,
together content,
time goes on endlessly.

I miss you so
when you're not
in my sight,
during the day
but mostly at night.

It makes me happy
when I say to you,
good night dear.
I love you.
And you say,
me too.

Wendell W. Copeland
Plainville, CT

[Hometown] Plainville, CT; [DOB] September 6, 1931; [Ed] high school graduate; [Occ] air craft machinist, playing guitar; [Hobbies] woodworking, painting; [GA] winner of the North Central Region 2012 Essay Contest

Born in New Britain, CT, I was raised in Canton Center, CT, by my grandparents. At that time, every house was a farm. I had a great child's life. I went in to the service and was in the 43rd Division. I was married for fifty-six years and we had three children, one boy and two girls. I have four grandchildren. I worked for an aircraft factory for thirty-one years. I enjoyed my wife and children. I had a good life with them. Now times have changed, the kids have families of their own and I'm retired. So I write and draw and play my guitar.

Dreamland's Door

The scent of forest in the air
A mist floats 'cross the pond
It brings an eerie quietness
As though with mystic wand
The air so thick with morning fog it saturates my being
Dampness chills me to the bone
I drift beyond my seeing
Though some might be unsettled
By the strangeness of this place
For me, I find a solitude—a lair to contemplate
My thoughts are carried far away
Into a world of dreams
Reality suspended there nothing's as it seems
Deep into a mystery vale this vale inside my mind
Should I drift deeper, deeper still
What answers might I find?
Absorbed in dreams and visions
That defy both time and space
Shall I abide—should I abide
This rapt, unearthly place?
Strange irony, a loon calls out as though to beckon me
"You cannot stay, you must return to your reality"
Endeav'ring to return again
Those mysteries to explore
Try as I might, I cannot find
The way to Dreamland's Door

Fred Plant
Saugerties, NY

A. F. Plant was born in Newburgh, NY January 20, 1954. He is a freelance writer, author, and consultant. Hobbies include distance running and playing guitar. He has a bachelor's degree from Albany State. His greatest achievement is his bachelor's degree in four years at age forty-five.

Silence in the Morning

Silence
In the early morning
And silence screams out loud
Loud and clear
Alive and kicking
I take myself out of the game
And look the other way
And wonder—perhaps?
Come what may
Silence screams loudly
And will not go away
Only to come close
The next day
Silence! Come what may
You reach out to me
And I fear what may be said
Some other day
Or silence speaks her mind
Out loud, then gone
And I shan't be here anymore

Holly Prince
Riverside, CT

Holly Prince lives in Riverside, CT. She has a bachelor's degree in English from the University of Connecticut and got her master's degree at Manhattanville College. She is an avid writer, writes poetry every day, and has kept a journal since she was a young child. She was a staff reporter for the UCONN newspaper. She is also working on her autobiography with hopes of publishing it.

My Mother's Love

As I look back upon my life
From the earliest of time,
I was always very proud to say,
You're my best friend, my mom, all mine.

You gave me so much more
Than I could ever give,
You were the best there ever was or is,
You showed me how to love and live.

I always knew I could count on you,
Dad too, for help, support and love,
I've been blessed with the greatest of moms,
Sent by an angel of God from above.

I can't say goodbye as it hurts way too much,
But as you leave please say for me, "Hi, I love you, Dad."
I know you're finally at peace, Mom, and want to join him now,
So go to Dad and leave behind all those days of being sad.

I'll never forget you, oh mother all mine,
Nor your awesome love for me.
When I need you now I'll close my eyes
And the Lord will show me thee.

Linda K. Webster
Riverview, FL

[Hometown] Omaha, NE; [DOB] May 11, 1949; [Ed] high school education to study business; [Occ] word processing, data entry, inventory control and asset management, administrative career path with IBM; [Hobbies] crocheting afghans; [GA] getting an "A" in Bible college after being out of a classroom setting for nearly forty years, then using that education as a life coach volunteer at a local pregnancy resource center since 2012

An Ethnobotanist's Devotion

I plaudit the shaman, esteeming the witch
Who've entrusted to us their erudition
They descried the forest's efficacy
Greeting humanity's continuity
I also witness the coppice winsomeness
Regarding its cultural worth
With flavored spices and oils to enrich and preserve
Of cinnamon barks, crocus stigmas, or orchid vanillins
Sustenance from flower, fruit, leaf, pod and seed
And bestowing to us vital solar energies
Rich fragrances that invigorate our mind and spirit
Utility in pesticide from chrysanthemum or raspberry leaves
And brilliant dyes for textiles and art
Maple purple, juniper yellow, mushroom red, and lichen green
Endowing us with lumber for structures and heat
And oh the alluring possibilities
From roses, tulips, and weeping willow trees
Fibered cordage, warm cotton, jute, straw and palm
Rich biomass servicing renewable energy
Pharmacognosy of willow aspirin, poppy morphine, or taxol of yew
Air purifying, soil enriching, and providing thriving biodiversity
The habitat for all living things, with secrets of communication and adaptability
Clever as if borne brains and powerful to kill
Teeming with immortal boundless mystery
Their pith is alive and sentient, deep within us anthropomorphically
This ethnobotanist's devotion is toward their entrancing inquiry

Amy Pinney
Juneau, AK

[Hometown] Juneau, AK; [DOB] June 1977; [Ed] BS in biology, MS in natural resources; [Occ] stay-at-home mom; [Hobbies] archery, hiking, sports, skiing, boating

As a teen I was entranced with biologists, obsessed with becoming one. I adored the work outside, exploring and studying the natural world. I aspired to tell people all about the land, plants and creatures around them. In college, I volunteered for biologists, enjoying it thoroughly, and soon became a biologist working in many fields, learning exponentially and experiencing so many adventures. I worked under a renowned ethnobotanist who stoked my fire for botany. I submitted this poem because it's a personal reflection of a time in my life and the many stories I have to share.

The Forgotten Garden

The dark rock walls, so old
Hold many stories of another time.
Tiny white flowers shine light
Into the cracks that is their home.

Brick and moss hold each other softly
To guide footsteps to a quiet place.
Small hedges, long overgrown
Stand in line with no place to go.

A small wooden bench waits patiently
For the company of lovers, but none are near.
Swollen bark bears the wounds of many
Who carved their young love here long ago.

Rain gently washes an old maple above.
Leaves turn and twist and fall.
Below, the one last rose petal holds on
For one more day of sun.

A song bird prays a litany of this day.
A tarnished wind chime answers.
It rings on and on and I wonder
If anyone else is listening.

Paul J. Lyons
Lake Oswego, OR

[DOB] February 21, 1943; [Ed] MBA, BS business; [Occ] MBA instructor on strategic planning, strategic consultant in technology, healthcare, real estate and non-profit organizations; [Hobbies] writing, photography, cooking, public speaking, volunteering, Irish history and gardening; [GA] marrying the woman I love almost fifty years ago

I Lost If You Lost

I lost if you lost. We lost everything but as long as we didn't lose each other then we never lost anything. Meaning we could've lost it all but as long as we are standing side by side we never lost at all. After all we been through we are still hanging in there. I don't think I could've walked on this path alone, and made it by myself because the reason is we were meant to go through it together. Mistakes were made and some things were so out of control but that is what made us stronger. We are still standing together, we never lost but we became winners. We can't control what is done, and all we can do now is learn from it. Only thing we can do now is live in the present, look to the future, and forget about the past. Only thing we can do now is pick up the pieces, and put our lives back together the best way we can. We got to hold on to what we have, and not allow anyone to tear us apart. Crooked people crossed our path, tried to break us down, and tear us apart. Nobody wanted to see us together it seemed because they can't stand to see anyone happy. It's sad it's that way anymore. I found out through our journey it made us stronger, so therefore they can't break us apart, we are still standing together, and we never lost.

Genevieve Razo
Cutbank, MT

Hi my name is Genevieve Razo. I've been writing poems since I was a teenager, and it's always been a dream of mine to become a writer—to write a book of poems, to write novels, and to become a song writer. Those are big dreams of mine, but you can't dream unless you dream big. I believe you can make it if you have faith and continue to put your best efforts towards your dreams. I am a Native American Indian from the Blackfeet Indian Tribe of Browning, MT but I grew up in Seattle, WA. My hobbies are writing, reading, and I like to do art work as in drawing, painting, and beading. Also, I like listening to music and going to movies.

The Joy of Music

In the living room stood an old upright piano
With its white and black keys in silence
Waiting for a little girl to discover
The beautiful melodies hidden there.
She was seven years old when lessons began,
Her excitement lured over the many keys
Entering the gateway, treble and bass.
Lines and spaces, notes and rests.

A journey in the wonderful land of Music,
All sorts of notes dancing on the page,
Half notes, quarter notes... legato and staccato,
Suddenly an arpeggio runs up and down the keys.
Capers in excitement, loud and soft,
Dainty little grace notes all in a flutter,
The old piano of wood that stood so quiet
Came alive with the beautiful sounds of music.

The journey of music through the years
Traveling the keyboard of the Piano,
The Classical music of the great Composers
Inspired by their inner emotions.
Sonatas, Preludes, Nocturnes and more,
Musical expressions reaching the heart.
Oh! the joy Piano and Music can bring
Never ending... lives on in mind and soul.

Joyce Ramey
Greeley, CO

[Hometown] Greeley, CO; [DOB] December, 1921; [Ed] business college, University Extension Conservatory, Sherwood Music School; [Occ] secretary and music teacher; [Hobbies] scrapbooking, crocheting; [GA] guild, approved music teacher, hall of fame

Music and poetry... what a joy! I began my music lessons when I was seven, gave piano lessons for forty-four years. I was an affiliated teacher of the Sherwood Music School. Upon retiring I attended crochet class for ten years, afghans winning many ribbons at fair. In recent years, I wrote a memoir of my life and some poems. I was inspired to write this poem as I reflected back to my early music years. I have always enjoyed poetry, but not written any. I was married almost sixty-nine years and have a wonderful, caring son.

Eber & Wein Publishing

Faded Love

I drew a heart
on the window
in the cold

the heart faded
slowly which reminded
me of the love I once

had for you.

Kirsten Knapp
Shawnee, KS

My name is Kirsten Knapp. I am from Shawnee, KS. I am seventeen years old. A couple of my hobbies are running, poetry and listening to music. What I enjoy the most is entering into poetry competitions.

Eternal

Watching the water turn from light green to dark blue is something you must do.
Sitting in the sun watching the waves roll by, time flows, as does the sky.
From brilliant blue to sea foam green, to orange, then yellow.
The sky and the sea change together.
At days end, the colors show hope and grandeur,
Then fade to black only to begin again.

Juliee Santos
Elk Grove, CA

[Hometown] Elk Grove, CA; [Ed] bachelor of arts in political science, California State University, Sacramento; [Hobbies] writing poetry, traveling, snow skiing, hiking, reading, cooking; [GA] my son, Joshua Taylor Santos, born June 26, 1999

Grief

When grief comes, it catches us unaware
And at such awkward times
Stealing fresh thoughts of the present
Never returning those skipped heart beats
Taking our words away for perhaps days
Never saying a word about how long it intends on staying
Or how long our heart will continue to ache

When grief comes, it never says excuse me
Nothing polite about its manner when bringing such sad news
Or even the depth of the wounds it leaves with us
It simply says, "I'm here, so how do you plan to pay?"
"Will you be using Master Card, Visa or American Express?"

Patricia Resnover
Las Vegas, NV

[Hometown] Indianapolis, IN; [DOB] November 9, 1946; [Ed] graduated from Crispus Attucks High in June 1965; [Occ] early retirement as senior clerk from the LAC/USC medical center after twenty-nine years of service; [Hobbies] writing, reading, crocheting; [GA] receiving my ministerial license in 2007

Eber & Wein Publishing

Hidden Thoughts

In my mind, I heard a song go softly by
It seemed to represent a strange melody
On the wind outside myself, it seemed to sigh
And, strangely, that song had an effect on me.

I thought I felt a zephyr whisper in the air
It made a strange like humming sound
And it prompted me to sit and kind of stare
And a clear thought concerning life was found.

I felt a wonderful stillness on the breeze
As quietness seemed to engulf the sky
My mind gave me a new idea to seize
And soon it made me want to give it a try.

I realized I had a session with the Host divine
A satisfactory intervention that stirred my soul
Like God had given me new venues to define
Dividing each special segment apart from the whole.

Each person will experience a chance like I
Since God will provide each of us a thought of ease
Letting one solve little things and know the reason why
Mankind will experience such hidden thoughts as these.

So, let such hidden thoughts come easily into view
It will be a privilege for one to interpret its meaning
And as you accept such hidden thoughts inside of you
Those hidden thoughts will become a part of your learning.

Ray E. Brewer
Grover Beach, CA

I am a professor emeritus in education (from Fresno State University). I have been married to Rose nearly sixty years. We have six grandchildren and one great-grandchild, who bring us no end of pleasure. I write poetry for personal pleasure and family occasions.

I Saw Her Smile

My friend has always been loud
She stands a head over most of us
When she's happy nothing can bring her down
But when she's down you don't want to show up on her radar
She has been a single mom,
(she is a tiger you don't want to tangle with her
when it comes to her children)
for most of the time I have known her
She thought she found someone to share her life and children
It didn't work out, the damage to her pride and self-esteem nearly did her in
She suffered through the humiliation, the embarrassment
She walked the floors at night alone
She questioned, "Why me, what did I do or not do?"
I recently saw her at a cookout
There was something different…
I couldn't quite put my finger on it at first
Then I saw him, he came over and sat down at the same table
Nothing that would trigger anyone to think
maybe there was something going on there
But then… I saw it! Slowly, shyly
spreading across both their faces as they talked
They are building a relationship
He helps her with tasks that she cannot tackle alone
The smile she had not been able to put on
her face for so long was visible once again
Slowly, cautiously, she treasures the moments
Her heart she will protect at all costs
But he must be pretty special to her, because
when she thought no one was looking…
I saw her smile!

Pamela Griffin
Rockingham, NC

[Hometown] Sanford, NC; [Hobbies] reading, knitting projects, crocheting, word search puzzles

Always putting events and things in her life to word, several hundred poems were lost in a house fire, so things that cannot be replaced at any cost were replaced by new poems and short stories. One summer I knitted enough dishcloths to replace all the appliances in my home! I can read printed words upside down, and I absolutely love word search puzzles and create them for children. Words used to describe the beauty and pizazz found around us, to share with others—if nothing else I would like to be remembered for this!

373

The Little Things

A cool, gentle breeze on a warm summer day
Playful waves roll, splashing you with spray
A pink and orange sky falls to the sea
Children playing, laughing so free
A colorful rainbow fills the sky
Hello from a stranger who passes you by
A pat on the back for a job well done
Sitting on the beach, soaking up sun
A sincere smile from a distant face
A soft white dress made from lace
Shadows dancing from a fire lit
The taste of cider upon your lips
A whispering kiss from the one you love
While stars twinkle from the sky above
Snow falling, covering angel white
While the moon smiles, clear and bright
Each of these, what a smile it brings
For it truly is the little things

Dawn M. Kilgore
Largo, FL

White Cloud Teddy Bear

For my granddaughter Allison

I'm your guardian angel
I guide you as you dare.
When you cry reach to the sky
And hug your "white cloud teddy bear."

As you grow I shall know
Your thoughts and dreams we'll share.
Ups and downs all of life's clowns
Remember to hug your "white cloud teddy bear."

When you are grown and prosper
On your shoulder I will be there.
When you're sad I'll try to make you glad
Look and reach up hug your "white cloud teddy bear."

When you're a senior citizen person
You have a guided path you wear.
Memories surround you everywhere
It's my privilege to have been your "white cloud teddy bear."

I'm your guardian angel
I guide you as you dare.
When you cry reach to the sky
and hug your "white cloud teddy bear."

James Horton
Sutherlin, OR

[Hometown] Sutherlin, OR; [DOB] June 8, 1948; [Ed] high school graduate, some college; [Occ] retired; [Hobbies] car and airplane mechanics, writing, cooking; [GA] retiring from the US Air Force and having my poetry published

Irene

Do you remember
when we first met
and you said to me
"I don't want to play
with you
Nigger?"
And those times
when you called me
bitch
slut
and hoe?
I never
had the chance
to tell you
Thank you.

Kimberly James
Jamaica, NY

Kimberly James is a native of New York City who loves Jesus, singing, dancing, reading and teaching English to New York City's students.

The Boy Scout & The Dreamer

A boy scout and a dreamer
Set out on adventure.
With light in sight,
They lived to fight—for freedom.
Armed with love,
They soared above
The earth's magic cities.
With nothing to fear, he called her near
And whispered ancient truths.
Awakening her vibrant flame,
She transformed into night.
Where she could shine her guiding light
And heal the world below.
Bestowed upon him, a badge of honor
So all the souls would know,
That a boy scout and a dreamer could
Inspire them all to grow.

Christine Dennis
Los Angeles, CA

My name is Christine Dennis and I am from Eagle Rock, CA. I graduated from USC with a BA in Communication and Cinematic Arts. I am a spiritual healer, teacher and artist. My hobbies include reading, theological research, crystal healing, reiki, painting, dancing and community service. My greatest achievement is Wind Song *(2013), a film about healing and transformation.*

Caregivers

Caregivers are people who
love doing wonderful, wonderful things for you.
Helping others who need your care,
watchin' over them with love and extreme care.
Help giving them life to enjoy their day,
being their guide through life each day.
Showin' you care makes their day,
prayers to God to help you through the day.
Angels up high watchin' down from above.
Blessin' you with guidance, strength, and love.
Never knowing what hour of the day
God will come and take them away.
You keep them safe like a bird in a nest,
watchin' them not getting much rest.
Growin' to love them more each day,
never a dull moment, Lord, I pray.
Keep me alive, Lord, to continue my work,
to keep caring for them for better or worse.
Being there for them until the end,
a caregiver's job will never end.

Barbara McDonald
Westland, MI

[Hometown] Westland, MI; [DOB] September 5, 1952; [Ed] high school graduate, CNA program; [Occ] personal caregiver; [Hobbies] watching movies, reading, writing; [GA] taking care of seniors

I worked as a personal assistant for the last fifteen years. I love my (babies) clients; they bring joy to my life, as I bring to theirs. I write short poems down when I have time to relax and when there is free time at work. I am a caregiver. There's time when there's nothing to do. That's when I write down things that are on my heart.

Your Kiss

Oh what passion beheld in your kiss,
You and I together forevermore.
Our hearts now melt together in bliss,
Our love for each other will surely soar.
Life has put us each through a test,
But need be, to find what love hold be true,
To strive through the seamless rest,
As we climb towards skies—forever blue.
The way I feel towards you and you towards I,
Like a dream become real; hearts greatest appeal,
Destiny has been swift to time passing by,
Our fate comes together, as that a holy seal,
So with that be it known between you and I, forever your tender kiss,
I shall know as you should too, true love to the heart—never miss.

Ryan Shea
Plymouth, MA

[Hometown] Plymouth, MA; [DOB] September 22, 1990; [Ed] AA in English; [Occ] student; [Hobbies] writing, learning new things, meeting new people, good conversation, Netflix, spending time with my girlfriend; [GA] overcoming my difficult past and creating a path for a bright future

Ghost Ship

A ghost ship stands alone amidst a silent sea.
Trapped! The ugly grasp of the doldrums refuses
to release its strangling grip.
Alone! Lost! Drifting aimlessly! A dream caught in the fog!
Is there hope in such a despondent setting?
Silence shouts its lonely call.
Confusion flusters a waiting sail.
Years of storms! Raging seas!
Messengers assigning naked seams in a sleepy hull.
Slowly. Leisurely. Salty brine wanders into worn-out cracks.

Watching! Hoping! Tear-stained eyes! Hopeful sentinels!
Whimpers whine as a lonely ghost ship
Soundlessly slips beneath a muted sea.

Walt Riopel Jr.
Chaplin, CT

What happens when a life grows empty? Discouragement settles in and it does become tough. My life came crashing down on me and I ran into a time where I wrote much poetry. I was stuck in the doldrums with a ship that had many prosperous times. I endured many storms and now the Ghost Ship begins to show those scars as water leaks into weathered seams. The ship belongs to me, or maybe it would be better to say that I am the ship. The last three lines are set apart to describe those that are trying to help me. I am fifty-two years old and disabled. As the poem infers I am a lonely guy, just trying to weather out the storms. I wish each of you luck with the poems you have written.

Snowflake, Snowflake

Blow away. You make
everything cold your way.
You're pretty in a way.
You make the snow look
like cotton candy and like
clouds in the sky.
And you sparkle like a
diamond and you shine
in the sunlight. But
spring is coming and it's
time to make hay.
So it's time to go on
your way.

Jack Johnson
Charlotte, MI

[Hometown] *Charlotte, MI;* [DOB] *April 25, 1925;* [Ed] *tenth grade;* [Occ] *barber;* [Hobbies] *arts, painting pictures;* [GA] *cutting hair*

I grew up in a small town called Potterville, MI. My dad was the town barber—25¢ for a hair cut. We didn't have much. The Depression hurt everybody. If you found a penny you were lucky. I left home when I was sixteen, and when I turned seventeen I joined the Navy. World War II had started. When the war was over I was honorably discharged. From there I returned home. I went to barber college. I was on Main Street sixty-one years when I retired. Now I'll have time to paint pictures and write poetry. They call me Jack the barber.

I Am a Mother

I am a mother, my strength is beyond my expectation
Going through life without hesitation
My mind and body keeps going without reservation

Being a mother comes with plenty of demands
Reaching out to my family and others with fifty hands
Remembering these simple words, yes I can

The mothering in me was instilled at birth
Set for life, as long as I am on this earth
There is no price for what a mother is worth

I am as strong as a tree that has taken roots for years
When it comes to mothering I have no fears
Yet the feminine side of me helps me shed my tears

Ella M. Allen
Galveston, TX

My name is Ella Mae Allen. I was born in Monroe, LA. My home town now is Galveston, TX. I am a certified notary public. My training is a supervisor for housekeeping. My hobbies are writing poetry, plays and making jewelry, etc. My greatest achievement is raising four wonderful children, Dimetris, Cleveland, Nedra and Cliffton, as a single parent.

Untitled

I don't remember asking for permission to come to Earth
and if I did ask for permission to come here, I probably would have asked to come in a slightly
different configuration. Since having arrived, I've learned and am continuing to learn our
Creator makes no mistakes. The joy in learning is continual learning, releasing that which
you've learned that is untrue, and striving to learn something new each day, sometimes in a
different way. No experience is ever as unpleasant as it may appear to be, or as pleasant as it
seems to be. Paint your own Earth canvas!

Ted Brown
Las Cruces, NM

[Hometown] Hampton, VA; [DOB] March 1, 1945; [Ed] associate's degree in aviation maintenance; [Occ] spiritual adviser; [Hobbies] reading, writing, driving; [GA] participating in birth of children

I am a retired United States Air Force Chief Master Sergeant, a retired General Electric mid-level manager, a retired Honeywell manager, an ordained Baptist minister (I've since left organized religion or perhaps it left me), and I find having an open mind about anything facilitates learning about everything, regardless of any prior Earth successes.

Mystical

I walk the trail through the pine
I held the forest's breath in mine
The purest scent
Filled me with content

Gazing upon the jutting cliff so steep
And the canyon so deep
I listened to the thunderous mountain call
Of the glistening waterfall

The white foam churning at the base
The bank holding it all in its wild embrace
Dampness from the misty spray
Caused a multicolor display
Beside I stand
Grasping for the rainbows with my hand

Tina J. Clifford
Lewisburg, TN

[Hometown] Lewisburg, TN; [DOB] April 21, 1965; [Ed] English major; [Occ] homemaker; [Hobbies] reading, writing, drawing; [GA] my children and grandchildren

I have been writing poetry since the age of fifteen. My inspiration comes from many things—the beauty of the outdoors, art, the people I love, and a teacher I met when I was ten years old. I went and spent a summer with her. At age eighteen I showed her my collection of poetry and asked for her help with corrections in punctuations and form. Her advice was to leave it the way it was—"Let it become your style." I love to write story poems—a meaning, a story to tell. This contest doesn't allow that long of a poem. This coming April I will be fifty, and my dream is to have a book published to hand down to my children. I acknowledge my style is different. I am a down-home country girl.

My Babies

Faith, my beautiful daughter with blue eyes and blonde hair
A little girl that looks like me that was my prayer
Bringing love and joy, you are growing up so fast
and as far as daughters go, you are the best

James, I felt you in me for only five months
You came too early and we were all so crushed
I held you in my arms and watched your life fade away
I hope to see you grow up in a world with no more pain

Eleven months later to the day, along came Manly to
brighten our days
Handsome and smart and so full of life
I get down on my knees and thank God for you every night

I know as far as mothers go, I haven't been the best
But having you all in my life, I know I've been blessed
Had you guys not been given to me
Lord only knows the mess I would be

Amber Stetson
Natchitoches, LA

[Hometown] Natchitockes, LA; [DOB] September 7, 1979

I am a military wife and mother.

I Wonder

I wonder—I wonder—I wonder,
where all the memories went
I keep in my heart—
and try to remember them all.

But the memories fade away
as I am getting older and forget the days
I used to know—
to remember what life it was
when I was young and brave,
many years ago.

Now, only the days remain
I try to remember with little smile
over my wrinkled face—
and the sad tears in my eyes
and the trembling hands and wonder,
where have all the memories gone
I never will know at all.

Otto Valnoha
Fox Lake, IL

[Hometown] Fox Lake, IL; [DOB] July 2, 1926; [Ed] elementary school; [Occ] retired from school; [Hobbies] woodcarver, painter, poet; [GA] received certificate from Illinois Board of Education for those who excel

Many years passed by since I defected from my country, Czechoslovakia, in 1948 to Austria—because of my anti-Communist oppression with warning of arrest by the police. With difficult conditions, I managed to go to West Germany where I stayed nine years in refugee camps and had the chance to emigrate to Canada, in 1957, and later, in 1961, to America. One of my latest jobs was working at one school district in Des Moines for twenty-five years as head custodian, and I received from the Illinois Board of Education a certificate for those who excel, at the end of my retirement. I wrote a book, Return to Yesterday, and have done some paintings and wood carvings. I donated large pieces—panoramas of towns—to museums. Now I write poems. And I am proud to be an American—in the land of freedom—but never forget my country and those I lost.

Pocket Gems

At times I ache to reach out
and zealously seize
those beauties of life,

warm colored lights
that wink from
Christmas trees,

flickering candles
burning brightly
to an end,

red-gold embers and
the quiet crackling
on a fire.

If I seized quickly enough,
I would gather them
and tuck them into some
back pocket of
my jeans—
saving them to pull
out on gray cloudy days,

savoring their brightness
and warmth
to tuck away again
knowing that I alone
carry such gems.

Joyce M. Grosko
Shawnee, KS

I was born on January 10 in Kansas City, MO and live in Shawnee, KS, a suburb of Kansas City. I have a BS in education with an emphasis in English and a minor in speech and theatre from the University of Central Missouri. I also have an MEd in special education for crippled and health impaired from the University of Kansas. I have been an educator in inner-city schools teaching English, reading, learning disabilities and behavior disorders. I have also been a behaviorist for juvenile offenders, was a materials development specialist for a genetics project, a statewide training program for respite care for the developmentally disabled, and the state-wide coordinator for a Centers for Disease Control-funded project through the Kansas State Department for Education on Human Sexuality and AIDS Education, and have been a graphic designer and grant writer for not-for-profit agencies.

Only One Shoe

Without laces and with a mashed tongue
    In the mangled grass
    Lay one Nike mud-splattered shoe
    partnered with my Hawaiian walking path.
As sunrise broke open each morning for fifty-seven days,
    with a lava flow of curiosity,
    the forgotten shoe coffin called to me.
Whose foot was once embraced by this shoe?
Had he run a New York marathon with steady determination?
Had she ridden a wild horse across the plains of South Dakota?
Did he stop at a Farmers Market and taste the home-grown tomatoes?
Had she run away from a lover after an argument about buying a house?
Had he knelt with both shoes at his father's funeral
    to meet the one shoe each morning on the walking path?
My heart was heavy with loneliness each morning
    As I felt rejected by a beloved
    As I felt forgotten by a family member
But most completely I felt grateful
    To have walked this luscious earth...
Even for one shoe-filled step.

Phyllis Tyler
El Monte, CA

At sixty-nine years of age, I am a retired United Methodist clergy of the California Pacific Annual Conference. It was my privilege to serve forty years as pastor to several congregations plus eight years with the General Board of Discipleship of the United Methodist Church in Nashville, TN. My husband, Marshall Mock, and I have four sons and five grandchildren who make their homes in various places of Southern California, Hawaii and Oregon. South Dakota is my state of origin and formation from which I was adopted as a small child and raised through high school. My schooling includes a BA from Morningside College in Iowa, a master of divinity from Wesley Seminary of Washington, DC, and a doctor of ministry from Claremont School of Theology in California. My passion at this time in my life is "to savor the moments" wherever that takes me. I love to learn. I love people. I love plants and animals, rocks, the moon, the vast ocean and night sky. My delights include sunrises, sunsets and rainbows. To live each day is an honor, and death intrigues me. This is just a glimpse of me.

Becoming

We knew you without regret; tested
but unnerved, a cause without action.
Surely seen and surely blessed, closely
Watched at work or rest; Becoming.

Once we cried, felt remorse
Slowly sighed…if only…
maybe. Watched the fall and then the rise.
Walking, running, resting; Becoming.

James Albion Crumly
Page, NE

[Hometown] Page, NE; [DOB] April 30, 1947; [Ed] BS in biology, MS in economics, graduate of Nlebr LEAD program; [Occ] production agriculture; [Hobbies] singer/songwriter and outdoors man; [GA] singing "Amazing Grace" to the Thai Delegation at the war memorial at the bridge over the River Kwai

I wrote this after visiting the World War II Allied War Memorial under the bridge on the River Kwai in Thailand. The memorial is a tribute to the soldiers who survived the "horrific Burma march." "Becoming" is a written tribute to these soldiers' spirit and self-determination.

The Lost Street

Where is the street of dreams?
That street where there are no screams?
I don't want to lose sight of it,
I'm tired of my plight.
Those dreams seem to get lost
At a pretty high cost.
The vision of my life without hope,
Can cause me to mope.
I try to keep my life on an even keel,
And still continue to feel
A sense of the fleeting dreams,
And hope, without inner screams.
Where is that street?
Oh wait, maybe it's at my feet.
Some of my dreams can still come true,
The direction to take if I only knew.
My life belongs to God, I know,
The way He will show.
I think the street corner is Faith and Hope,
A place where with His help I can go beyond cope.

Carol Daugherty
Temple City, CA

[Hometown] Dayton, OH; [DOB] 1941; [Ed] two courses from Longridge Writers School in CT; [Occ] semi-retired office jobs, drove school bus, housewife; [Hobbies] writing

I married my high school sweetheart, Hoyt Daugherty, in March of 1961. Three children were born to us: Ruth, James and Glenn. As each one married, grandchildren were born: David, Desiree, Jeannette and James. A great-granddaughter, Jeannette, was born in 2011, and another great-granddaughter is expected. During these years, I began writing stories and other articles and stories about life in general, and then poetry came into my life. I've been featured in several anthologies and have published my own book, From the Heart, in 2013, with a variety of themes in the poems. I write poetry because it is a release of all those thoughts that run circles in my head and mind, that are always taking my world around me and my outside activities.

The Other Woman

He stood before me tall and lean
Was I ready for this scene?
I knew it was coming for quite some time
She must be young and in her prime
Suddenly his face lit up—he was all aglow
He said, "She's lovely" and "I love her so"
Together for many a year
Trying not to shed a tear
I give him to you, his future wife
With love from his mom, who gave him life.

Bev Levine
Cincinnati, OH

[Hometown] Cincinnati, OH; [DOB] February 17, 1929; [Ed] high school, business college; [Occ] retired; [Hobbies] painting, writing; [GA] living so long

An immediate reaction prompted me to write this poem. I am eighty-seven, widowed, the mother of two daughters and one son, grandmother of seven, and great-grandmother of five. I count my blessings every day.

Chest

When my grandpa was old and gray,
In a hospital bed he had to stay.
He told me of his secret chest,
where he saved all things best.
I asked where this was hid,
But he said, "I can't tell you kid!"

I asked him this day after day,
But still my grandpa wouldn't say.
And on the day we laid him to rest,
I told my grandma about this chest.
She said she heard this when they met,
But this mystery she could never forget.

Until today, she wasn't smart,
To realize all things best were in his heart.

Melissa Barry
Colchester, VT

[Hometown] Mattituck, NY; [DOB] January 5, 1994; [Ed] currently studying biology at the University of Vermont; [Hobbies] writing/reading (of course), running, Irish dancing, working as an EMT

The End Is Just the Beginning

In the evening hours
From five fifteen to five thirty
The sun is leaving

Bright, the pink orange hue
Against the tan mountains face
With purple and blue

A yellow haze falls down
God kisses Earth good night
With a gentle hug

Dark gray the shadows
Climbing up the mountainside
Racing to the top

As darkness covers all
God winks at Earth, through the clouds
Bright white, the moonlight

Twelve months to each year
Spring, summer, fall and winter
The last month is here

December is cold
Snowing or raining sometimes
Most vivid sunsets

Bye 2014
As God promised, a new day
Hi 2015

Debbie Zimnock
Tucson, AZ

I was born in Philadelphia, PA and grew up in Norristown, PA. After moving around some years, I currently live in Tucson, AZ. I am disabled but work part time as a security officer. When one door closes, God opens a window! I chose the title of my poem because it defines everything in life. The theme of my poem ends a day, a month, a year, but, as God promised, a new day!

Progress

I hate to see that evening sun go down
When I know there's hungry kids around;
Who feeds them while we build this town,
In the name of Progress?

Those who have get more, by and by,
The rich get richer, while the poor still cry.
Sitting in the way and asking, "Why?"
Do we really need Progress?

Lives are discarded "for the greater good!"
High rises come from a charred neighborhood,
Muraled in contrailed skies and blood,
This is Progress?

Fifty story skyscrapers shade homeless missions;
Hundreds every day eat from soup kitchens,
In the coldest of winters, there are those with no mittens;
They are paying for Progress.

Instead of knowledge, we use a machine
To do our thinking, destroying the dream,
Graying the earth that once was green,
All in the name of Progress.

Garry Owens
Lebanon, TN

[Hometown] Lebanon, TN; [DOB] July 12, 1933; [Ed] AS in general studies, BSEE equivalent Navy schools; [Occ] USN, ATC, retired electronic engineer; [Hobbies] writing, designing inventions, genealogy, fraternal organizations; [GA] patented electronic bingo game

My early years were spent in full-time church work. I led music thirty-five years and was an ordained Baptist deacon and minister. I've been married sixty-one years and have one son and daughter. I wrote my first poem in an English class contest in the ninth grade. I have been writing poems and stories and editing newsletters periodically in the sixty years since.

My Hero, My Villain

There is so much you never told me...
About heroes, and villains, and of damsels in distress.
You, who were the master story-teller...
Who never said that none of it really mattered.

You were my teacher... my brother...
And you twisted and destroyed everything!

What you told me to be, the wicked games we played...
I was a damsel in distress for too many years!

My big brother, my hero, turned out to be...
Nothing more than an evil villain, a big bad wolf...
Who kept me hidden away from any challengers,
Who discarded me when I learned the truth.

So many tears I cried over you,
So many hours I spent wishing you'd care.

But do I want to go back?
If you are the past... then *no!*

Heroes can be villains...
Villains can be heroes...
Damsels in distress can break free...
I...am...free.

Carolanne Geissler
Branford, CT

[Hometown] Branford, CT; [DOB] August 14, 1983; [Occ] stay-at-home mom; [GA] giving birth to my daughter Aurora.

I have been writing poetry since my Naunny first told me to use it as a way to purge my sorrows at the age of twelve. This poem was a purging of my past, burning me to ash so that I could finally rise up from those ashes as a new woman, full of determination and hope! I finally let go of some of my most powerful demons and moved on into the life I know I was always meant to live. I am a wife, a mother, a writer... and I am finally free.

The Rock of Salvation

Time is as shifting sand
That falls through an hourglass
Though it shifts and swirls
It finally finds its end

The hourglass is then flipped over and the cycle repeats
There seems to be no ending to the ticking of the clock
We cannot waste the time that we have
We must stand upon The Rock

The Rock of Salvation alone holds the key
To understanding an infinite eternity
To stand upon The Rock we first must kneel
We must accept His Truth revealed.

Jesus Christ, our Morning Star
The One who traveled from afar
Opens the gates for us to stand
Upon The Rock of Salvation in The Promised Land

Vernon Ray Cook III
McEwen, TN

My name is Vernon Ray Cook III. Most of my friends and family call me Trey. I was born in Dickson, TN and was raised in McEwen, TN. I was born on January 24, 1997 to Vernon Ray Cook Jr. and Ann Marie Cook. I am currently a senior at McEwen High School and am planning to go into Christian Ministry after college. Throughout the last few years of my life I have experienced many things that have helped shape who I am. My family, my best friend Marisa Hagen, and most importantly Jesus Christ, have helped me to become who I am today. I would be nowhere without them. Proverbs 3: 5-6 tells us to "trust in the Lord with all your heart and lean not on your own understanding; in all your ways submit to him, and he will make your paths straight." In the end, no matter what we have to go through, if we trust in God and His Word, we will never be alone and we will always achieve our purpose.

Listen!

I'll keep my ears open
In the quiet of the day
Keep my ears open
Listening for what the breeze would say

Beautifully spoken words
Spoken into my spirit, like lips sweet with syrup
Tasting like honey to me
Saying things that only my soul can conceive
Words that spell out love
Embracing me with healing
Singing life to my soul
Teaching me to dance
To move about and to beautifully prance
In my honest truths

Bearing witness
To the conscious mind
I won't be afraid to live
I won't be afraid to pray
No matter what circumstances say
For my life is a gift
A beautiful treasure
It's time for me to live
Live without measure

Robin Harris
Atlanta, GA

My name is Robin Denise Harris, and I am the fourth of nine children. I am forty-nine (as of August 30, 2014), and I have five beautiful children and nine grandchildren of my own. I'm from Akron, OH; however, I am currently living in Atlanta, GA. I have recently acquired my MBA (specialization in management) and my greatest achievement is in becoming a published poet; this will be my fourth publication. In my leisure time, I love to read material that aids me in my venture to become a better-rounded individual and I am currently in the process of completing my first book. Writing is my first love.

Ode to Music

When I hear the music play
I feel as if it surrounds me, covers me, protects me
For without that beautiful sound, I can't live a day
When I'm anything but happy, 'tis my elixir, 'tis my key

Music is what makes my life livable, my heart lovable, myself alive.
Without it, my world would be empty, my world would seem dead.
Music to me is my own personal sea.

Music helps me live, love, forget, to take the risk, to take a dive.
If music was lost so would be my head
For music is my life, my passion, my reason to be.

Kaitlyn Maczko
Murrieta, CA

[Hometown] Poway, CA; [DOB] July 19, 1995; [Ed] currently studying psychology and criminology at Cal State, San Marcos; [Occ] working part time as a sales associate at EXPRESS; [Hobbies] loves to read, write and spend time at the beach with boyfriend

Suits and Ties

They wear wool suits and silken ties,
A few more words, too many lies,
Pandering to masses with slickness and thickness,
Meaningless nothings
Are seen through dark glasses.
Self-serving and greedy,
The watchwords of power,
Exploiting the workers,
While living in towers,
They know not the people,
And care even less,
Their visions corrupted,
Their souls in distress.
But the outcome is certain,
Strong wills shall prevail,
With wrongs to be righted and spirits unbroken,
The people set sail,
And suit-ties will fail.

Richard A. Sano
Sammamish, WA

I am from Albany, NY and have a BS in education from SUNY Oneonta and a MA in liberal studies from Wesleyan University. I am retired and play traditional jazz piano.

Walking with Angels, My Dear

For Nik McCarson

At night, I stare out into space
Recalling every feature of your face
With brilliant blue eyes, perfect in every way
And that gleaming smile with me to stay

Your enjoyment for every ounce of life
The memory of that I shall always hold tight
Saying the Lord's Prayer for you broke my heart
When the time is right, we'll have a new start

To finally be together and get it just right
Loving one another through day and night
So until then, work with the angels and play
On the clouds of the Goddess as they stay

You are always in my heart, even today
Because with every memory of you, it's your day
Don't' worry about me while walking with angels, my dear
Despite the strife of late, I'll be fine, have no fear!

Just remember that for you I will always care
I love you for eternity, this I gladly share
Handsome protector of mine always
Be my angel and in my heart until my last days

Lynette Murry
Jefferson City, MO

[Hometown] Salem, MO; [DOB] November 9, 1972; [Ed] attending SNHU; [Occ] student; [Hobbies] crafts, cooking, reading, writing; [GA] raising funds for HIV/AIDS treatment and research

The Resurrection Hope

When I go, don't weep for me
For I have only gone to sleep
No more can Satan do to me
For I have gone through death
and I am free
No more tears, sorrow or pain
Soon I will come to life again
The resurrection is a grand
Reward for all the faithful
That has endured
And for all our loved ones that
Have gone before
When I awake then I can sing
Death where is your victory
Where is your sting
Jesus died to conquer death
And Satan too
The victory is for me and you

Virginia Sanders
Chapmanville, WV

[Hometown] Chapmanville, WV; [DOB] July 30, 1936; [Ed] finished ninth grade in eight years; [Occ] housewife; [Hobbies] writing poetry, gardening, birdwatching; [GA] raised three children with the help of my husband

I was born July 30, 1936 on top of Kaford Mountain in Kanawha County of West Virginia. I was named Virginia Mae Miller. I am the oldest of six children. I grew up in the coal fields of West Virginia. I am a coal miner's daughter. I made good grades in school. I loved reading, writing, spelling and math. I have been writing poetry almost all my adult life. I was inspired to write about the resurrection because I have lost many loved ones in death and I hope to see them again.

Peace on Earth

When life comes at you hard and fast,
Do you cry out against the darkness,
"How long will this last?"
Or do you hear a whisper deep inside your soul
That comforts you in the night;
And feel an invisible arm hold you tight?

When you stand at the head of a casket,
And watch it go deep into the ground,
Does your heart harden?
Do you wear a permanent frown?
Or is there a Light that guides
Along an unknown path,
And frees you from bitterness and wrath?

There's a choice we make at some point in life
That determines which way it will go.
If you have chosen Jesus as Lord, you can know —
    Real peace in tragedy
    Real love through forgiveness, and
    Real hope for eternity.

The world can be a scary place
Without His hand to hold.
So, if you know Him, act like it. Be bold.
For without His Love in your heart, Earth can be dark and cold.

Kathleen Highley
Big Spring, TX

I was born in Carlsbad, NM, but got to Texas by the ripe old age of one. I have trained in many different fields, but always gravitate back to the legal field as an administrative assistant. I do all my writing with a mechanical pencil, on a short yellow legal pad before I type a word. I sing for the Lord at every opportunity, lead a prayer ministry at church, and do some public speaking. I have been published in numerous anthologies, published four Christian novels and one non-fiction book on divorce recovery for women. My greatest achievement would have to be the blessing of children and grandchildren. Between us, my husband and I have five children and ten grandchildren.

Untitled

The purpose of writing this
Is to give that one girl bliss.
Even if she was the one no one knew,
She still spent every day trying to figure out what's true.
In the end, the purpose is not finding the truth.
It is not finding answers to questions you asked in your youth.
It is trusting that there are answers to everything asked.
It is trusting the future and forgetting the past.
Don't satisfy the human race, for everything will be searched.
For happiness is still resting, peacefully perched.

Hannah Roberts
Ringgold, GA

[Hometown] Ringgold, GA; [DOB] August 29, 2001

Waves of Time

Waves lapping at the beach,
Erasing imprints from various feet,
Filling the holes dug deep,
Breaking down castle's keep.

Time lapping at our lives,
Smoothing over hardship times,
Erasing intense emotional lines,
Softening thickened heart's rinds.

Ebb and flow everlasting,
Stopping for none, no one.
As long as the Earth shall spin
Waves will be lapping at the sands.

P. Clauss
Mesquite, TX

P. Clauss lives in Dallas, TX area with her husband and two children. Born March 29, 1962, she graduated with a DVM degree from Oklahoma State University in 1987 and has been working in the veterinary medicine field since. She enjoys crochet, crafts, and reading as well as writing. She considers the most important thing in life is to continually learn to trust God in all things.

Lost

Lost like a sailor, in deep ocean dark; your sails be tattered, ne'er make yard.
Strong men do fall, down to their knees, begging the sky for help, if you please.
Hearts are heavy, hearts that do long, need only just
Heed Siren's song.

Lost like a child, deep in wild meadow, trees be looming, casting dark shadow.
Smart men do bow, down in the dust; begging to take them, now if you must.
Hearts that are moaning for one last chance, need only just
Ask Fairy to dance.

Lost like an urchin, deep in dark streets, naught in your pockets, no meal to eat.
Wise men falter, then they pray; are there none who can save today?
Hearts that only wish to lie, need only ask
The Specter why.

Bash your life on rocks below, may your wreckage be sight to behold.
Dance until your feet do bleed, may the children one day take heed.
Follow the dead into the mist, may you someday get your wish.
Heed the warnings of the lost, may you never know the cost.

Wise men pray, for they dismay. They cry only; outlast the fray.
Hearts that blunder, hearts in pain, need only ask,
The Lord to save.

Felicia Kelly
Corbin, KY

[Hometown] Corbin, KY; [DOB] December 27, 1995; [Ed] currently a freshman at Morehead State University; [Occ] student; [Hobbies] reading, writing, hiking, camping; [GA] being the first in my family to attend a four-year college

For Robin

A thousand faces, a million voices,
You could make me laugh and make me cry,
But that power couldn't change your choices
And now I'm left here wondering why.
You saw the good that you did for others,
How couldn't that have been joy enough?
To think of life's pains that must have plagued yours
I can't begin to imagine how rough.
It pains my heart to look back and see
I never met you, nor know what you went through.
But you have no idea what you meant to me.
I loved what you could be and what you could do.
O captain, my captain, the screen's turned black.
And not even Genie could bring you back.

Jacob Diller
Natrona Heights, PA

[Hometown] Natrona Heights, PA; [Occ] college student; [Hobbies] karate, hockey, fishing, reading

Heart's Content

This paradise breathes an Adam and Eve feeling.
God's retreat beneath a leafy, sky-less ceiling,
Eden's temple, giant pillars of gray-green bark,
Holds heavenly pleasure for an October lark.

Quiet, quivering ferns dance to a faithful breeze
As we wanderers are dwarfed by towering trees.
Our sylvan saunters within virgin Penn entrails
Startle transit chipmunks scampering on log rails!

A hollow tree with wooden reddish-brown decay
Frames our friendship in backdrop of primeval play;
Offering musty moss aroma, dampened leaves
To content our hearts as ageless silence relieves.

Mary Anne Shay
Conneaut Lake, PA

[Hometown] *East Brady, PA;* [DOB] *December 1, 1948;* [Ed] *BS in special ed/elementary ed;* [Occ] *retired elementary school teacher;* [Hobbies] *writing poetry about nature and family, walking, gardening, scrapbooking, preserving foods—especially jelly, volunteering with husband in care and documentation of game reserve birdhouses;* [GA] *choosing the father of our miraculously born daughter and son*

I was born the eldest of Ronald and Rita Seybert's loving family of fifteen children. I married my sister's best man and moved to a small resort town between two small lakes near the Great Lakes. I finished my college degree thirty years after high school graduation while working part time at a local winery. I joined a vibrant church and volunteered as a twenty-year preschool teacher. I resigned when hired in a local school. Health problems shortened my late-blooming teaching career to ten years. My ultimate goal is to have many more family visits to places like Heart's Content, Warren County, PA—a section of old forest dating back to the mid-1880s, preserved within the Allegheny National Forest.

Doc, You Got It Wrong!

Heed me, prod this vessel no further.
This organic domain of mine is beyond your imagination.
A universe of misunderstood anomalies, rarely explored.
Doc, you got it wrong and I'm turning down the volume on gibberish!
Push my fear button, make me weep, and forward me to further prodding.
I will not expire at present!
'Cause, I'm full of purpose and motivated forward.
Heed me; my soul discards that negative thought of yours.
Quit yanking my ear, 'cause I'm not listening!
Suspend all prodding, 'cause you've stumbled over Fool's Gold!
No daisies sprouting between these toes; so cease sowing your seeds here!
"Reaper," remove yourself from my shadows; you've been misinformed!
Mind the weak and weary please; this gal's goin' nowhere, but forward…
Look through my amber windows; do you see a quitter, in here?
Doc, you got it so wrong…
Next!

Lauri J. Gerace
Fabius, NY

Inspiration comes from the most amazing places. For this poem, my inspiration emerged from the deepest recess of my soul. There are moments when we face the reality of our mortality, and for me this is one of those moments. I have an infinite "bucket list" and have no intention of leaving this realm anytime too soon. So to my doctors… thank you, but no thank you! Now, back to my creative little corner; I have intense faith in my infinite tomorrows.

Thanksgiving Day

A family gathers around the table
Bowing their heads in prayer
Giving thanks for their food
No worries, no cares.

For it was Thanksgiving Day
Football games, turkey, pies
Parades and shopping for great buys

In a distant land,
A soldier sits on foreign sand,
No football, no turkey, or pies
Bowing his head, he cries,
"Deliver me, Lord, please don't let me die."

So remember those soldiers
This Thanksgiving Day,
When you gather around your table to pray,
Thank God for their service and lives today.

Joann Gallagher
Inverness, FL

I was born and raised in Long Island, NY. I moved to Florida in 1987, and I presently live in Inverness, FL with my husband Joseph. I am a Christian, and I have been writing poetry and some songs for several years now. "Thanksgiving Day" was written to honor all our men and women who serve our nation. Because of their dedicated service, we can live free and protected lives. I enjoy reading and writing, as well as singing, cooking, baking, and gardening. I especially enjoy spending time with my husband, fishing and boating. Our children are all grown and married with children of their own. We have three granddaughters and one grandson. All live in Long Island, NY.

Magic

If the world was full of magic and wishes could come true
I would wish to spend my life being in love with you.
If man could love a rainbow and have it love him too
Then you would be my rainbow and I'd love only you.
If the world was full of magic and we could pick our grace
I would love to spend my life gazing at your face.
If I could hug a soft, warm breeze and kiss a bright sunbeam
Then all I'd dare to think of you would be more than a dream.
If the world was full of magic and we could choose our time
I would choose to spend my days making you all mine.
With magic I could wrap your heart in the soft blanket of night
And light the corners of your soul with stars that shine so bright
But there's no magic in this world and wishes don't come true
So I will just content myself with being friends with you.

Ernest Walwyn
N. Las Vegas, NV

[Hometown] Bronx, NY; [DOB] February 2, 1939; [Ed] BA in resources management from Troy University, BA in systems management from University of Maryland; [Occ] retired from the Air Force in 1986 and Civil Service in 2003; [Hobbies] bicycling, writing, reading, walking and fitness training

She Writes

A poet she is
Words dance for her

She writes about the world
Observations, how the world changes

She writes about thoughts
Challenges the way society thinks

She writes about pain
Unyielding, unforgiving, ever broken

She writes about love
Relationships, friends, family, and that not-so-quite love

She writes about hope
Empowering, fleeting, but ever present

She writes about courage
Letting the world know who she is

She writes about loneliness
Being in a crowd and feeling like no one sees you

She writes about life
Human nature and imperfection

She wants to believe her words inspire
But her words are for herself
Reminding her that nothing will ever be better
Than the moment she's in.

Emily Martell
Ashaway, RI

[Hometown] Ashaway, RI; [DOB] May 25, 1993; [Ed] BS in pharmaceutical sciences; [Occ] student; [Hobbies] beading, reading; [GA] acceptance into a research fellowship supported by a federal grant

Sheryl Kay

She was a darling little girl
By the name of Sheryl Kay
Whom God loaned us for a while
Until He called her home one day
In the few short years she spent
With us we grew to love her so
And when we had to say goodbye
It broke our hearts to see her go
But she will always be with us
In the happy memories we share
Of that pretty little girl
With green eyes and auburn hair
She would wrap her arms around
My neck and say, "Mommy, I love you,"
Then she would run to her daddy
And happily say, I love my daddy too.
She thought it was her duty
To correct her two older brothers
Sometimes she would chide and scold them
Just like a little mother
Yes, we have precious memories
Time can never take away
So thank You, Lord, for lending us
That darling angel Sheryl Kay!

Lou A. Carey
Vian, OK

[Hometown] Vian, OK; [DOB] March 31, 1935; [Ed] high school; [Occ] retired business owner: carpet and upholstery cleaning; [Hobbies] hiking and photography; [GA] getting our troops and veterans the thanks and appreciation they deserve

I wrote this poem about my daughter, Sheryl Kay, not long after losing her in a car accident shortly after her fifth birthday. She was such a sweet, pretty little girl, and we missed her so much. What inspired me to try and get the troops and veterans the thanks and appreciation they deserved was seeing that lone soldier coming out of that empty, lonely depot with no signs of life around, until the veteran came up to him with a big smile and shook his hand. Then the whole city came alive. That played over and over on TV and made me feel so sad. I was just a young girl during the second world war and just about everyone went all out to show the troops and veterans how much they were appreciated. So I decided to write a long letter to a top government official and I ended my letter by saying, "What if this, our country, is ever invaded and our troops refuse to stand up and fight for such thankless, ungrateful people?" I never did receive a reply to my letter, but it was only a few short weeks after that I started seeing on TV and hearing on radio our troops and veterans being given thanks and appreciation, which they very much deserve.

Unspoken

She speaks with frailty,
her words half formed
lost in her quivering mouth.
Speaking causes her
to stumble over fragile phrases that…

when asked,
softly, she answers
and with each rising word a grimace is formed—
the silence she has made now broken by the stuttering sound of her
weak thoughts fashioned into

tentative utterings
stained with hollow-hearted humor,
dampened by unshed tears
that drown the voice
others need to strain to hear.

Lee Musho
Rye Brook, NY

[Hometown] Rye Brook, NY; [DOB] October 24, 1997; [Ed] high school; [Hobbies] reading, writing, watching film; [GA] surviving mental illness

First Snow

There's something magical
About the first snow
It makes your heart warm
And your face all aglow

But now and again
A cold wind blows
And freezes the marrow
Why? No one knows

To a cherry red blaze
The fires are stoked
We cuddle together
With stories and jokes

From out of the blue
A soft string of notes
Then another story
As off to sleep we float

Terry Lee Sporcic
Brant, MI

[Hometown] *Muskegon Heights, MI;* [DOB] *August 14, 1946;* [Ed] *associate's in small business management;* [Occ] *retail and caregiver;* [Hobbies] *writing, painting, embroidery, crocheting, drawing, singing, crafting, toothpick painting small ornaments, spending time with family;* [GA] *the poetry published through Eber & Wein Publishing and the book,* Cursed at Birth

I had ten brothers and sisters, but only one sister still lives. God blessed me with five sons, four daughters-in-law, one stepdaughter, fifteen grandchildren, fourteen great-grandchildren, and sixteen or so great-great-grandchildren. Life can be a great challenge, as it was for not only me but my mother as well. The book is a fiction based on her story, and the tragedies in it are the truth.

Butterflies for Carol, Daddy's Little Girl

To my new sweet escape, where pain can't penetrate,
butterflies take me there. Now free from life's cocoon,
safe forever. Finally taking my true form Breathtaking and
amazing, the butterflies take me home. God made this
day for me, flow now with me through clouds of stardust
from God's loving eyes. I flutter through Heaven brilliantly
sparkling as if drenched in morning's dew. At last I soar
among Him, the spirit I've longed to know, Jesus now
guides my flight through sunshine days and moonlit nights.
all at once I look beneath to see two shining feet, a
Second is all it takes for me to realize they're His.
My Savior's taking me home to His garden where I
can fly free and fast. I'll be coming each day from my
home far away. I'll visit often God's little angel butterfly,
see me in His hands, a most amazing miracle shining
in the sky like wings of an angel. Now, for reasons not
apparent to you, I'm with Him. He has told me His
stories, now I'm at peace with complete understanding
and love why my life has come to pass.
He needs me now to come with Him, I now fly alongside
the maker, the Spirit I've longed to know.
My love I leave to those left behind. Look for me,
I will never be far away.
Butterflies are free and *now so am I.*
P.S. I'll be the one in purple.

Cynthia Graham-Lemon
Ottawa, KS

[Hometown] Johnson County, KS; [DOB] December 19, 1961; [Ed] two years of college; [Occ] writer, artist, CNA; [Hobbies] living, loving, laughing, painting the whole world pink! [GA] John Kevin and Chloé Noelle

For my brother Marty's late wife. We dedicate this to Carol Graham and her Father, Bob Benson, who joined his little girl today. "Keep her safe, Dad." Poetry helps overcome and cope with sadness, loss, pain—darkness from the past. Jingling, grabbing my soul's inner balance, light and dark, somehow words come from there, bringing new light where there was just void. Yin or Yang, poetry's always beautiful to the heart it enters, bringing from that place inside you, sharing with someone else. I've closed another break in the chain. I've connected to another human being. Always laugh.

Within Your Favor (Presence)

At this moment there is a hush,
Which words just don't convey,
Rather a settling godliness,
Which happens at the end of each day.

When all my business of sorts
Seem to disappear into thin air,
I now attain pure silence and solitude,
That captivates me everywhere.

Oh God, my holy Father,
Release my work and labor,
Give me calmness of self,
As I rest within Your favor.

Paul A. Chromey
Plains, PA

[Hometown] Duryea, PA; [DOB] November 8, 1954; [Ed] BS in physics and math; DPM, Temple School of Podiatric Medicine; [Occ] surgical podiatrist, pedorthist, shoe repairman; [Hobbies] shoe and leather repair; [GA] married my wife, Susan, who also is my best friend and critic

The Lord's Touch

The Lord heals your spirit when you're cast down.
He puts a smile back on your face and takes the frown.
He mends every broken soul picks up all the pieces and
makes them whole.
The Lord retrieves you, if you've wandered too far.
He catches your falling star.
He is there when you are unsure, relieves you when you're hurt.
Brings comfort and lifts you when you're inert.
The Lord rescues when you're in danger, finds you when you are lost,
reveals a path of righteousness when the truth is glossed.
The Lord is with you, every step of your way,
Guarding every night, guiding every day.
Carrying you in times of despair,
The Lord does bless you and care.
Amen

Donna Hill
Union, NJ

[Hometown] Union, NJ; [DOB] March 12, 1965; [Ed] early childhood education; [Occ] pre-school teacher; [Hobbies] tennis, swimming, dancing, sewing; [GA] poetry publication

I truly feel that poetry has the ability to open the heart to possibilities we've never entertained before and thus enlightening us with recognition and grace, setting us on a path of understanding and change that is both meaningful and profound.

Divorcing Sin

I want to give sin a divorce
For Jesus has put me on the right course
For Jesus is my heavenly source

This is the time for me to grow up
I need the Lord to fill my cup
For in Jesus, being down is getting up

For sin is not how I want to relax
Knowing Jesus' word is a pure fact
Now that sin is gone, I know how to act

Heaven is a choice that many have found
For Satan can't keep us hellbound
Jesus is the key that I have found
I divorce you sin on every ground

I want to give sin a heavenly divorce
For I am not without remorse
Jesus is my energetic force
It feels good to be on the right course

For my beginning is a new ending
Jesus' word just keep on sending
It's time to stop playing and pretending

Theresa Neely
Cherryville, NC

[Hometown] Cherryville, NC; [DOB] January 4, 1955; [Ed] Gaston College, early childhood education; [Occ] self-employed, home daycare; [Hobbies] gardening, baking, writing poems and children's books; [GA] when my songs hit the number one chart on ReverbNation

During that time I was going through trying times, a bitter divorce and raising two children. I felt spiritually impaired until I came to my senses, brought about by releasing the true expressions of my heart that I was going to give sin a divorce. I thank God for the ability He has given me to express myself through writing. His inspiration turned my negative thoughts into positive thoughts. I believe this poem will help inspire others as well. I have two albums in process and wrote eleven songs on ReverbNation. com. I have poems published in three books: Aspiration of Pen and Thought, The Poetry Guild *(International Library of Poetry), and* Love and Luminaries *(International Library of Poetry).*

A Story of Music and Freedom

A heart full of music
And a
Bag full of books
A game without numbers
And a
Pawn with a rook
A metal violin
And an
Iron piano played
Music beyond measure
That
Cannot be explained
A beat to the drum
And a
Flight to the bird
Laughs with tears
And a
Peace to the word
Shelter with dim light
And
Rules all within
So play on, keep the song
So that
Freedom can begin

Charlotte George
Paola, KS

[Hometown] Paola, KS; [DOB] August 28, 2002; [Ed] secondary (seventh grade); [Occ] student; [Hobbies] playing the piano, reading; [GA] winning second place in the spelling bee

Reading and writing are both something that I've always enjoyed. My poem was inspired by those who have had the courage and confidence to encourage others through hard times. Those people are heroes to keep a spirit up with hope. Hope is an important thing to keep in our lives.

Laid Back

Sittin' on a creek bank, catchin' no fish
Hook ain't baited, just came here to wish
Back to a stump, pole on my toe
Got nothing to do and nowhere to go
Too lazy to work, too righteous to steal
I'm laid back letting life glow like it will
Pa said, take care of this old farm son
It'll take care of you when your day is done
I hustled this farm with sweat and toil
Crops wouldn't grow and I never struck oil
But if my mule hadn't died, I'd be farming still
Stead, I'm laid back lettin' life flow like it will
I had a job one time at an old saw mill
Cutting down trees, so folks could build
Never saw no sense in helping towns grow
'Cause life's a lot better when it goes real slow
So I left that job at the old saw mill
And I'm laid back lettin' life flow like it will
Shore hope my welfare check ain't late
Gettin' low on tobacco, need a hinge on the gate
But everything's going along just fine
House and barn and land's all mine
And on the back forty, I got a little still
And I'm laid back letting life flow like it will

James E. Kelley
Gray, GA

[Hometown] Gray, GA; [DOB] March 20, 1932; [Ed] high school graduate; [Occ] machinist at Keebler Bakery; [Hobbies] hunting and fishing; [GA] married sixty-two years, seven children

Country "Gem" Kelley was born in Randolph County, AL on March 20, 1932. He moved to Macon, GA in 1937 because Dad lost his farm during the Depression, and his son by a previous marriage got him a job at the cotton mill in Macon. He graduated Lanier Senior High School for Boys in 1950 and had his first poem published while in fifth grade. He has written several poems and songs randomly since then.

I Light the Candles of My Love

I light the candles of my love, peaceful light of my
Devotion's love, now burning brightly for Thee.
These candles bright, material form of my love,
Become the light of my love in flames of my
Devotion's joy I now light for Thee. Whisperings of
Joy of internal wonder in which my spirit now bows
To Thee, these candles bright behold Thy soothing
Light, lit now with the match of my devotion's
Flame, burning all lesser thoughts, save my one
Burning thought—my devotion's love for Thee. All
Sense of need is consumed in the fires of Thy love,
A love I sense only when these my candles I light
For the joy of loving Thee. Though a man be blind.
May he not yet see Thy light of love lit by the match
Of his spirit's love for Thee? For internal vision of
Spirit knows no barriers to Thy presence when he
Lights the candles of his love, never to be
Extinguished, save by Thee. I light the candles
Of my love upon the altar of my spirit's joy, now
Burning for Thee, and there my soul call to Thee
Suddenly heralds unto me—Thou hast suddenly
Appeared as the halo of burning light, caressing
My devotion's love to Thee, as I light the candles of
My love, peaceful light of my devotion's love
Now burning brightly for Thee.

Jaime H. Reyes Oquendo
San Francisco, CA

Born in Oakland, CA, I attended UC Berkeley, receiving a BA in Spanish literature in 1983. In 1997, I became a chiropractor, a major achievement in my efforts to support people to maintain their health in a natural way. I enjoy practicing Kriya Yoga meditation from India, which has enriched my inner life, the impetus for the mystical poetry I write in both English and in Spanish. Here is a prayer-poem to the Divine; the lighting of candles is a symbol of undying love for the Divine.

A Mother's Life Is Always a Heartbeat Away

For you I've longed all my life,
and now you're here in my life.
For you I've waited so long, so patiently,
and now you're here, I don't have to wait
anymore. You are worth so much more than
the agony and pain I have endured.
The wait for you has been a long,
beautiful road. The patience I have had
to have has been worth the wait all the
more.
Now I have you in my life, and I thank
the Lord, for it feels so right. Your little face
I love to kiss, those lovely hands that
touch me so softly in such an innocence.
My heart longs to love you forever and eternity.
You, my special children, you complete
me. I roe to you now and forever, to love,
cherish you all my living days, and to give
to you now my heart. For I pray to the
Lord we will never be apart.

Malinda S. Lewis
Livingston, TN

*[Hometown] Anderson, IN; [DOB] February 25, 1972; [Ed] high school, two years business
management; [Occ] writing a novel, making candles, owning a business; [Hobbies] writing, reading,
cooking, etc; [GA] having all three of my boys five years apart*

*Poetry is forever. I love to write. I have had five poems published. These two this year. The other three
back in 2001 and 2002 through the International Library of Poetry. Sometimes my feelings inspire
me to write on good or bad things going on in my life. My boys, Alex Rubenstein, Zachary Lewis, and
Justin Lewis, my husband Ryan, and my mother and father, all inspire me. This is a poem I wrote in
2002 about all three of my children. I'm blessed to be here and constantly give thanks for the things
I receive. I am very grateful for this chance for you to see my work in writing poetry. Thank you all.*

Reflection

I had a talk with my reflection
She told me to look, but do not speak
Her message was one of importance
The answers to the questions that I seek
She said thank God every morning
For He has blessed you with this life
She said remember He's always here
Especially when you're dealing with strife
She said hold your chin up high
Be proud of the reflection you see
Don't let others define you
Remember they don't know you like me
Make sure you wear your smile
It's beautiful, and oh so you
Love with all your heart
'Cause that's just what you do
Never look down or be disappointed
A strong woman is who you've become
Many challenges you have faced
And each one you've overcome
So hold that head up high
Be as proud as you can be
'Cause I know all the reasons
That I love you, being me

Cindy Frazier
Follett, TX

I have always loved poetry. My parents, Ray and Ellen Costenbader encouraged me at a young age to pursue my passion. They are the reason I still write today. This poem is about loving who you are every single day. It is so easy to get down on ourselves or see our many faults, but why look at them when there is so much beauty to be seen?

Today for Sale

The morning blessed the coming day with drops of holy dew.
The genuflecting sunbeams acquiesced.

The promise of a bold new life lay pregnant on a score of hours, unused, unsullied, unafraid, un-compromised as yet.

But sanctuary of the coin and fear of God knows what, then turned my face to yesterday, my hands to tasks well known.

And with a sigh I sold today for that which held no fear. The death throws of the promised day fell noiseless on my ear.

The bread is won, the home secure, the suit of clothes procured. Another repetitious day was grudgingly endured.

The sun is set, my song played out, recorded every note. Posterity may lift its ear, its judging voice may quote:

"Sung out again. His song of life was written in one day. A symphony in monotone, a rhapsody in gray.

J. Stephen Larsen
Ogden, UT

I am the writer of a novel, several novellas, and eighteen poems. In addition, I wrote a five-part book on a fifth alternate business strategy entitled The Epsilon Papers including "The Magnificent Worker," "The Involved Investor," "The Beneficent Manager," "The Considerate Customer," and "The Symbiotic Supplier." I also made an audio work entitled, "The Vision of Epsilon." I love to write. I love the world and its people.

Love of My Life

I see you in my thoughts and dreams,
when I awake,
how real it seems,

you aren't here beside me,
but soon I hope you will be,
no one truly knows or understands,

you have my heart in your hands,
my love is what you truly own,
come soon and make our house a home

Inside those walls you're doing your time,
not being here with me
is your only crime.

Others in your life may come and go,
but my love is true,
and I'm sure you know.

I may not be rich or the prettiest one,
but I love you so much,
you are my sun.
You light up my life
every time you call,
when the time is up,
I begin to fall.

Heather Cunnup
Bohemia, NY

I'm from Bohemia, NY. I was born on July 7, 1987. Some of my hobbies are going to art exhibits, museums, painting, and writing poetry. As per my occupation, I'm a published author and poet. Some of my greatest achievements are getting my book published, graduating high school, getting my cosmetology license, getting one of my poems published in the World Famous Book of World Poets *in Manhattan Library and setting goals for myself to achieve more.*

The Real Me

Can I ever really be the real me?
Will anyone ever truly see?
Why do I hide the best part?
Will I ever let anyone into my heart?
How come I close away the part that's real?
Will I ever tell them how I really feel?
I've done it for so long now.
I'm not sure that I know how
To unlock all the doors I've locked,
To unblock all the walls I've blocked.
Can it be done after all these years?
Am I able to chase away all these fears?
Will someone ever hold the key
To unlock all the secrets within me?
How will I ever know if the time is right?
I wish I had some kind of magical insight.
It's not easy to know when someone is being true.
I just wish I had some kind of clue.
To know that this time he won't hurt me.
Maybe then I could let him see
The absolute and complete real me.

Sonya Philbrick
Leavenworth, KS

[Hometown] Jonesboro, GA; [DOB] November 24, 1973; [Ed] high school; [Hobbies] writing, painting, sculptures, reading, playing games, puzzles, decorating cakes, collecting knives; [GA] my kids and my poems

Malala Yousafzai

A pint-size dynamo
An unlikely hero
An entity before her time
Promoting global education
Through the United Nations,
Around the web, and prime time
May Malala live to see
The blossoms of her mango tree

The activist from Pakistan
Who stood defiant against the Taliban
Shot in her forehead and left for dead
In a league of her own
Girl power strong,
And a global figurehead
May Malala live to see
The blossoms of her mango tree

Malala for Prime Minister!
A Nobel Prize contender,
A politician, a doctor and everything in between
Let the Pakistanis be forewarned
Look out here she comes!
One girl changing the world with her dreams
May Malala live to see
The blossoms of her mango tree

Sandra Penro
Shannon, MS

[Hometown] Shannon, MS; [DOB] January 15, 1956; [Ed] Itawamba Community College; [Occ] general office clerk, administrative assistant; [Hobbies] writing, quilting; [GA] book of poetry Revealed: A Personal Encounter with God

Once in a while, I see something in the news that needs to be expressed in a special way, and so the poem "Malala Yousafzai" was born. Malala is a sixteen-year-old activist from Pakistan. This poem was written October 2013 when Malala was a contender for the Nobel Peace Prize. The next year, October 2014, she was a recipient of the prize. My niece was also my inspiration for writing this poem. She is the founder and CEO of a global center for women's leadership and development. I shared this poem with her to be supportive of her work and because she and Malala have a lot in common. I knew that she could identify with this poem.

The Gifts My Mother Gave Me

She gave me a love of books
So I can hear the ancient kings
Cross the desert in caravans,
And feel the scorpion sting.

She gave me a love of poetry,
Those flowing words of rhyme,
From the epic tales of Byron
To simple ditties like mine.

She gave me a thirst for knowledge,
To learn all I possibly can
Of the splendid works of nature,
And complexities of man.

She gave me a sense of justice:
To hear the other side, too,
Not to be hasty in judgment,
And to give credit where it's due,

Mother gave me many gifts;
I've listed some, at length,
But the final gifts she gave to me
Were her courage, valor and strength.

Linda Neitzel
Kissimmee, FL

[Hometown] Farwell, MI; [DOB] January 7, 1942; [Ed] AA in liberal arts; [Occ] retired medical transcriptionist; [Hobbies] oil painting, poetry, reading; [GA] earning a degree at age seventy

As my mom lay dying of cancer, I began to think of all the gifts she had given me—not material gifts wrapped in tissue and ribbon, but characteristics that helped shape me into who I am. As I listed these I found them taking the shape and sound of a poem. The poem wrote itself, and when finished, I gave it to my Mom. I was so glad that I had thought of writing it while there was still time for her to read it. And I read it to friends and family at her funeral.

Forgiveness Is for You

Telling someone you messed up is not easy.
A good place to start is to use God as your measuring rod.
Forgiveness takes meekness, humbleness, and greatness too.
Remember forgiveness is really for you.
Keeping in mind we have all missed the mark.
This is always a great place to start.
You might be sorry, but it comes with no guarantees.
Just say you're sorry and keep moving forward until another life bell rings.
The roads of life are narrow, short and quick.
Choose your path wisely. There are many choices
and negative voices.
Never delay forgiveness.
To receive it, you must give it.
Be diligent in what you say or do,
forgiveness is really for you.

Daisy Kincheloe
Dallas, TX

[Hometown] Chicago, IL, but I have lived and traveled all over the world (France, three years; Hawaii, three years); [Ed] graduated magna cum laude with three degrees: BA in psychology, BA in philosophy, BA in journalism; [Occ] author, broadcast media television; [Hobbies] reading, traveling, writing; [GA] being a published poet, having a television program, authoring three books to be released in 2015, family, my relationship with God

Writing poetry that inspires, encourages, and uplifts others is an honor and a privilege. My goal is to write poetry made simple: easy to read, easy to relate. I feel motivated to share poems with the world, family and friends. Every place I go, and in all the people, places and things I see, there is a poem. Forgiving people can be challenging. The power of prayer can help with the steps to forgive. I am humbled and grateful to be a published poet with poems being read all over the world. If you need forgiveness, just say you are sorry. It will make you feel better!

Hero

You kissed my hand before you left to get on the plane,
and I said tell them bad guys you don't play any games.
Tell them you kick ass and you take names.
You weren't Hercules,
you were just some boy in army green
with his mind made up to be a marine.
I met you when I was just fifteen.
Little did I know, you'd be the hero
I once saw in my dreams...
You picked me up, and you spun me around
when you returned, and I said missing you months
at a time is worth the feeling to know
your father's honor is earned.
You weren't Superman;
you were just some boy in faded pants
with his mind made up to fight for what makes sense.
I fell in love with you when I was just sixteen.
Little did I know, you'd be the hero
I wouldn't just see in my dreams...
Your dream is to be someone's hero,
if you die being their hero then you're satisfied,
but your dream has already been achieved because
you've been my hero since your lips met mine.
You weren't Hercules. You weren't Superman.
You were more realistic than Cinderella's prince.

Shayla Mayhugh
Chickasha, OK

[Hometown] Chickasha OK; [DOB] October 16, 1995; [Ed] USAO; [Occ] full-time college student; [Hobbies] songwriting; [GA] recognition for one of my songs from Oklahoma's House of Representatives

In December of 2012, I wrote this song about a boy named Steven. All he ever talked about was joining the military, and I fell in love with his heroic charm. I thought the world of him, but I found out the hard way that even a hero can only save you once.

Beyond Time, Beyond Space

Through the end of time
Through the end of space
I shall always, always,
Always see your face...
Through the end of time
Through the end of space
As you are my only love.
Beyond the river of time
To a land full of grace
Beyond time, beyond space
I shall wait for you there,
Though it may take me
Far beyond my years I fear.
Yet love will surely win
Your heart one day my friend
And love shall take us to that place
Beyond time, beyond space.

Debra Stuart
Houston, TX

I have a bachelor of arts degree from the University of Kentucky, Lexington, in art studio, as well as a teaching certification from Western Kentucky University in Bowling Green, KY. I have always had a deep passion for the arts and have been writing since childhood. I love to write sonnets, and Shakespeare had a profound influence on me. I am currently in graduate school at Capella University and working full time in healthcare.

Of the Abyss: Chapter 1

You there, that wanders so innocently and aimlessly
Permit me to speak to you as a shepherd of a lost lamb
You seek something, yes. I see it in your heart
Fortune favors and curses you, traveler, as it has been found
Here I stand before you, a guide, naked and covered in blood
Should you choose to follow
I will protect you from all except myself
I will show you a journey that will forever change you
How, I will not say
For if I told all who passed through then you'd wish to never know me
And I'd therefore know no one
Intriguing, isn't it? All before you certainly thought so
I can entertain, jest and bring comfort. But you shall not know me
My mind, ears, arms and tongue are yours but not my heart
Why, you ask? Oh lamb, you are kind but foolish
I am bound here forever as I am bound to you, for now
All of me you will have, you will become drunk with it
Only to be easily seduced further
All your dreams will come true at equal cost of nightmare
As nothing in this realm comes without a price
Be not afraid for I am not. I have no room in my heart for it
I promise you nothing, only that should you descend into darkness
You will be in good company
So I say to you, follow lamb… follow
For the way up is down and I am your fall
So, tell me, will you choose to rise and tell me stories of the sun?

Elisabeth Evans
Danville, CA

[Hometown] Danville, CA; [DOB] August 22, 1991; [Ed] BS in abnormal psychology Saint Mary's College; [Occ] PhD student and writer; [Hobbies] writing, reading, gaming, nature, being a nerd; [GA] surviving

This poem is actually a first chapter of a series of poems that I've been creating over time. Each poem is a fable for the reader who is on a journey with this naked, blood-soaked guide. Mysterious and dangerous, the discovery of who she is and what your journey truly is about, is revealed in her story. This is her introduction, this is the first step of the journey. She, the spirit of suffering, will show you truth in a sea of lies, should you choose to search for them. "All suffering begins and ends in blood. And when you find a story that does not belong in my river, it will find its place along the shore," Spirit of Suffering.

Commencement

Aimlessly wandering around,
Bound to these four years.
The weak die out long before now,
The strong make it through.

They don't make us fight each other
Just their equation.
If we succeed
We get released.

Our chains are unlocked,
And our papers signed.
We get released to the real world.

Nothing but paper in hand,
We have to find a way to survive.
Our sentence is over.

Beth Shiller
Youngstown, OH

Poetry

Poetry is an untimely true friend
Of the incessant friend of the friendless
Poetry sticks with you through thick
And a never ending attitude called thin

Poetry with its throbbing free verse swings
And deep seated rhythmic beats
Brings great joy to its avid readers
Poetry is not a fair weather friend
Rather
Poetry wants to give its avid patrons a
Literary shoulder to lean on
Poetry brings a soothing-tenderhearted relief
To the trapped minds of uptight souls suffering
From the blues in the night

Poetry is an invincible gift from Jehovah
The omnipotent Holy Spirit created
Everything and everybody
For this reason alone—
He spiritually encourages the sensitive ones
To thoroughly enjoy and write poetry about
His magnificent Beauty of Nature
Draw ever so close to Jehovah
He is a poet of poets

Naomi Abdulrahman
Joppa, MD

[Hometown] Joppa, MD; [DOB] January 30, 1944; [Ed] BS in history; [Occ] retired; [Hobbies] writing poetry, painting, drawing; [GA] publication of my poetry in five books

I was inspired to write this poem for two primary reasons. First of all, I want to keep poetry alive and moving. Second, I want poetry patrons to know that poetry will always be there for them in good times and in bad times. Poems (reality) that they can relate to will often bring peace of mind and solace to the reader. Poetry is a friend (literary) that will always be there when you need it most. I graduated from Towson University with a BS degree in history in 1999.

If I Thought

If I thought for just one
moment that this would be
my last breath, I'd tell you
I'll love you forever, even beyond death.

If I thought for just one
moment that your face would
be the last I'd see, I'd take
a million pictures and save them
just for me.

If I thought for just one
moment that your voice would
be the last I'd hear, I'd listen
attentively and promise not to
shed a tear.

If I thought for just one
moment that your touch would
be the last I'd feel, I'd embrace
you and know that this has
all been real.

If I thought for just one
moment that my heart would
beat its last beat, I'd thank the
Lord for allowing you and me
to meet.

Dana Smith
Camdenton, MO

[Hometown] Camdenton, MO; [DOB] January 8, 1984; [Ed] high school; [Hobbies] writing, photography, fishing, being outdoors and being with my family; [GA] becoming the mother of two wonderful children, army veteran

Beneath the Flame

Oh, there is much to be said
For passion and for flame
And nary a soul will deny a hero cannot be tame
When senses writhe or love still burns
When rapture heats and anger churns
Great strivings can indeed ensue
And mighty men and not too few
Might accomplish and indeed imbue
The world with all the mighty goals we knew

But once attained it fails to linger
The passion and the flame
Not like the gentle love beneath
That will forever remain
That still gives the gentle swell of happiness
When someone mentions to me your name
It's like the hush of twilight on a calm and sandy shore
Or a gentle breeze on the grasses
When the raindrops are no more
It's making me feel like a flower
Sprinkled with morning dew
When each loving gesture drew my whole soul through
Oh, men will always justly pursue with
Passion and with flame
But I will always remember the love that still lingers
When someone mentions to me your name

Eleanor Gilchrist
Wake Forest, NC

Lovely Paradise

Like the night sky,
we're full of mysteries with our curious eyes,
possessing the elegance of a blooming rose
in a field of ungracious souls.
We are pearls of an extraordinary paradise,
though most of us are blinded by the earthly cries.
I write of such matter
in the deepest state of poetry.
Such a graceful art,
that's written cursively across my heart.
In a paralyzation of beauty,
this earth inevitably stuns me,
leaving each flower to grow
in a cardiac arrest of a fanciful field unknown.
Each day is an adventure; grasp the exhilaration
resting gracefully at your awaiting.

Courtney Casteel
Hillsboro, MO

Eber & Wein Publishing

Happy Holidays

Our pockets are nearly empty,
The checkbook funds are low.
The gas tank's getting lower,
And the tires need to go.

The tree is a little shabby
The electric lights are sparse.
The decorations are a'falling down
In a heap of broken glass.

But our cupboard's full of groceries
And our hearts are full of cheer.
The wishes are abundant—
The reason is so clear!

As we reflect on this whole year
We remember friends of old.
It is time to tell them once again—
If we are not too bold.

With these friends in mind, we know
They are worth their weight in gold.
This season, lets make it very clear,
For this you must be told—

We wish you a very Merry Christmas
And a Happy New Year full of cheer,
With health, and wealth, and happiness
To be with you all next year!

Arthur C. Elvin
Greenville, TN

[Hometown] Readfield, ME; [DOB] 1933; [Ed] Readfield and Kent Hill School; [Occ] accountant;
[Hobbies] photography, camping

I was born and brought up on a farm outside August, ME, and served in the US Conflict. I worked in retail management and retired with the Florida County government in their accounting departments. I retired to Greenville, TN in 2006, where I enjoy watching the birds and animals play in the back yard. I enjoy poetry and my two Boston terriers.

God's Guardian Angels

When illness comes your way
Put your faith in God
Strength and hope will never die
If you nourish them with faith

They will soar with the angel wings
They will walk and not grow faint
They will run and not grow weary

God gives us angels
With or without wings
To make sure we know
The kind of care He brings

Juanita Turner Mullins
Abingdon, VA

I was born on September 8, 1927 in Backbone Ridge, VA in Southern Appalachia, and moved to Abingdon, VA in 1977 after a flash flood took my home in Haysi, VA. I am one of ten children, the only high school graduate, educated at University of Virginia and Virginia Community College. I have worked in retail management, substitute teaching, being a teacher's aide, and as a published poet. I also worked over thirty years as a non-profit volunteer in the Women's Prison Ministry. My greatest achievement is using my spiritual gifts given to me by the Holy Spirit and honed from the tragedy of losing my three-year-old son in an accidental fire and my husband to murder by the time I was twenty-seven years old. Faith born of these tragic situations made me a survivor. My children are Jimmy, Linda, Myra, Charlotte, and Christopher. I have six grandchildren and eight great-grandchildren. My legacy will live on as they go into the world with strength of purpose and love.

My Brother

Heaven has called for you today,
Leaving so many words left to say.
But now it's too late, for the time has come.
Words unspoken, surely there are some.

Regrets and wishes are there too,
But lasting forever are memories of you.
I was there when you had a word to say,
Just like you would be there night or day.

There have been times that we disagreed,
But we were there for each other in time of need.
Now it's time for me to say goodbye
Until we meet again in Heaven to fly.

Betty Morris
Barnwell, SC

[Hometown] Barnwell, SC; [DOB] September 5, 1944; [Ed] high school and one year of vocational school; [Occ] retired home health assistant; [Hobbies] fishing, taking long walks; [GA] raising two wonderful children

My brother passed in 2013. We were raised by our grandparents. He always watched over me. He was my protector. I could always count on him. We were very close. I raised two wonderful children. One saves souls and one helps to save lives. At age seventy, I am very proud.

Early Morning About Five

Early morning, about five, lightning outside flashes through the blinds.
Eyes half awoke, flutter to see the dawn.
Another day to begin, eyes open wide, with a listening ear.
Ears tuned to noise outside, hearing new sounds pleasant to the ears.
The day goes by hour by hour, gathering dreams about families and friends,
Doing things that make their day.
Late night at ten, time to rest our thoughts, rest our bodies and brains.
Thinking of things to be done, family talks to be held.
Getting a new start for the next day.
Day goes by faster than lightning in the skies.
Thoughts are slow to admit to the brain.
Time to really turn into our soft beds and rest.
Early morning, again, about five.

Pauline Wright
Dearborn, MI

The Night Nurse

Together, we are one,
Somehow caring, somehow sharing,
And loving only one,
The Patient.

In the still of the night,
We carry our light,
Hoping they might have a restful night,
The Patient.

If, per chance, we heard a sigh of pain,
We were there to alleviate the same,
The Patient.

When morning came, and the sun shone through,
Remembering that the nurse took care of you,
The Patient.

I thank you, God, for giving me the friendship
Of the nurse who helped me through the night,
The Patient.

Elizabeth Mylod
Oradell, NJ

Your Smiling Face

Your smiling face is my sunshine.
It rained the other day.
Your warmth and beauty
Brightened through
And chased the clouds away
Your glowing eyes,
Your tenderness
Your charm and kindness too
All help me to realize
Why I'm so fond of you
And should some clouds
Appear again
And darken my sunlit skies
I'll think of you, and you alone,
And watch the clouds drift by.

John Van Ness
Tuxedo, NY

[Hometown] Tuxedo, NY; [DOB] February 1, 1948; [Ed] two years of college; [Occ] retired custodial worker; [Hobbies] many; [GA] being published in Best Poets of 2010

My name is John Van Ness. I had had a fight with my girlfriend and as a result I thought that the situation was my fault. So as an act of apology I wrote the poem. My poetry instruction came from my English 101 instructor at Rockland Community College in Suffern, NY. He was a published poet and is currently the Poet Laureate of Rockland County, NY.

Index of Poets